THE LETTERS OF JOHN

In this commentary, Duane F. Watson provides a careful verse-by-verse interpretation of the Letters of John that foregrounds the author's rhetorical strategy. He emphasizes the means that the Elder uses to persuade the churches he addresses to continue affirming the Johannine tradition and to resist secessionists who corrupt it. While illuminating the sophistication of the author's rhetorical approach, Watson also explores traditional exegetical questions, demonstrating how many issues of interpretation are clarified or resolved by rhetorical analysis. He also sheds new light on the relationship between the author, his audience, and opposition in their original context. This commentary features "closer look" sections giving more detail on related subjects and "bridging the horizons" sections that suggest how these epistles address our world. The commentary is aimed at educated laity, clergy, college and graduate students, and scholars interested in the Letters of John, the history of the churches addressed, and the social formation and location of these early Christians.

Duane F. Watson is Professor Emeritus of New Testament Studies at Malone University in Canton, Ohio. He is most known for his pioneering work in the rhetorical analysis of the New Testament. His works include *Invention, Arrangement, and Style: Rhetorical Criticism of Jude and 2 Peter* (1988); "The Second Letter of Peter" and "The Letter of Jude" in *The New Interpreter's Bible* (1998); editor, *The Intertexture of Apocalyptic Discourse in the New Testament* (2002); *First and Second Peter* (with Terrance Callan) in the Paideia Commentaries on the New Testament (2012); editor, *Miracle Discourse in the New Testament* (2012); and editor (with Alan Hauser), *A History of Biblical Interpretation*, 3 volumes (2003, 2009, 2017).

NEW CAMBRIDGE BIBLE COMMENTARY

GENERAL EDITOR: Ben Witherington III

HEBREW BIBLE/OLD TESTAMENT EDITOR: Bill T. Arnold

EDITORIAL BOARD
Bill T. Arnold, *Asbury Theological Seminary*
James D. G. Dunn, *University of Durham*
Michael V. Fox, *University of Wisconsin–Madison*
Robert P. Gordon, *University of Cambridge*
Judith M. Gundry, *Yale University*

The New Cambridge Bible Commentary (NCBC) aims to elucidate the Hebrew and Christian Scriptures for a wide range of intellectually curious individuals. While building on the work and reputation of the Cambridge Bible Commentary popular in the 1960s and 1970s, the NCBC takes advantage of many of the rewards provided by scholarly research over the last four decades. Volumes utilize recent gains in rhetorical criticism, social scientific study of the Scriptures, narrative criticism, and other developing disciplines to exploit the growing advances in biblical studies. Accessible jargon-free commentary, an annotated "Suggested Readings" list, and the entire *New Revised Standard Version* (NRSV) text under discussion are the hallmarks of all volumes in the series.

PUBLISHED VOLUMES IN THE SERIES
The Pastoral Epistles, Scot McKnight
The Book of Lamentations, Joshua Berman
Hosea, Joel, and Amos, Graham Hamborg
1 Peter, Ruth Anne Reese
Ephesians, David A. deSilva
Philippians, Michael F. Bird and Nijay K. Gupta
Acts, Craig S. Keener
The Gospel of Luke, Amy-Jill Levine and Ben Witherington III
Galatians, Craig S. Keener
Mark, Darrell Bock
Psalms, Walter Brueggemann and William H. Bellinger, Jr.
Matthew, Craig A. Evans
Genesis, Bill T. Arnold
The Gospel of John, Jerome H. Neyrey
Exodus, Carol Meyers
1–2 Corinthians, Craig S. Keener
James and Jude, William F. Brosend II
Judges and Ruth, Victor H. Matthews
Revelation, Ben Witherington III

The Letters of John

Duane F. Watson
Malone University

CAMBRIDGE
UNIVERSITY PRESS

Shaftesbury Road, Cambridge CB2 8EA, United Kingdom

One Liberty Plaza, 20th Floor, New York, NY 10006, USA

477 Williamstown Road, Port Melbourne, VIC 3207, Australia

314–321, 3rd Floor, Plot 3, Splendor Forum, Jasola District Centre, New Delhi – 110025, India

103 Penang Road, #05–06/07, Visioncrest Commercial, Singapore 238467

Cambridge University Press is part of Cambridge University Press & Assessment, a department of the University of Cambridge.

We share the University's mission to contribute to society through the pursuit of education, learning and research at the highest international levels of excellence.

www.cambridge.org
Information on this title: www.cambridge.org/9780521813952

DOI: 10.1017/9781139045865

© Duane F. Watson 2024

This publication is in copyright. Subject to statutory exception and to the provisions of relevant collective licensing agreements, no reproduction of any part may take place without the written permission of Cambridge University Press & Assessment.

First published 2024

A catalogue record for this publication is available from the British Library

Library of Congress Cataloging-in-Publication Data
NAMES: Watson, Duane Frederick, author.
TITLE: The letters of John / Duane F. Watson.
DESCRIPTION: Cambridge ; New York, NY : Cambridge University Press, 2024. | SERIES: New Cambridge Bible commentary | Includes bibliographical references and index.
IDENTIFIERS: LCCN 2023014400 (print) | LCCN 2023014401 (ebook) | ISBN 9780521813952 (hardback) | ISBN 9780521891059 (paperback) | ISBN 9781139045865 (epub)
SUBJECTS: LCSH: Bible. Epistles of John–Commentaries.
CLASSIFICATION: LCC BS2805.53 .W38 2024 (print) | LCC BS2805.53 (ebook) | DDC 227/.9407–dc23/eng/20230504
LC record available at https://lccn.loc.gov/2023014400
LC ebook record available at https://lccn.loc.gov/2023014401

ISBN 978-0-521-81395-2 Hardback
ISBN 978-0-521-89105-9 Paperback

Cambridge University Press & Assessment has no responsibility for the persistence or accuracy of URLs for external or third-party internet websites referred to in this publication and does not guarantee that any content on such websites is, or will remain, accurate or appropriate.

Dedicated to the memory of my grandmother, Mary Lovice Halsted Watson (1900–1983), who always encouraged and gently advised me, and my grandfather, Harold Frederick Watson (1902–1999), for whom being an engineer was the dream, but being a farmer was the reality.

The Letters of John

This commentary is a careful interpretation of the Letters of John. Its distinctive feature is a focus on their rhetorical dimensions, which have been neglected or only briefly discussed in previous interpretations. The author of these letters used Greco-Roman, Jewish, and general rhetoric in their composition to make them persuasive to their recipients. He struggled to convince them to adhere to the theology and ethics of the Johannine tradition against challenges posed by secessionists from their own ranks. His rhetorical arsenal is rich and varied, employing everything from grammatical changes of person, to figures of speech and thought, to repetition and amplification, to simple argumentation. He employs invention (constructing arguments), arrangement (arranging rhetorical units), and style (figures of speech and thought) to enable the recipients to recognize the situation he addresses, assess them as he does, and respond to them as he deems most advantageous to them. These rhetorical dimensions provide numerous insights that enrich and clarify traditional interpretation.

Contents

List of Supplemental Elements	*page* xiii
Acknowledgments	xiv
List of Abbreviations	xv

THE LETTER OF 1 JOHN	1
I INTRODUCTION TO THE LETTER OF 1 JOHN	3
Authorship	3
Audience and Situation Addressed	4
Rhetorical Constraints Bearing on the Situation	7
The Rhetoric of 1 John	9
Rhetorical Insights into the Situation of the Letter	12
II SUGGESTED READINGS ON THE LETTERS OF JOHN	14
Commentaries	14
Monographs, Essays, and Articles	14
Studies in Greco-Roman Rhetoric	16
III COMMENTARY ON THE LETTER OF 1 JOHN	17
1:1–4: Letter Opening or *Exordium*	17
1:5–5:12: An Overview of the Rhetoric of the Letter Body or *Probatio*	27
1:5–2:2: God as Light and Its Implications	30
1:5: The Governing Proposition	31
1:6–7: First Secessionist Claim, Its Refutation, and Counterclaim	33
1:8–9: Second Secessionist Claim, Its Refutation, and Counterclaim	35
1:10–2:2: Third Secessionist Claim, Its Refutation, and Counterclaim	36

ix

2:3–11: What It Means to Know the God Who Is Light	41
2:3: The Governing Proposition	42
2:4–5a: First Secessionist Claim, Its Refutation, and Counterclaim	44
2:5b–6: Second Secessionist Claim, Its Refutation, and Counterclaim	46
2:7–8: A Parenthesis	48
2:9–11: Third Secessionist Claim, Its Refutation, and Counterclaim	51
2:12–14: A Digression Affirming the Positive Spiritual State of the Faithful	56
2:15–17: Exhortation Not to Love the World	62
2:18–27: Beware the Antichrists and Affirm Jesus as the Christ	66
2:18–19: First Negative Characterization of the Secessionists	68
2:20–21: First Affirmation of the Faithful	71
2:22–23: Second Negative Characterization of the Secessionists	72
2:24–25: Second Affirmation of the Faithful	73
2:26: Third Negative Characterization of the Secessionists	75
2:27: Third Affirmation of the Faithful	76
2:28–3:10: The Identity of the Children of God	79
2:28: Opening Exhortation	82
2:29–3:4: First Antithetical Pair	84
3:5–6: Second Antithetical Pair	89
3:7–8: Third Antithetical Pair	90
3:9–10: Fourth Antithetical Pair	92
3:11–24: Love One Another	94
3:11: Proposition: Love One Another	96
3:12: Opposite by Example: Cain	96
3:13: Exhortation: Do Not Be Astonished	98
3:14: Syllogism: Love as a Sign of Life	98
3:15: Proposition: Hatred Is Murder	99
3:16: Example and Exhortation: Christ's Love Obligates the Same	100
3:17: Rhetorical Question	100
3:18: Exhortation to Fully Love	101
3:19–22: Love in Deed and Truth Brings Reassurance and Boldness Before God	102
3:23–24: Definition of the Commandment and Benefit of Obeying It	104
4:1–6: Distinguishing the Spirit of God from the Spirit of the Antichrist	107
4:1–3: First Test of the Spirits: Confession as Sign	108

4:4–6: Second Test of the Spirits: Listening to the World versus Listening to God	110
4:7–5:5: Obligations Incurred and Blessings of God's Love for Us	114
4:7–10: God's Love as the Source and Imperative of Our Love of One Another	116
4:11–16a: Loving Others and Confessing the Son as Assurance of Abiding in God	118
4:16b–21: Perfect Love Casts Out Fear	121
5:1–5: Conquering the World through Faith	126
5:6–12: Divine Testimony That Jesus Christ Came in Water and Blood as a Gift of Life from God	130
5:6–8: The Testimony of the Johannine Tradition, Water, Blood, and the Spirit	131
5:9–12: The Testimony of God	136
5:13–21: The Conclusion or *Peroratio*	141
5:13: Calculation	143
5:14–15: Enumeration	144
5:16–17: First Proposal of Policy	145
5:18–20: Threefold Enumeration	146
5:21: Second Proposal of Policy	148

THE LETTER OF 2 JOHN — 153

I INTRODUCTION TO THE LETTER OF 2 JOHN — 155

Author — 155
Audience and Situation Addressed — 156
Literary and Rhetorical Genres — 157
   As a Letter — 157
   As Rhetoric — 158

II SUGGESTED READINGS ON THE LETTER OF 2 JOHN — 160

III COMMENTARY ON THE LETTER OF 2 JOHN — 161

Verses 1–3: Letter Opening — 161
   Verses 1–2: Prescript — 162
   Verse 3: Greeting/Blessing — 164
Verses 4–5: Exhortation to Obey the Love Commandment — 165
Verses 6–11: Beware the Dangers of the Secessionist Deceivers — 167
Verse 12: Body Closing — 174
Verse 13: Letter Closing — 175

THE LETTER OF 3 JOHN	179
I INTRODUCTION TO THE LETTER OF 3 JOHN	181
Author	181
Audience and Situation Addressed	181
Literary and Rhetorical Genres	182
As a Letter	182
As Rhetoric	184
II SUGGESTED READINGS ON THE LETTER OF 3 JOHN	186
III COMMENTARY ON THE LETTER OF 3 JOHN	187
Verses 1–4: Letter Opening	187
Verse 1: Letter Prescript	187
Verses 2–4: Health Wish and Expression of Joy	188
Rhetorical Function as *Exordium* and *Narratio*	191
Verses 5–8: The Hospitality of Gaius	191
Verses 9–10: The Inhospitality and Hostility of Diotrephes	196
What Are the Dynamics of the Situation?	197
Honor Challenge and Possible Visit	199
Verses 11–12: Exhortation to Imitate Good versus Evil and a Recommendation of Demetrius	201
Verses 13–14: Letter Closing	203
Verse 15: Letter Postscript	204
Index of Greek and Roman Rhetorical Handbooks	208
Index of Deuterocanonical and Early Christian Writings	211
Index of Scripture and the Apocrypha	213

Supplemental Elements

A Closer Look: Life/Eternal Life	page 25
Bridging the Horizons	26
Bridging the Horizons	40
A Closer Look: Abiding	54
A Closer Look: The Love Commandment	55
Bridging the Horizons	55
A Closer Look: The Evil One	61
A Closer Look: The World	65
Bridging the Horizons	66
A Closer Look: The Antichrist	76
Bridging the Horizons	78
Bridging the Horizons	93
Bridging the Horizons	106
Bridging the Horizons	113
Bridging the Horizons	125
Bridging the Horizons	129
A Closer Look: Water and Blood in 1 John 5:6	138
Bridging the Horizons	141
A Closer Look: Nondeadly and Deadly Sins	150
Bridging the Horizons	150
A Closer Look: Letter Writing	176
Bridging the Horizons	176
A Closer Look: The Virtue of Hospitality	205
Bridging the Horizons	206

Acknowledgments

A manuscript never depends upon the efforts of just one person. I want to thank my first class in Johannine Epistles at Malone University, fall 1989, which probed the depths of Johannine thought with me: Mark Barnes, Matthew Evangelista, Jerry Fetters, Johanna Moody, Terri Norcia, Christopher Radcliffe, Brenda Rentsch, Daniel Schultz, and Tom Showalter.

I would also like to thank Ben Witherington III, who invited me to produce this commentary, and for the work of the staff at Cambridge University Press in producing it.

Finally, Raymond Brown's commentary on the Epistles of John (Anchor Bible) has had a strong influence on my thinking about these letters. I found it to be a sterling example of thorough scholarship, readable prose, and responsible stretching of interpretive boundaries. It piqued my interest in these letters in my student days and continues to do so today.

All quotations of Greek and Roman sources are from the latest editions in the Loeb Classical Library.

Abbreviations

PRIMARY SOURCES

Apoc. Ab.	Apocalypse of Abraham
Aristotle, *Poet.*	*Poetica*
Aristotle, *Rhet.*	*Rhetorica*
Aristotle, [*Rhet. Alex.*]	*Rhetorica ad Alexandrum*
Aristotle, *Top.*	*Topica*
Augustine, *De doct. chr.*	*De doctrina christiana*
2 Bar.	2 Baruch
Barn.	Barnabas
CD	Cairo Genizah copy of the Damascus Document
Cicero, *Brut.*	*Brutus*
Cicero, *De or.*	*De oratore*
Cicero, *Inv.*	*De invention rhetorica*
Cicero, *Opt. gen.*	*De optimo genere oratorum*
Cicero, *Or. Brut.*	*Orator ad M. Brutum*
Cicero, *Part. or.*	*Partitiones oratoriae*
Cicero, *Top.*	*Topica*
1 Clem.	1 Clement
2 Clem.	2 Clement
Clement of Alexandria, *Strom.*	*Miscellanies*
Demetrius, *Eloc.*	*De elocutione*
Did.	Didache
Diogn.	Diognetus
1 En.	1 Enoch
Eusebius, *Hist. eccl.*	*Ecclesiastical History*

Gk. Apoc. Ezra	Greek Apocalypse of Ezra
Gregory of Nazianzus, Or. Bas.	Oratio in laudem Basilii
Herm. Mand.	Shepherd of Hermas, Mandate(s)
Herm. Sim.	Shepherd of Hermas, Similitude(s)
Herm. Vis.	Shepherd of Hermas, Vision(s)
Ign., *Eph.*	Ignatius, *To the Ephesians*
Ign., *Magn.*	Ignatius, *To the Magnesians*
Ign., *Phld.*	Ignatius, *To the Philadelphians*
Ign., *Smyrn.*	Ignatius, *To the Smyrnaeans*
Ign., *Trall.*	Ignatius, *To the Trallians*
Irenaeus, *Haer.*	*Against Heresies*
Josephus, *Ant.*	*Jewish Antiquities*
Josephus, *J.W.*	*Jewish War*
Longinus, *Subl.*	*De sublimitate*
1 Macc	1 Maccabees
2 Macc	2 Maccabees
Philo, *Embassy*	*On the Embassy to Gaius*
Philo, *QG*	*Questions and Answers on Genesis*
Philo, *Spec. Laws*	*On the Special Laws*
Plato, *Phaedr.*	*Phaedrus*
Polycarp, *Phil.*	*To the Philippians*
Pss. Sol.	Psalms of Solomon
1QH	Thanksgiving Hymns
1QS	Rule of the Community
Quintilian, *Inst.*	*Institutio oratoria*
Rhet. Her.	Rhetorica ad Herennium
Sir	Sirach
T. Benj.	Testament of Benjamin
T. Jud.	Testament of Judah
T. Levi	Testament of Levi
T. Mos.	Testament of Moses
T. Sim.	Testament of Simeon
Tob	Tobit

SECONDARY SOURCES

AB	Anchor Bible
AnBib	Analecta Biblica

List of Abbreviations

ANTC	Abington New Testament Commentaries
AUSS	*Andrews University Seminary Studies*
BDAG	F. Danker, W. Bauer, W. F. Arndt, and F. W. Gingrich. *Greek-English Lexicon of the New Testament and Other Early Christian Literature*, 3rd edition. Chicago: University of Chicago Press, 2000.
BDF	F. Blass and A. Debrunner. *A Greek Grammar of the New Testament and Other Early Christian Literature*. Revised and translated by R. W. Funk. Chicago: University of Chicago Press, 1961.
BETL	Bibliotheca Ephemeridum Theologicarum Lovaniensium
Bib	*Biblica*
BT	*The Bible Translator*
BZNW	Beihefte zur Zeitschrift für die neutestamentliche Wissenschaft
CBQ	*Catholic Biblical Quarterly*
DLNT	*Dictionary of the Later New Testament and Its Developments.* Edited by R. P. Martin and P. H. Davids. Downers Grove: Intervarsity Press, 1997.
ECL	Early Christianity and Its Literature
EKKNT	Evangelisch-katholischer Kommentar zum Neuen Testament
EvQ	*Evangelical Quarterly*
ExpTim	*Expository Times*
HNTC	Harper's New Testament Commentaries
HUT	Hermeneutische Untersuchungen zur Theologie
ICC	International Critical Commentary
JBL	*Journal of Biblical Literature*
JSNT	*Journal for the Study of the New Testament*
JSNTSup	Journal for the Study of the New Testament Supplement Series
JTS	*Journal of Theological Studies*
LEC	Library of Early Christianity
MGNTG	J. H. Moulton, *Grammar of New Testament Greek*, 4 vols. Edinburgh: T. & T. Clark, 1908–1976.
MNTC	Moffatt New Testament Commentary
MTZ	*Münchener theologische Zeitschrift*
Neot	*Neotestamentica*
NICNT	New International Commentary on the New Testament
NovT	*Novum Testamentum*
NovTSup	Supplements to Novum Testamentum

NRTh	La nouvelle revue thèologique
NTL	New Testament Library
NTS	*New Testament Studies*
RB	*Revue biblique*
RSR	*Recherches de science religieuse*
SBJT	*Southern Baptist Journal of Theology*
SBLDS	Society of Biblical Literature Dissertation Series
SJSJ	Supplements to the Journal for the Study of Judaism
SNTW	Studies of the New Testament and Its World
SP	Sacra Pagina
TDNT	*Theological Dictionary of the New Testament.* Edited by G. Kittel and G. Friedrich. Translated by G. W. Bromiley. 10 vols. Grand Rapids: Eerdmans, 1964–1976.
TynBul	*Tyndale Bulletin*
TZ	*Theologische Zeitschrift*
WBC	Word Biblical Commentary
ZNW	*Zeitschrift für die neutestamentliche Wissenschaft und die Kunde der älteren Kirche*
ZTK	*Zeitschrift für Theologie und Kirche*

The Letter of 1 John

I Introduction to the Letter of 1 John

The Letters of John have received a lot of attention in the past few decades and many fine works have resulted. However, these works have not provided an examination of how the author carefully employed rhetoric to persuade his audience. While addressing the standard issues expected in a commentary, this one seeks to do so with the author's rhetorical construction as the primary focus. He designs every word, phrase, and sequence to move his audience to maintain its course or to redirect it according to what he deems most advantageous to it. This commentary seeks to show how detailing his rhetorical strategy helps us to interpret and apply these letters for today.

AUTHORSHIP

Most scholars assume that the Gospel of John, the Letters of John, and the Book of Revelation are all products of the bearers of the Johannine tradition centered in Ephesus at the close of the first and beginning of the second centuries AD. The Gospel of John is a collaborative effort of the Apostle John and his disciples, who created the core of this tradition. The prescripts of 2 and 3 John state that the letters are written by the "Elder," while 1 John does not disclose its author. This commentary assumes that all three Johannine Epistles are composed by the Elder, a primary bearer of the Johannine tradition (1:1–5; cf. 4:6).[1] This commentary also assumes

---

[1] For detailed discussion of authorship, see R. E. Brown, *The Epistles of John*, AB 30 (New York: Doubleday, 1982), 14–30; J. Painter, *1, 2, 3 John*, SP 18 (Collegeville: Liturgical Press, 2002), 44–51. P. Trebilco (*The Early Christians in Ephesus from Paul to Ignatius* [Tübingen: Mohr Siebeck, 2004/Grand Rapids: Eerdmans, 2007], 264–67) argues that the Elder wrote the Gospel as well as the Epistles of John.

that the Johannine Epistles were written in the order in which they are presented in the canon and address consecutive, developing events.[2]

AUDIENCE AND SITUATION ADDRESSED

Constructions of the situation addressed by the Johannine Letters are as diverse as those devised for the Johannine literature in general. This commentary constructs the situation from points of broad consensus and in dialog with rhetorical features of the letters.[3] The situation that the Elder addresses is rooted in a schism within the Johannine churches in Ephesus and elsewhere in Asia Minor at the end of the first century to the early second century AD. This schism resulted in two distinct groups: the Elder and his audience and the secessionists, who left the Johannine churches to be independent (2:18–19; 2 John 7).[4] First John is written to "the 'mother' Johannine group that spawned the Johannine churches in the outlying areas."[5] Although it has lost members to the secessionists (cf. 4:5), the churches have not changed their allegiance (2:12–14; 4:4).[6] Differing interpretations of Johannine tradition as represented in the Gospel of John (circa AD 90) caused the schism. As Brown states, "every idea of the secessionists (as reconstructed from the polemic of I and II John) can be plausibly explained as derivative from the Johannine tradition as preserved for us in GJohn [Gospel of John]."[7] Since the Johannine Letters do not

---

[2] Brown, *Epistles of John*, 30–35.
[3] For further discussion of the situation of 1 John, see Brown, *Epistles of John*, 47–115; R. E. Brown, *The Community of the Beloved Disciple* (New York: Paulist Press, 1979), 93–144; Painter, *1, 2, 3 John*, 79–94; S. S. Smalley, *1, 2, 3 John*, WBC 51 (Waco: Word Books, 1984), xxiii–xxxii; Trebilco, *Early Christians in Ephesus*, 268–92; U. C. von Wahlde, "Raymond Brown's View of the Crisis of 1 John: In the Light of Some Peculiar Features of the Johannine Gospel," in R. A. Culpepper and P. N. Anderson, eds., *Communities in Dispute: Current Scholarship on the Johannine Epistles*, ECL 13 (Atlanta: SBL Press, 2014), 19–45; J. M. Lieu, "The Audience of the Johannine Epistles," in *Communities in Dispute*, eds. Culpepper and Anderson, 123–40.
[4] In agreement with most commentators, I am assuming that there is only one group opposing the Elder. For discussion of attempts to identify the secessionists with known groups in antiquity, see Brown, *Johannine Epistles*, 47–68; J. Painter, "The Opponents in 1 John," in *The Quest for the Messiah*, 2nd edition (Nashville: Abingdon, 1993), 437–64.
[5] Brown, *Epistles of John*, 89. For further information on the nature of the audience of 1 John, see Brown, *Epistles of John*, 100–03; Smalley, *1, 2, 3, John*, xxxii.
[6] For a detailed study of the opponents of 1 John, see D. R. Streett, *They Went Out from Us: The Identify of the Opponents in First John*, BZNW 177 (Berlin: de Gruyter, 2011).
[7] Brown, *Epistles of John*, 72. The secessionists' claims are derivative of topics of the Gospel of John: being sinless, knowing God, abiding in God, and walking in the light (1:8, 10; 2:4, 6, 9; John 3:21; 8:12; 14:7; 17:22, 23, 26). Brown, *Epistles of John*, 69–86; Smalley, *1, 2, 3 John*, xxvi–xxx.

quote the Gospel of John, it may not have been used by the Elder. However, the Johannine tradition that the Gospel explicates is the basis of both the Elder's and the secessionists' interpretation.[8]

The Elder considers the secessionist interpretation of Johannine tradition to have diverged from the true understanding (2 John 9) to become deceitful lies (2:22; 3:7; 5:10; 2 John 7). The secessionists refuse to give authority to him and other tradition-bearers (4:6) and instead promote their own interpretation of Johannine tradition (2:26–27; 4:5; cf. 2 John 9–11). They successfully gather members from the neighboring region and elsewhere in the Johannine churches (1 John 4:5; 2 John 10) and pose the further threat of potentially adding even more converts to their number (2:26–27; 3:7; 2 John 9–11).

The differing interpretations of Johannine tradition derive from the closely related topics of Christology and ethics (3:23; cf. 2 John 5–11). The secessionists draw out the implications of the high Christology of the Johannine tradition, particularly of incarnation based on the preexistence of the Son of God. One such implication is to minimize the salvific significance of the earthly life and death of Jesus. The secessionists deny that Jesus is the Christ, the Son of God, come in the flesh, and come by water and blood (2:22–23; 4:2–3, 15; 5:1, 5–6, 9–13, 20; cf. 2 John 7). Rather, the baptism of John initiated the revelation of God's glory in Jesus, and the crucifixion was merely the continuation of this initial revelation (cf. John 1:14; 7:18; 8:50; 11:40; 14:9; 17:5, 24).[9] In response, the Elder stresses the salvific nature of Jesus's earthly life (1:7–9; 2:2, 12; 3:5, 8, 16; 4:9–10, 17) and death (5:6).

> The struggle in 1 John is still for a proper faith in Jesus as 'the Christ' and 'the Son of God' (5:1, 5); but now the stress is on the human career of God's Son: a 'Jesus Christ come in the flesh' (4:2; II John 7), a Jesus Christ who 'came ... in water and in blood' (1 John 5:6). The struggle is against those who 'negate the importance of Jesus' the man (4:3), against those who are too 'progressive' (II John 9).[10]

---

[8] For an in-depth study of the use of the Johannine tradition in the Letters of John, see R. Kakola, "The Reception and Development of the Johannine Tradition in 1, 2, 3 John," in T. Rasimus, ed., *The Legacy of John: Second-Century Reception of the Fourth Gospel*, NovTSup 132 (Leiden and Boston: Brill, 2010), 17–47.
[9] Brown, *Epistles of John*, 75.
[10] Brown, *Epistles of John*, 29. For further discussion of Christological problems, see Brown, *Epistles of John*, 50–54, 73–79.

From the high Christology of the Johannine tradition the secessionists also draw out implications for ethics. Minimizing the salvific importance of the life and ministry of the earthly Jesus led to moral indifference. Contributing to this moral indifference is the lack of emphasis upon ethics or moral teachings in Johannine tradition. Moral indifference does not mean that the secessionists are antinomian or libertines, for they consider themselves begotten by God, in fellowship and communion with God, and to abide in and love God (1:6; 2:4, 6; 4:20). The Elder does not accuse the secessionists of any vice, and his silence is unusual if vices were present. In ancient rhetorical practice, vices of opponents were emphasized to ruin their ethos or authority, and in early Christianity this emphasis took the form of vice lists (e.g., 2 Pet 2:12–22). The closest that the Elder comes to incriminating the secessionists' ethics is insinuating that they love the world (2:15–17) and do not help the needy (4:20).[11]

The secessionists also claim that they are free from the guilt of sin and have not sinned (1:8, 10). Apparently, they denied the possibility of sin after redemption on analogy of the sinlessness of Jesus. The claim of sinlessness in imitation of the sinlessness of Jesus is probably derived from Johannine tradition (John 3:18; 5:24; 8:46; 13:10; 20:22–23). The Elder does not refute these claims outright, later making similar claims himself (3:6, 9; 5:18). Rather, he conditions them, making it clear that sin is still a possibility in the Christian life and the secessionists should take it very seriously (1:6–2:2, 4, 6, 9).[12]

The secessionists are guilty of not loving fellow Johannine Christians (2:9–11; 3:10–18, 23; 4:78, 20). The presence of passages in the Johannine Letters that deal with the commandment to love (2:7–11; 4:7–21; 5:1–5; 2 John 4–6) suggest that the Elder speaks specifically of the love commandment when he claims that the secessionists do not keep the commandments (2:3–5; cf. 3:22). In the Gospel of John, every time Jesus mentions the commandment(s), love is at the forefront (13:34–35; 14:15; 15:10, 12, 17). In Johannine tradition, the brothers and sisters to be loved are members of the churches whose beliefs and practices conform to those of the group. Therefore, the secessionists do not love the Elder's group because of their secession over these very matters.[13]

---

[11] For further discussion of ethical issues, see Brown, *Epistles of John*, 54–55, 79–86.
[12] Brown, *Epistles of John*, 81–83.
[13] Brown, *Epistles of John*, 83–86; Smalley, *1, 2, 3 John*, xxvi–xxvii.

The Elder perceives the situation to be acutely negative. The secessionists do nothing but lie and deceive (1:6, 10; 2:4, 22; 3:7; 5:10; 2 John 7). Their doctrine is a lie and characteristic of the antichrist (2:22; 4:1–3), and their sinning makes them children of the devil (3:8). Christ will shame their followers at his coming (2:28). The Elder expects the situation to continue. It is a fulfillment of the expectation of the antichrist (2:8, 18, 22; 4:1–3) and, as such, a precursor of the second coming of Christ in the end-times already underway (2:8). It will remain until the end (2:18, 28; 4:17). However, the effects of the situation can be minimized by the faithful if they remain loyal to the Johannine tradition (4:4). To that end the Elder continually affirms the knowledge of the faithful and warns against being deceived (2:3, 24, 26–28; 3:7, 19–22; 4:13).

RHETORICAL CONSTRAINTS BEARING ON THE SITUATION

Rhetors seek to persuade using rhetorical constraints to direct the decisions and actions of their audiences to modify the situations addressed as the rhetors desire. Such constraints are of two main types: those inherent in a situation and those created by the rhetor. The former include traditions, beliefs, interests, and images familiar to their audiences, and the latter include the rhetors' proofs from ethos (authority), pathos (emotion), and logos (argumentation).[14]

The Elder uses several inherent and created rhetorical constraints as he tries to persuade his audience to navigate the situation with the secessionists as he deems most advantageous to it. While he does not appear to rely directly upon the Gospel of John to construct his letter,[15] he depends on Johannine tradition as originally understood by the Johannine tradition-bearers, of which the Gospel of John is a primary expression (1:1–3; 2:7, 24; 3:11; cf. 2 John 5–6).[16] One element of tradition with particular constraining force is the expectation that the antichrist will appear and signal the

---

[14] L. F. Bitzer, "The Rhetorical Situation," *Philosophy and Rhetoric* 1 (1968): 8.

[15] R. Bultmann (*The Johannine Epistles* [Philadelphia: Fortress, 1973], 1) argues that the author uses the Gospel, though "not slavishly." Brown (*Epistles of John*, 86–100) argues that "the genre, polemic, argumentation, and even structure of 1 John depends essentially on GJohn" (p. 86). See his chart on pp. 757–59, which shows the similarities between the Gospel of John and 1 John. Smalley (*1, 2, 3 John*, xxvii–xxx) argues that the author is consciously expounding the theology and tradition of the Gospel of John for the benefit of the opposition and occasionally relies directly on the text.

[16] Brown, *Epistles of John*, 97–100.

imminence of the return of Jesus Christ, something the Elder assumes has already occurred (2:18–19, 28; 4:1–6, 17). Any exhortation based on this fulfilled expectation takes on an added urgency because the right response of the faithful is tied directly to their fear of judgment and hope of eternal life.

The interests of the audience are also constraints. These interests include fellowship with the Johannine tradition-bearers and the Johannine churches as a whole (1:3, 7), cleansing from unrighteousness (1:9), abiding in the light (2:10), eternal life (2:17, 25; 3:14), mutual abiding in the Son and Father (2:24; 3:9, 24; 4:15), confidence in judgment at the return of Christ (2:28), being born of God (5:1), overcoming the world (5:4–5), and obtaining answers to prayer (5:14–15). The Elder upholds these interests as realities restricted to those who adhere to the traditional Christology and moral behavior of the Johannine churches.

The constraining power of images is prevalent and particularly strong in the portrayal of the secessionists as antichrists (2:18, 22; 4:3), false prophets (4:1–3), spirits of deceit and error (4:6), and liars and deceivers (1:6, 10; 2:4, 22, 26; 3:7; 4:20; 5:10; cf. 2 John 7). These images associate them with the forces of evil and with the final conflagration of good and evil. The Elder insinuates that to align with the secessionists is to be duped by their deceit and to be loyal to the powers of darkness.

The Elder's proofs function as constraints, particularly the proofs of ethos and logos. Ethos is moral character and conduct, the course of life (Aristotle, *Rhet.* 1.2.1356a.3–4; 1.8.1366a.6; Cicero, *De or.* 2.43.182–84; Quintilian, *Inst.* 6.2.8–19).[17] It "is related to men's nature and character, their habits and all the intercourse of life" (Cicero, *Or. Brut.* 37.128). Ethos acts as proof when the rhetor's goodness, moral righteousness, and goodwill are demonstrated throughout a discourse and enhance the persuasiveness of the message (Aristotle, *Rhet.* 1.8.1366a.6). The Elder shares the ethos of the revered Johannine tradition-bearers, the authoritative transmitters and interpreters of the Johannine tradition and witness to Jesus Christ as given by the Beloved Disciple (1:1–5; cf. 4:6).

Proofs from logos involve example and argument – induction and deduction, respectively (Aristotle, *Rhet.* 1.2.1356b.8; Cicero, *Inv.* 1.31–41). Deductive arguments include the enthymeme, which is an

---

[17] For a discussion of ethos, see G. A. Kennedy, *The Art of Persuasion in Greece* (Princeton: Princeton University Press, 1963), 91–93; J. Wisse, *Ethos and Pathos: From Aristotle, to Cicero* (Amsterdam: Adolf M. Hakkert, 1989).

"imperfect syllogism" (Quintilian, *Inst.* 5.14.2), "a proposition with a reason" (Quintilian, *Inst.* 5.10.2). The Elder's use of enthymemes to refute his opponents and present his own positions offers the constraint of logic (e.g., 2:8, 19).

There does not seem to be an ecclesiastical structure with authority analogous to the later presbyter–bishop that the Elder can use as a constraint. The source of truth in the Johannine Community is the Paraclete (John 14:15–17; 15:26–27; 16:13). This requires the Elder to appeal to the inner constraint of the knowledge of the truth obtained from the divine anointing of the Holy Spirit that provides guidance and discernment to each audience member (2:20, 27; 4:1).[18]

THE RHETORIC OF 1 JOHN

J. M. Lieu comments, "although 1 John does at times appear to use rhetorically effective strategies, the letter as a whole is not easily analyzed in these terms."[19] This assessment is certainly true regarding the arrangement of 1 John, which does not conform to Greco-Roman rhetorical conventions. However, it is not true of its invention and style, which can be analyzed according to those rhetorical conventions. The Elder did not necessarily study rhetoric or use rhetorical handbooks in the composition of this letter, but his rhetorical approach shares much with the rhetoric of his time as taught and found in those handbooks. Whatever his background, his letters are rhetorically sophisticated. I will use Greco-Roman rhetoric as a primary tool of interpretation in this commentary.

The three species of rhetoric are judicial (forensic), deliberative, and epideictic.[20] Simply put, these concern accusation and defense, persuasion and dissuasion, and praise and blame, respectively. First John is best classified as epideictic rhetoric.[21] The Elder seeks to increase the audience's commitment to the just and honorable values it already holds (Aristotle, *Rhet.* 1.9; [*Rhet. Alex.*] 3, 35; Quintilian, *Inst.* 3.7; Rhet. Her., 3.6–8) and the

---

[18] Brown, *Epistles of John*, 70, 93–94.
[19] J. M. Lieu, *I, II, & III John*, NTL (Louisville: Westminster John Knox, 2008), 36. For more on the rhetoric of 1 John, see H.-J. Klauck, "Zur rhetorischen Analyse der Johannesbriefe," *ZNW* 81 (1990): 205–24.
[20] G. A. Kennedy, *The Art of Rhetoric in the Roman World: 300 B.C.–A.D. 300* (Princeton: Princeton University Press, 1972), 7–23.
[21] T. C. Burgess, *Epideictic Literature*. University of Chicago Studies in Classical Philology 3 (Chicago: University of Chicago Press, 1902), 3.89–261 (reprinted London and New York: Garland, 1987).

proper understanding of and response to the Johannine tradition regarding Christology and ethics.[22] His choice of epideictic rhetoric indicates that he considers his audience to share the values he is espousing and not to have been led astray by the secessionists.

Using epideictic rhetoric, "[t]he speaker tries to establish a sense of communion centered around particular values recognized by the audience..."[23] This is the Elder's approach, for he begins by stating that fellowship with God and Jesus Christ is dependent upon acceptance of the values of the Johannine tradition-bearers, as well as fellowship with them and the faithful churches (1:3). Throughout the letter, the Elder encourages a community of shared values by using the topics of abiding in God, Christ, light, and love (*menō*; 2:6, 10, 14, 24, 28; 3:6, 24; 4:13, 16) and obeying or keeping God's word, Christ's word, and the commandments (*tereō*; 2:3, 4, 5; 3:22, 24; 5:3).

Epideictic rhetoric also calls upon universal values, eternal truths, and a god that vouches for these.[24] The Elder continuously appeals to principles and truths deemed by his community to be universal because they derive from God in the tradition received from Jesus through the Beloved Disciple (1:1–3, 5) and the anointing of the Spirit (2:20, 27). He affirms that the audience heard this tradition from its beginning (*akouō*; 2:7, 24; 3:11; cf. 2:18; 4:3) and knows it (*oida*; 2:20–21; 3:2, 5, 14, 15; 5:18–20; cf. 2:29).

Amplification, the main means of proof in epideictic rhetoric (Aristotle, *Rhet.* 1.9.1368a.38–40), is found in abundance in 1 John, as will be demonstrated throughout the following analysis.[25] Also, as is true of the style of epideictic rhetoric, 1 John is characterized by metaphor, frequent repetitions of parallels, similes, contraries, and doublets (Cicero, *Part. or.* 21.72).

Epideictic rhetoric praises and blames others to increase or decrease their ethos or authority (Quintilian, *Inst.* 3.4.6–9, 12–14). The Elder blames the secessionists because their Christology and ethics veer from the received tradition (2:22–23; 4:2–3; 5:10). They are without the Father and the Son (2:22–23; 3:6) and thus without life (5:12). They love the world (2:15–17) and hate their fellow Christians (2:9, 11; 3:10, 13, 15, 17; 4:20).

---

[22] Brown, *Epistles of John*, 47, 90–92; Smalley, *1, 2, 3 John*, xxviii.
[23] C. Perelman and L. Olbrechts-Tyteca, *The New Rhetoric: A Treatise on Argumentation*, trans. J. Wilkinson and P. Weaver (Notre Dame: University of Notre Dame Press, 1969), 51.
[24] Perelman and Olbrechts-Tyteca, *New Rhetoric*, 51.
[25] D. F. Watson, "Amplification Techniques in 1 John: The Interaction of Rhetorical Style and Invention," *JSNT* 51 (1993): 99–123.

They are liars without the truth (1:6, 8, 10; 2:4, 22; 4:20; 5:10) and try to deceive the churches as they do themselves (1:8; 2:26; 3:7). They make God a liar by denying their sin and God's testimony to the Son (1:10; 5:10). They are of the darkness (2:9, 11) and the spirit of error (4:6), false prophets (4:1) with human testimony (5:9), children of the devil (3:8), antichrists (2:18–19, 22; 4:3), part of the lawlessness of the last days (3:4), idolators (5:21), and mortal sinners (5:16–17). All this vituperation is itself amplification.

It is typical to find all three species of rhetoric in a single work, with one predominating and the other two supporting (Aristotle, [*Rhet. Alex.*] 5.1427b.31ff; Quintilian, *Inst.* 3.4.16). While 1 John is primarily epideictic rhetoric, it also contains portions of deliberative rhetoric. This combination is expected because epideictic and deliberative rhetoric are related, for what epideictic praises and blames, deliberative advises and dissuades (Quintilian, *Inst.* 3.7.28). First John is not deliberative rhetoric per se because it is not primarily intended to advise and dissuade the audience regarding a particular course of action.[26] Although the secessionists have been actively pursuing them (2:26; 3:7) and their faith may be shaken (2:3, 26–28; 3:19–22; 4:13–16a), the audience has not been persuaded to leave the Johannine churches and follow the secessionists (2:12–14; 4:4; 5:13; cf. 5:4–5).

However, there is still a deliberative posture throughout the argumentation. Deliberative rhetoric aims to persuade and dissuade an audience about what is advantageous, expedient, and necessary and their opposites – aims present in 1 John. The Elder deems the audience's adherence to the traditional understanding of Johannine tradition to be advantageous because the secessionist interpretation of the tradition is not salvific, and their appearance is a sign of the last days (2:18–19; 3:4; 4:1–3). Adherence to the tradition is necessary to be found faithful at the return of Christ (2:28; 4:17; cf. 3:2).

As is characteristic of epideictic rhetoric, the stasis or basis of the case laid out by 1 John is one of quality (Quintilian, *Inst.* 3.7.28; 7.4.1–3). With the stasis of quality, a claim is made that what is proposed is the best course of action to take under the circumstances, or there is an inquiry into the nature of something, as to whether it just, right, true, and profitable or their

---

[26] For a discussion of deliberative rhetoric, see D. F. Watson, *Invention, Arrangement, and Style: Rhetorical Criticism of Jude and 2 Peter*, SBLDS 104 (Atlanta: Scholars Press, 1988), 9–10.

opposites (Cicero, *Inv.* 1.9.12; Quintilian, *Inst.* 7.4.1-3).[27] The deceptive nature of the secessionists' doctrine and their immoral behavior are the subjects of inquiry. Based on traditional Johannine Christology and ethics, the Elder inquires into the true nature of Jesus Christ and the necessary and beneficial course of action or ethical walk to follow considering that nature. He exhorts his audience to adhere to the original understanding of Johannine tradition on matters of Christology and ethics.

RHETORICAL INSIGHTS INTO THE SITUATION OF THE LETTER

The rhetorical features of 1 John inform us about the rhetorical situation of the letter. This information can supplement and refine the reconstruction of the situation made by historical criticism. The Elder's choice of epideictic rhetoric indicates that he assumes that the churches he addresses agree with him about the matters addressed. If they did not agree with him, deliberative rhetoric of dissuasion and persuasion would have been more appropriate. Also, the Elder does not debate the secessionists directly as if they were in the churches or refute their teaching in detail as if they were posing a more immediate threat. For such a situation judicial rhetoric would have been imperative.

Two features of the *exordium* or introduction (1:1-4) indicate that the Elder assumes that the churches he addresses are favorable to him. First is the use of a brief introduction, one that takes the direct approach reserved for causes the audience perceives to be honorable. Second is the heavy reliance upon the teaching of the Johannine tradition-bearers of which the Elder is a member rather than dependence on formal proof.

The need to begin the *probatio* or the body of the epistle (1:5-5:12) with refutation (1:5-10) indicates that the Elder perceives the secessionists' teachings to present some challenge to his churches' loyalty. The fact that the Elder lists the teachings chosen for refutation and refutes them sequentially rather than all at once indicates their cumulative strength. However, his rebuttal of these teachings with simple objections based on personal authority as a member of the Johannine tradition-bearers rather than a more complex refutation indicates that the churches have not given their

---

[27] For a full discussion of stasis, see Kennedy, *The Art of Persuasion in Greece*, 303-14; G. A. Kennedy, *Greek Rhetoric under Christian Emperors* (Princeton: Princeton University Press, 1983), 73-86.

approval to secessionist teachings. The Elder treats the secessionists' teachings as threats only until their weaknesses are exposed.

There is much discussion about just what content in 1 John is derived from the secessionists and is polemical versus what content the Elder wished to cover that was unrelated or marginally related to the secessionists. This is particularly true of antitheses, which can be interpreted as refuting secessionist positions or as rhetorical teaching tools.[28] There is always the danger of mirror-reading, which Raymond Brown, whose polemical reading of 1 John I follow, has pointed out about his own reading. A rhetorical reading of 1 John demonstrates that the Elder has a primarily polemical agenda that he carries out with great subtlety by refining the tradition, amplifying topics, utilizing antithesis, and insinuating.

---

[28] For detailed discussion and a conclusion that 1 John is not primarily polemical, see Trebilco, *The Early Christians in Ephesus*, 273–90; B. Witherington III, *Letters and Homilies for Hellenized Christians. Volume 1: A Socio-Rhetorical Commentary on Titus, 1–2 Timothy and 1–3 John* (Downers Grove: IVP Academic, 2006), 427–31.

II Suggested Readings on the Letters of John

COMMENTARIES

A. E. Brooke. *A Critical and Exegetical Commentary on the Johannine Epistles*. ICC. Edinburgh: T. & T. Clark, 1912.
R. E. Brown. *The Epistles of John*. AB 30. Garden City: Doubleday, 1982.
R. E. Brown. *The Gospel According to John*, 2 vols. AB 29. New York: Doubleday, 1966, 1970.
R. Bultmann. *The Johannine Epistles*. Translated by R. P. O'Hara et al. Edited by R. W. Funk. Philadelphia: Fortress, 1973.
C. H. Dodd. *Johannine Epistles*. MNTC. New York: Harper & Brothers, 1946.
J. L. Houlden. *A Commentary on the Johannine Epistles*. HNTC. New York: Harper & Row, 1973.
H.-J. Klauck. *Der Erste Johannesbrief*. EKKNT 23/1. Zürich and Braunschweig: Benziger/Neukirchen-Vluyn: Neukirchener, 1991.
H.-J. Klauck. *Der Zweite und Dritte Johannesbrief*. EKKNT 23/2. Zürich and Braunschweig: Benziger/Neukirchen-Vluyn: Neukirchener, 1992.
J. M. Lieu. *I, II, & III John*. NTL. Louisville: Westminster John Knox, 2008.
I. H. Marshall. *The Epistles of John*. NICNT. Grand Rapids: Eerdmans, 1978.
J. Painter. *1, 2, and 3 John*. SP 18. Collegeville: Liturgical Press, 2002.
G. L. Parsenios. *First, Second, and Third John*. Paideia. Grand Rapids: Baker, 2014.
D. Rensberger. *1 John, 2 John, 3 John*. ANTC. Nashville: Abington, 1997.
R. Schnackenburg. *The Johannine Epistles*. Translated by R. Fuller and I. Fuller. New York: Crossroad, 1992.
S. S. Smalley. *1, 2, 3 John*. WBC 51. Waco: Word, 1984.
G. Strecker. *The Johannine Letters*. Translated by L. M. Maloney. Edited by H. Attridge. Hermeneia. Minneapolis: Fortress, 1996.
U. C. von Wahlde. *The Gospel and Letters of John: Volume 3: Commentary on the Three Johannine Letters*. Eerdmans Critical Commentary. Grand Rapids: Eerdmans, 2010.
B. F. Westcott. *The Epistles of St. John*. Grand Rapids: Eerdmans, 1966. First edition 1883.
B. Witherington III. *Letters and Homilies for Hellenized Christians. Volume 1: A Socio-Rhetorical Commentary on Titus, 1–2 Timothy and 1–3 John*. Downers Grove: IVP Academic, 2006.

MONOGRAPHS, ESSAYS, AND ARTICLES

R. J. Bauckham. *The Testimony of the Beloved Disciple*. Grand Rapids: Baker Academics, 2007.
J. Bogart. *Orthodox and Heretical Perfectionism in the Johannine Community as Evident in the First Epistle of John*. SBLDS 33. Missoula: Scholars Press, 1977.
M.-E. Boismard, "La connaissance de Dieu dans l'alliance nouvelle d'après la Première Lettre de Saint Jean." *RB* 56 (1949): 365–91.
R. E. Brown. *The Community of the Beloved Disciple*. New York: Paulist, 1979.

G. M. Burge. *The Anointed Community: The Holy Spirit in the Johannine Tradition.* Grand Rapids: Eerdmans, 1987.
J. Byron. "Slaughter, Fratricide and Sacrilege: Cain and Abel Traditions in 1 John 3." *Bib* 88 (2007): 526–35.
A. D. Callahan. *A Love Supreme: A History of the Johannine Tradition.* Minneapolis: Fortress, 2007.
J. C. Coetzee. "Life (Eternal Life) in John's Writings and the Qumran Scrolls." *Neot* 6 (1972): 46–62.
H. Conzelman. "Was von Anfang war." Pp. 194–201 in *Neutestamentliche Studien für R. Bultmann.* Edited by W. Eltester. BZNW 21. Berlin: Alfred Töpelmann, 1954. Repr. pp. 207–14 in his *Theologie als Schriftauslegung: Aufsätze zum Neuen Testament.* Munich: Kaiser, 1974.
O. Cullmann. *The Johannine Circle.* Translated by J. Bowden. Philadelphia: Westminster, 1976.
R. A. Culpepper. *The Johannine School.* SBLDS 26. Missoula: Scholars, 1975.
R. A. Culpepper. "The Pivot of John's Gospel." *NTS* 27 (1980): 1–31.
R. A. Culpepper and P. N. Anderson, eds. *Communities in Dispute: Current Scholarship on the Johannine Epistles.* ECL 13. Atlanta: SBL Press, 2014.
M. de Jonge, "Analysis of 1 John 1.1–4." *BT* 29 (1978): 322–30.
I. de la Potterie, "La notion de 'commencement' dans les écrits johanniques." Pp. 379–403 in *Die Kirche des Anfangs (FS Heinz Schürmann).* Edited by R. Schnackenburg, J. Ernst, and J. Wanke. Leipzig: St. Benno, 1977.
I. de la Potterie, *La vérité dans saint Jean.* 2 vols. AnBib 73–74. Rome: Biblical Institute Press, 1977.
P. J. De Plessis. *Teleios: The Idea of Perfection in the New Testament.* Kampen: Kok, 1959.
F. O. Francis. "The Form and Function of the Opening and Closing Paragraphs of James and 1 John." *ZNW* 61 (1970): 110–26.
B. E. Gärtner. "The Pauline and Johannine Idea of 'to Know God' against the Hellenistic Background." *NTS* 14 (1968): 209–31.
C. Haas, M. de Jonge, and J. L. Swellengrebel. *A Translator's Handbook on the Letters of John.* Helps for Translators. London: United Bible Societies, 1972.
J. Hills. "'Little Children, Keep Yourselves from Idols': 1 John 5:21 Reconsidered." *CBQ* 51 (1989): 285–310.
R. Kakola. "The Reception and Development of the Johannine Tradition in 1, 2, 3 John." Pp. 17–47 in *The Legacy of John: Second-Century Reception of the Fourth Gospel.* Edited by T. Rasimus. NovTSup 132. Leiden and Boston: Brill, 2010.
H.-J. Klauck. "Zur rhetorischen Analyse der Johannesbriefe." *ZNW* 81 (1990): 205–24.
C. R. Koester. "The Antichrist Theme in the Johannine Epistles and Its Role in Christian Tradition." Pp. 187–96 in *Communities in Dispute: Current Scholarship on the Johannine Epistles.* Edited by R. A. Culpepper and P. N. Anderson. ECL 13. Atlanta: SBL Press, 2014.
W. S. Kurz. "Intertextual Permutations on the Genesis Word in the Johannine Prologues." Pp. 179–90 in *Early Christian Interpretation of the Scriptures of Israel: Investigations and Proposals.* Edited by C. A. Evans and J. A. Sanders. JSNTSup 148. Sheffield: Sheffield Academic Press, 1997.
J. M. Lieu. "The Audience of the Johannine Epistles." Pp. 123–40 in *Communities in Dispute: Current Scholarship on the Johannine Epistles.* Edited by R. A. Culpepper and P. N. Anderson. ECL 13. Atlanta: SBL Press, 2014.
J. M. Lieu. *The Second and Third Epistles of John.* Edited by J. Riches. SNTW. Edinburgh: T. & T. Clark, 1986.
J. M. Lieu. *The Theology of the Johannine Epistles.* New Testament Theology. Cambridge: Cambridge University, 1991.
E. Malatesta. *Interiority and Covenant: A Study of einai en and menein en in the First Letter of Saint John.* AnBib 69. Rome: Biblical Institute Press, 1978.
B. M. Metzger. *A Textual Commentary on the Greek New Testament,* 3rd edition. New York: United Bible Societies, 1971.
J. Painter. *The Quest for the Messiah: The History, Literature and Theology of the Johannine Community,* 2nd edition. Nashville: Abingdon, 1993.
G. Richter. "Blut und Wasser aus der durchbohrten Seite Jesu (Joh 19,34b)." *MTZ* 21 (1970): 1–21. Repr. pp. 120–42 in *Studien zum Johannesevangelium,* Edited by J. Hainz. Biblische Untersuchungen 13. Regensburg: Pustet, 1977.
D. M. Scholer. "Sins Within and Sins Without: An Interpretation of 1 John 5:16–17." Pp. 230–46 in *Current Issues in Biblical and Patristic Interpretation.* Edited by G. F. Hawthorne. Grand Rapids: Eerdmans, 1975.

F. F. Segovia. *Love Relationships in the Johannine Tradition.* SBLDS 58. Chico: Scholars, 1982.
J.-L. Ska. "'Petits enfants, prenez garde aux idoles' 1 Jn 5,21." *NRTh* 101 (1979): 860-74.
G. S. Sloyan. *Walking in the Truth: Perseverers and Deserters.* New Testament in Context. Valley Forge: Trinity Press International, 1995.
D. R. Streett. *They Went Out from Us: The Identity of the Opponents in First John.* BZNW 177. Berlin: de Gruyter, 2011.
M. M. Thompson. "Intercession in the Johannine Community: 1 John 5.16 in the Context of the Gospel and Epistles of John." Pp. 225-45 in *Worship, Theology and Ministry in the Early Church: Essays in Honor of Ralph P. Martin.* Edited by M. J. Wilkins and T. Paige. JSNTSup 87. Sheffield: Sheffield Academic Press, 1992.
P. Trebilco. *The Early Christians in Ephesus from Paul to Ignatius.* Tübingen: Mohr Siebeck, 2004/ Grand Rapids: Eerdmans, 2007.
D. G. Van der Merwe. "Experiencing Fellowship with God According to 1 John 1:5-2:28: Dealing with the Change in Social Behavior." *Acta Patristica et Byzantina* 18 (2007): 231-62
D. G. Van der Merwe. "Family Metaphorics: A Rhetorical Tool in the Epistle of 1 John." *Acta Patristica et Byzantina* 20 (2009): 89-108.
U. C. von Wahlde. *The Johannine Commandments: 1 John and the Struggle for the Johannine Tradition.* New York: Paulist Press, 1990.
U. C. von Wahlde. "Raymond Brown's View of the Crisis of 1 John: In the Light of Some Peculiar Features of the Johannine Gospel." Pp. 19-45 in *Communities in Dispute: Current Scholarship on the Johannine Epistles.* Edited by R. A. Culpepper and P. N. Anderson. ECL 13. Atlanta: SBL Press, 2014.
D. F. Watson. "1 John 2:12-14 as *Distributio, Conduplicatio,* and *Expolitio*: A Rhetorical Understanding." *JSNT* 35 (1989): 97-110.
D. F. Watson. "Amplification Techniques in 1 John: The Interaction of Rhetorical Style and Invention." *JSNT* 51 (1993): 99-123.
D. F. Watson. "Antichrist." Pp. 50-53 in *Dictionary of the Later New Testament and Its Developments.* Edited by R. P. Martin and P. H. Davids. Downers Grove: InterVarsity Press, 1997.
D. F. Watson. "'Keep Yourselves from Idols': A Socio-Rhetorical Analysis of the *Exordium* and *Peroratio* of 1 John." Pp. 281-302 in *Fabrics of Discourse: Essays in Honor of Vernon K. Robbins.* Edited by D. B. Gowler, L. G. Bloomquist, and D. F. Watson. Harrisburg: Trinity Press International, 2003.
R. A. Whitacre. *Johannine Polemic: The Role of Tradition and Theology.* SBLDS 67. Chico: Scholars, 1982.

STUDIES IN GRECO-ROMAN RHETORIC

L. F. Bitzer. "The Rhetorical Situation." *Philosophy and Rhetoric* 1 (1968): 1-14.
T. C. Burgess. *Epideictic Literature.* University of Chicago Studies in Classical Philology 3. Chicago: University Press, 1902, 3.89-261 (reprinted London/New York: Garland, 1987).
G. A. Kennedy. *The Art of Persuasion in Greece.* Princeton: Princeton University Press, 1963.
G. A. Kennedy. *The Art of Rhetoric in the Roman World: 300 b.c.-a.d. 300.* Princeton: University Press, 1972.
G. A. Kennedy. *Greek Rhetoric under Christian Emperors.* Princeton: Princeton University Press, 1983.
H. Lausberg. *Handbook of Literary Rhetoric.* Edited by D. E. Orton and R. Dean Anderson. Translated by M. T. Bliss, A. Jansen, and D. E. Orton. Leiden: Brill, 1998.
J. Martin, *Antike Rhetorik.* Munich: C. H. Beck, 1974.
C. Perelman and L. Olbrechts-Tyteca. *The New Rhetoric: A Treatise on Argumentation.* Translated by J. Wilkinson and P. Weaver. Notre Dame: University of Notre Dame Press, 1969.
D. F. Watson. *Invention, Arrangement, and Style: Rhetorical Criticism of Jude and 2 Peter.* SBLDS 104. Atlanta: Scholars Press, 1988.
J. Wisse. *Ethos and Pathos: From Aristotle, to Cicero.* Amsterdam: Adolf M. Hakkert, 1989.

III Commentary on the Letter of 1 John

1:1–4: LETTER OPENING OR *EXORDIUM*

> 1:1 We declare to you what was from the beginning, what we have heard, what we have seen with our eyes, what we have looked at and touched with our hands, concerning the word of life –
>
> 1:2 this life was revealed, and we have seen it and testify to it, and declare to you the eternal life that was with the Father and was revealed to us –
>
> 1:3 what we have seen and heard we also declare to you so that you also may have fellowship with us; and truly our fellowship is with the Father and with his Son Jesus Christ.
>
> 1:4 We are writing[1] these things so that our joy[2] may be complete.

First John 1:1–4 is the letter opening. It exhibits the double, repetitive nature of some letter openings with the theme initially given (vv. 1–2) and then reformulated (v. 3), followed by a transitional verse alluding to joy (v. 4).[3]

---

[1] There is a choice between the readings "we (*graphomen hēmeis*) are writing" (emphatic) and "we (*graphomen*) are writing to you (*hymin*)." I agree with the *New Revised Standard Version* (NRSVue) in choosing the former because the latter is an assimilation to *hymin* in vv. 2 and 3, providing an object for the verb ("we write") and eliminating the awkward placement of the emphatic "we" (*hēmeis*) after the verb (B. M. Metzger, *A Textual Commentary on the Greek New Testament*, 3rd edition [New York: United Bible Societies, 1971], 709). This reading also allows the Elder to speak emphatically as a member of the Johannine School, the "We."

[2] *Hēmōn* ("our") is replaced in some manuscripts by *hymōn* ("your"), possibly under the influence of John 15:11 and 16:24 and due to the fact that a reference to "your" (the audience's) joy rather than the joy of the writer would be more typical at the end of the prescript (Metzger, *Textual Commentary*, 709). Also, this reading further allows the Elder to speak as a member of the Johannine tradition-bearers.

[3] F. O. Francis, "The Form and Function of the Opening and Closing Paragraphs of James and 1 John," *ZNW* 61 (1970): 110–26, esp. 121–24. Cf. Brown (*Epistles of John*, 176–78), who denies 1 John is an epistle.

It has been demonstrated elsewhere[4] and is the case here that the letter opening has many affinities with the rhetorical *exordium*, the initial element of rhetorical arrangement in which the rhetor prepares the audience for what will be addressed.[5] The *exordium* of epideictic rhetoric is often drawn from the person discussed, the audience, or the main subject (Aristotle, *Rhet.* 3.14.1414b.1–1415a.4; Rhet. Her. 3.6.11–12). The *exordium* of 1 John introduces the main subject: the word of life. The "word of life" (*logos tēs zoēs*) has been identified as Jesus Christ himself as Word (cf. John 1:1, 14)[6] and as the message about Jesus who is eternal life revealed (1:1–3, 5).[7] However, there is no need to be so precise: "[T]he life-giving word of the gospel is essentially a proclamation about Jesus who is the living Word of God."[8]

The length of the *exordium* is determined by the case being addressed. Simple cases require a brief introduction, while complicated, suspect, or unpopular cases require longer ones (Quintilian, *Inst.* 4.1.62). If the case is truly honorable, the *exordium* may be hastily set aside with just the introduction of the main subject (Aristotle, [*Rhet. Alex.*] 29.1437b.33ff; Cicero, *Inv.* 1.15.21). The brevity of the *exordium* and the introduction of the main subject in 1 John indicate that the Elder assumes that the case is simple and that the churches consider his case to be honorable.

The *exordium* aims to make the audience attentive, receptive, and well disposed.[9] The ethos of the speaker is central in this endeavor (Aristotle, *Rhet.* 3.14.1415a.7). Ethos is moral character demonstrated by the speaker's personal conduct through life and throughout a speech (Aristotle, *Rhet.* 1.2.1356a.4). The audience's perception of the speaker as a good person was considered the strongest influence in rhetorical presentation and central to obtaining the audience's goodwill in the *exordium* (Quintilian, *Inst.* 4.1.7; 5.12.9).

---

[4] Watson, *Invention, Arrangement, and Style*, 40–43, 95–96.
[5] For a full discussion of the *exordium*, see H. Lausberg, *Handbook of Literary Rhetoric*, eds. D. E. Orton and R. Dean Anderson; trans. M. T. Bliss, A. Jansen, and D. E. Orton (Leiden: Brill, 1998), 121–36, §§263–88.
[6] Bultmann, *Johannine Epistles*, 8; R. Schnackenburg, *The Johannine Epistles*, trans. R. Fuller and I. Fuller (New York: Crossroad, 1992), 59; G. Strecker, *The Johannine Letters*, ed. H. Attridge, trans. L. M. Maloney, Hermeneia (Minneapolis: Fortress, 1996), 10–11; cf. Smalley, *1, 2, 3 John*, 5–6.
[7] C. H. Dodd, *The Johannine Epistles*, MNTC (New York: Harper & Brothers, 1946), 4–5; Painter, *1, 2, 3 John*, 127–28.
[8] Smalley, *1, 2, 3 John*, 6; cf. Brown, *Epistles of John*, 164–67.
[9] For a detailed discussion of ethos, see Lausberg, *Handbook*, 113–17, §257.

1:1-4: Letter Opening or Exordium

In the *exordium* of 1 John the Elder's main concern is to establish his ethos and that of his message. The "we" of the *exordium* is a genuine plural.[10] It does not refer to the Johannine churches[11] since the Elder alternates back and forth from "we" to "you" throughout the *exordium*. This alternation places him in a separate category from the churches he addresses. Neither does "we" refer to the actual eyewitnesses of the ministry of Jesus,[12] nor to the Elder's prophetic self-consciousness as appropriating the experience of an eyewitness.[13] It is a distinctive we[14] and refers to "the tradition-bearers and interpreters of the larger Johannine Community who preserved a witness of auditory, visual, and manual contact with Jesus, probably stemming from the Beloved Disciple."[15] The Elder emphasizes his role as an official tradition-bearer in the Johannine churches and that his message is in agreement with the testimony of actual eyewitnesses of the revelation of the word of life from the baptism of Jesus onwards. The shift from the plural "we write" (*graphomen*) in the *exordium* (1:4) to the singular "I write" (*graphō*, 2:1, 7-8, etc.) or "I wrote" (*egrapsa*, 2:14, 21, etc.) after the *exordium* indicates that "the author of this Epistle is conscious of himself as having a personal authority, i.e., as being a representative of the bearers of the tradition."[16] In v. 1 he also aligns himself with the Paraclete, for the witness of the Paraclete was to "what was from the beginning" (John 15:26-27).[17] The Elder assumes the authority of the tradition-bearers of the Johannine churches and the divine origin and eyewitness nature of the tradition he is proclaiming.

---

[10] For a discussion of all the possibilities of the referent of "we," see Schnackenburg, *Johannine Epistles*, 51-56.

[11] A. von Harnack, "Das 'Wir' in den Johanneischen Schriften," *Sitzungsberichte der preussischen Akademie der Wissenschaften Philosophisch-historische Klasse* 31 (1923): 96-113. Smalley (*1, 2, 3 John*, 8) understands the referent of "we" more specifically as those in the Johannine churches that affirm apostolic witness as opposed to the secessionists.

[12] Marshall, *Epistles of John*, 106-07.

[13] Schnackenburg, *Johannine Epistles*, 55.

[14] With the possible exception of "our" (*hēmōn*) in v. 4, which may be inclusive of the Johannine tradition-bearers and churches addressed, used to emphasize the union that results from proclamation of the "we" in v. 3 (Bultmann, *Johannine Epistles*, 13; M. de Jonge, "Analysis of 1 John 1.1-4," *BT* 29 (1978): 327). However, it is unlikely that the strong distinctive "we" of vv. 1-3 and 5 would suddenly shift here.

[15] Brown, *Epistles of John*, 175 (cf. John 19:35; 20:31; 21:24). Brown, *Epistles of John*, 158-61, 172-73, 175; Bultmann, *Johannine Epistles*, 9-12; Painter, *1, 2, 3 John*, 130; Strecker, *Johannine Letters*, 11-12.

[16] Bultmann, *Johannine Epistles*, 11. Also, Brown, *Epistles of John*, 172-73.

[17] Brown, *Epistles of John*, 183-84.

It might be questioned how the Elder and the Johannine tradition-bearers, as recipients of eyewitness testimony, can talk in terms of hearing, seeing, and touching the revelation of the word of life in Jesus Christ. What is heard, seen, and touched is not the resurrection body of Christ as in the case of the Apostle Thomas (John 20:26-29). In antiquity followers of a religion could speak of vicariously experiencing the key moments of their religious heritage. Later generations understood themselves to share the religious experience of their forerunners in the faith (Joshua 24:7; Amos 2:10-11; Irenaeus, *Haer.* 5.1.1; Polycarp, *Phil.* 9:1; Gregory of Nazianzus, *Or. Bas.* 39.14).[18] The Elder has a physical connection with Jesus through the Beloved Disciple. Later the Elder includes the recipients of the letter in this more physical connection: "And we have seen and do testify that the Father has sent his Son as the Savior of the world" (4:14; cf. John 1:14).[19]

The Elder used the Prologue of the Gospel of John to create his *exordium*, further establishing his authority and that of his message. His modifications of the Prologue of John's Gospel place the revelation of Jesus Christ and its interpretation within the control of himself and the Johannine tradition-bearers who testify to Jesus using his own testimony about himself (John 3:31-32) through the Paraclete (John 15:26-27).[20] His modifications begin to establish the theological basis for his refutation of the secessionists who are misinterpreting Johannine tradition. In the comparison below, the Prologue of the Gospel of John is first and the *exordium* of 1 John is second in each grouping:

The "beginning" is the beginning before creation (1:1).
The "beginning" is the start of Jesus's public ministry (1:1).
All the apostles, including John, have "seen" (*theomai*) Christ's glory incarnate (1:14).
The Johannine tradition-bearers have "seen" (*theomai*) the revealed Christ (1:1).

---

[18] Dodd, *Johannine Epistles*, 13-16; Brown, *Epistles of John*, 160.
[19] Painter (*1, 2, 3 John*, 130) points out that this weakens the understanding of a distinction between "we" and "you" in the Prologue because both the Elder and other tradition-bearers and the members of the churches addressed have had this experience.
[20] For a more detailed discussion of the Elder's use of the Prologue of the Gospel of John, see Brown, *Epistles of John*, 176-87; Smalley, *1, 2, 3 John*, 5-6; A. Feuillet, *Le prologue de quatrième èvangile* (Paris: Desclée de Brouwer, 1968), 210-17; W. S. Kurz, "Intertextual Permutations on the Genesis Word in the Johannine Prologues," in C. A. Evans and J. A. Sanders, eds., *Early Christian Interpretation of the Scriptures of Israel: Investigations and Proposals*, JSNTSup 148 (Sheffield: Sheffield Academic Press, 1997), 179-90.

The "we" seeing (*horaō*) are all members of the Johannine Community (1:18).

The "we" seeing (*horaō*) are the Johannine tradition-bearers only (1:1-3).

The "word" (*logos*) is the preexistent Word (1:1, 14).

The "word" (*logos*) is the message preached by Jesus during his ministry and that message as proclaimed by the Johannine tradition-bearers (1:1-3).

Life (*zōē*) is revealed to the world by the Word (1:4).

Life (*zōē*) is personified and revealed to the Johannine tradition-bearers (1:2).

John the Baptist testifies (*martyreō*) to the light coming into the world (1:6-8, 15).

The Johannine tradition-bearers testify (*martyreō*) to eternal life revealed (1:2).

The *exordium* also briefly indicates some or all of the *topoi* or topics and propositions to be developed in the *probatio* or body of the work (Quintilian, *Inst.* 4.1.23-27). The Elder states that his main reason for writing is to proclaim the eyewitness testimony of the word of life to facilitate the churches' fellowship with the Johannine tradition-bearers, the Father, and the Son and to increase the joy of the Johannine tradition-bearers. The *exordium* also introduces several specific topics that the Elder will develop subsequently. In order of introduction, these include "beginning" (*archē*, 1:1), "hear" (*akouō*, 1:1, 3), "see" (*horaō*, 1:1-3), "eye" (*ophthalmos*, 1:1), "touch" (*theamai*, 1:1), "word" (*logos*, 1:1), "life" (*zōē*, 1:1, 2), "reveal" (*phaneroō*, 1:2), "testify" (*martyreō*, 1:2), "declare" (*apangellō*, 1:2, 3), "before (*pros*) the Father" (1:2), "Father" (*pater*, 1:2, 3), "fellowship" (*koinonia*, 1:3), "Son" (*hyios*, 1:3), "Jesus Christ" (*Iesous Christos*, 1:3), and "write" (*graphō*, 1:4).

The *exordium* establishes the groundwork for the polemic to be presented in the body of the letter. In 1:3, the wording "and truly our fellowship [i.e., the Johannine tradition-bearers] is with the Father and with his Son, Jesus Christ" is emphatic.[21] Allegiance to the tradition given by the Elder and the other tradition-bearers is presented as a prerequisite for fellowship not only with them, but also with the Father and the Son.

---

[21] The *kai ... de* construction and the possessive adjective form of "ours" (*hemeteros*) are emphatic. C. F. D. Moule, *An Idiom Book of New Testament Greek*, 2nd edition (Cambridge: Cambridge University Press, 1959), 165.

Fellow Christians, the Father, and the Son are a unity in Johannine thought (1 John 2:22-24; 2 John 9; John 14:9; 17:3, 10-11, 21). This emphasis is strong because the secessionists teach what the Elder deems to be a nonsalvific interpretation of Johannine tradition that is destroying this fellowship, especially through the schism with the churches that it promotes. Also, the stress upon the physical nature of the manifestation of the eternal life – that it could be heard, seen, and touched – lays the foundation for the polemic against the secessionists' denial that Jesus Christ came in the flesh (4:2-3; 2 John 7) by water and blood (5:6).

The ancient world attributed greater authority to older tradition, and to tradition with an authoritative source or broad support of custom. This is especially obvious in the authority accorded maxims and judgments (*kriseis*), "opinions which can be attributed to nations, peoples, wise men, distinguished citizens, or famous poets" (Quintilian, *Inst.* 5.11.36). The Elder's emphasis that his message is "from the beginning" and his use of the distinctive "we" of the Johannine tradition-bearers stress the age and the authoritative origin of his tradition about the word of life. This undergirds the following polemic, which seeks to undermine the secessionists' newer interpretation of the tradition.

The initial portion of the *exordium* (vv. 1-3) is a single sentence, with the main subject and verb, "we proclaim" (*apangellomen*), located near the beginning of v. 3. The object of the sentence, the word of life, is located near the end of v. 1; that is, before the subject and verb, which is the reverse of the usual. This grammatical reversal places the focus on the message proclaimed rather than the proclamation of the message.[22] In addition, the intervening v. 2 is an example of the figure of parenthesis (Quintilian, *Inst.* 9.3.23-26), which offers a brief explanation. Here the parenthesis explains the relationship between the object of the word of life and the subject of the Johannine tradition-bearers who proclaim it – the word was seen and revealed to them; that is, it gives them direct revelation and authority.

The *exordium* opens with the phrase "what was from the beginning" as the content of the proclamation. The initial neuter relative pronoun "what" (*ho*) that was from the beginning is used five times and refers comprehensively to Jesus, his person, his ministry, and his works.[23] What is proclaimed is from the "beginning" (*archē*), a term that has legal and

---

[22] I. H. Marshall, *The Epistles of John*, NICNT (Grand Rapids: Eerdmans, 1978), 100.
[23] Brown, *Epistles of John*, 154; Smalley, *1, 2, 3 John*, 6-7; Strecker, *Johannine Letters*, 10-11.

1:1-4: Letter Opening or Exordium

rhetorical functions in the Greco-Roman world where it was used to promise a full rendition of circumstances. In this case, the Elder is promising to fully explain the proclamation.[24] A big question is: What is the beginning being proclaimed?

The beginning has been identified as the beginning before creation, as in the Prologue of the Gospel of John (1:1) upon which this *exordium* is modeled and as later in this letter in 2:13-14, or as the beginning of creation as in Genesis 1:1 upon which the opening of both the Gospel of John and this letter are modeled.[25] It has also been defined as the beginning of the revelation of the word of life with the incarnation of Jesus (John 1:14)[26] or the beginning of his public ministry at his baptism and as he revealed himself to his disciples (1 John 2:7, 24; 3:11; 2 John 5, 6; John 15:27).[27]

All of these identifications make perfect sense. Jesus the word was in the beginning before creation and at creation and was revealed as the word at his incarnation and the beginning of this ministry. Ambiguity in rhetoric and in the Johannine literature is common and may very well be at play here.[28] Also, in the Prologue of the Gospel of John there is swift movement from the preincarnation of Jesus the Word in the beginning before creation to Jesus the incarnate Word (John 1:1, 14). This shift cautions us about too finely determining the meaning of "the beginning."

The word of life from the beginning proclaimed by the Johannine tradition-bearers was revealed (v. 2). Johannine tradition uses the verb "reveal" (*phaneroō*) of revelation that can be perceived through action, not revelation by words (John 2:11; 3:21; 7:4; 9:3; 1 John 2:19, 28; 3:2, 10; 4:9).

---

[24] G. L. Parsenios, *First, Second, and Third John*, Paideia (Grand Rapids: Baker, 2014), 39-40.

[25] H. Conzelmann, "Was von Anfang war," in W. Eltester (ed.), *Neutestamentliche Studien für R. Bultmann*, BZNW 21 (Berlin: Alfred Töpelmann, 1954), 194-201; repr. in his *Theologie als Schriftauslegung: Aufsätze zum Neuen Testament* (Munich: Kaiser, 1974), 207-14; Marshall, *Epistles of John*, 100-01; Strecker, *Johannine Letters*, 8-11.

[26] Bultmann, *Johannine Epistles*, 9; Schnackenburg, *Johannine Epistles*, 56-58; Painter, *1, 2, 3 John*, 132-33.

[27] I. de la Potterie, "La notion de 'commencement' dans les écrits johanniques," in R. Schnackenburg, J. Ernst, and J. Wanke, eds., *Die Kirche des Anfangs* (FS Heinz Schürmann) (Leipzig: St. Benno-Verlag, 1977), 379-403; Brown, *Epistles of John*, 155-58.

[28] For ambiguity in the Greco-Roman rhetorical tradition, see Cicero, *Inv.* 1.13.17; 2.40.116-41.121; Rhet. Her. 1.11.19; 1.12.20; 2.11; Quintilian, *Inst.* 3.6.43-46, 88; 7.9; Lausburg, *Handbook*, 96-97, §222-23; J. Martin, *Antike Rhetorik* (Munich: C. H. Beck, 1974), 44, 50-51. For ambiguity in Johannine literature, see E. Richard, "Expressions of Double Meaning and Their Function in the Gospel of John," *NTS* 31 (1985): 96-112.

It describes Jesus's earthly ministry to take away sin (1 John 3:5) and destroy the works of the devil (3:8), his resurrection appearances (John 21:1, 14), and his promised return (1 John 2:28). Here eternal life that was with the Father is revealed in the incarnation and ministry of Jesus (cf. John 1:1, 14). The Elder emphasizes that the proclamation of the Johannine tradition-bearers is rooted in the incarnation that was seen, touched, and heard.[29]

In v. 3, "fellowship" (*koinonia*) is between those who are in Christ and remain faithful to him. It is grounded in the fellowship of God and Jesus Christ, between a Father and Son, which only the Son can make possible for believers (John 14:6–11). Adherence to the eyewitness testimony passed on by the Johannine tradition-bearers, a testimony that is the proper understanding of the person and work of Jesus Christ, sustains this fellowship (cf. John 17:20–21). As the Elder will explain later, to deny the nature of Jesus as the Christ is to veer from their testimony and not have the Son or the Father (2:22–24). The same is true for not accepting God's offer of life through the Son (5:11–12). Christology is not an abstract enterprise for scholars but the bedrock for fellowship with other Christians, Jesus Christ, and God. This is an indirect attack on the secessionists who departed from the Christology of the Johannine churches and from their fellowship (2:19) and consequently from fellowship with God and Christ as well.

The concept of having fellowship with God is only found in Johannine literature in 1:3 and 6–7. As such, it is possible that this is a claim of the secessionists that the Elder denies is possible for anyone not in fellowship with the Johannine Community (1:3) and walking in darkness (1:6–7). Fellowship with God is synonymous with: "to be in God" (2:5; 5:20); "to have" the Father (2:23) or the Son (5:12), "Father and the Son" (2 John 9), or God (2 John 9); "to know God" (2:3, 13, 14; 3:6; 4:6–8); and "to see God" (3 John 11). It is also to abide: in God through obedience (2:6) and proper confession of Jesus as the Son of God (4:13–16); in the Father and the Son through obedience to the tradition (2:24); and in Jesus through the teaching of the Holy Spirit (2:27–28) and not sinning (3:6). Fellowship with God is also synonymous with God living in us (4:12), God's seed in us (3:9),

---

[29] In Johannine literature, outside the prefaces of the Gospel of John (1:1, 14) and 1 John (1:1), "word" (*logos*) refers to a message. Thus, some interpreters understand the referent of the "word" revealed here as a message only, not Jesus as the word of life. Considering Johannine ambiguity, this understanding of *logos* cannot be ruled out (Parsenios, *1 John, 2 John, and 3 John*, 45–46).

God's love (3:17) and eternal life in us (3:15), and Jesus in us through obedience to the love commandment (3:24).[30]

In v. 4, the Elder's use of joy is like the Apostle Paul's rejoicing over the health of the Christian communities he addresses (2 Cor 2:3; 7:13; Phil 1:4; 1 Thess 3:9) and the Elder's expressions of joy elsewhere (2 John 12; 3 John 4). The joy of fellowship is completed or perfected by adhering to the traditional teaching of the faithful community and maintaining fellowship with it, for the faithful have the fellowship with the Father and Son.[31]

Verse 4 contains the epistolary motivation-for-writing formula that gives a statement of authorship, reference to the act of writing, and reiteration of the reason for writing. It marks a major transition in a letter and here marks the end of the letter opening or *exordium* and the beginning of the letter body or *probatio*.[32] This formula will recur in 5:13 at the beginning of the letter closing to form an *inclusio* for the entire letter.

> ### A CLOSER LOOK: LIFE/ETERNAL LIFE
>
> Life (*zōē*) or eternal life (*zōē aiōnios*) is a rich and central topic in Johannine thought. Sin leaves humanity in darkness and death, excluded from life (1 John 5:11–13). God is the only one who can bestow life and bring humanity back to light and life. God's gift of life in the Son is an expression of God's love (1 John 4:9; John 3:16). Jesus the Son is life (1 John 1:1–2; 5:20; John 14:6), the resurrection and the life (John 11:25), the truth and life (John 14:6), bread of life (John 6:35, 48), and light of life (John 8:12). He came to the world to bring it life (John 3:16; 6:50–51; 10:10).
>
> The word mediates life (1 John 1:1–3), and believing Jesus's words brings life (1 John 5:11–13; John 3:14; 5:24; 6:40, 47, 68; 11:25–26; 20:31). Failure to believe in Jesus Christ leaves one in darkness and

---

[30] For further detail on fellowship with God, see D. G. Van der Merwe, "Experiencing Fellowship with God According to 1 John 1:5–2:28: Dealing with the Change in Social Behavior," *Acta Patristica et Byzantina* 18 (2007): 231–62.

[31] Typically, a letter opens with a wish for the joy of the recipients, but here it is the joy of the Johannine tradition-bearers that is wished for. This uncommon usage led some scribes to change the reading to "your joy" so that the verse complies with letter conventions.

[32] J. L. White, *The Body of the Greek Letter*, SBLDS 2 (Missoula: Scholars Press, 1972), 3, 5, 27, 33, 41, 62–63, 84–86, 97–98; J. L. White, *Light from Ancient Letters*, FF (Philadelphia: Fortress, 1986), 204–05.

death (1 John 5:16). Life requires knowing God and Christ (John 17:2–3). This new life also requires an ethical walk of obedience to Jesus Christ (John 8:51–52; 12:25–26), especially loving others as an expression and extension of that life (1 John 3:14–18).[33]

BRIDGING THE HORIZONS

The letter opening or *exordium* of 1 John illustrates the importance of church tradition as faithfully passed down from the eyewitnesses through faithful interpreters. It is a tradition based on apostolic eyewitness testimony whose interpretation cannot be significantly altered and still be called traditional or even Christian. Jesus is the Christ who is life revealed to humanity in his incarnation and earthly ministry and by the Holy Spirit. Any Christology that contorts or lessens this revelation veers from apostolic witness, which anchors that tradition. The Elder assumes the church proclaims the gospel, not reinvents it. It molds its proclamation to best reach the ears of its hearers as he does, but the content remains rooted in the tradition.

Christology has implications for fellowship with other Christians and with God. Fellowship with God is intimate and only through the Son. Such fellowship is not limited to moments of worship or spiritual highs but is permanently the possession of believers who have eternal life. There are theological and ethical criteria for fellowship with God including accepting the proclamation of the Johannine churches and its love commandment, the need for a pure ethical walk, and observing the teaching of the Holy Spirit.

It is in this fellowship that the joy of the Christian community is complete. Individual and corporate joy are intertwined in faithful response to the word of life as proclaimed from tradition. That word of life includes God's love in giving the Son as an atoning sacrifice to create a joyful community in loving fellowship with God and the Son and each other.

---

[33] Strecker, *Johannine Letters*, 16–19; J. C. Coetzee, "Life (Eternal Life) in John's Writings and the Qumran Scrolls," *Neot* 6 (1972): 46–62.

1:5–5:12: AN OVERVIEW OF THE RHETORIC OF THE LETTER BODY OR *PROBATIO*

The body of the letter is 1:5–5:12. Here the Elder elaborates the main topic of the word of life and other topics briefly introduced in the opening of the letter, and he also introduces new topics. From a rhetorical perspective, this section is the *probatio*, which has the same purposes as the body of a letter with a focus on how an audience hears the letter when it is read aloud to them much like a speech, as was the custom. The *probatio* of 1 John is rhetorically sophisticated, and what follows is an overview of its rhetorical features and strategies.

The *probatio* is that element of arrangement where writers/rhetors muster arguments to support their propositions and refute those of their opposition (Quintilian, *Inst.* 5.1–14).[34] These propositions can be given in a list (*partitio*; Quintilian, *Inst.* 4.5.1–28), implicitly or explicitly stated in a narrative of the facts of the case (*narratio*; Quintilian, *Inst.* 3.9.7; 4.2.54, 79), or placed at the beginning of every proof (Quintilian, *Inst.* 4.4.1). Epideictic rhetoric, such as 1 John, needs neither a *partitio* nor a *narratio* (Rhet. Her. 3.7.13), and we find neither in 1 John. The propositions in this letter are typically found at the beginning of each proof, often as part of the refutation of secessionist claims.[35]

Epideictic rhetoric needs some proof if the matter being discussed is incredible (Aristotle, *Rhet.* 3.17.1417b.3) or practical matters are being addressed for which some defense is needed (Quintilian, *Inst.* 3.7.4–6). The entire matter of 1 John is incredible – distorting the tradition upon which the Johannine churches were founded. There are also practical and ethical matters arising from the secessionist break with the Johannine churches that their modification of tradition spawned, especially in matters of Christology. The Elder employs proof as he seeks to encourage his churches to hold on to the tradition and Christian practice as it was originally proclaimed and taught.

If proof is used in the *probatio* of epideictic rhetoric, it must be ethical (based on ethos) and/or demonstrative (such as enthymemes, a proposition with a supporting reason; Aristotle, *Rhet.* 3.17.1418a.11–1418b.12). As is already clear in the *exordium* (1:1–4), the ethos of the Elder plays a

---

[34] For a detailed discussion of the *probatio*, see Lausberg, *Handbook*, 1.160–204, §§348–430.
[35] For a full discussion of the *probatio* of epideictic rhetoric, see Aristotle, *Rhet.* 3.17.1417b.3; Rhet. Her. 3.7.13–15.

key role throughout 1 John. The Elder states many propositions without formal proof, indicating that he assumes that the churches agree with his propositions and the values they espouse. There are also several enthymemes scattered throughout therobation that draw out the ethical implications of a proposition more than try to convince the churches of its truth, the latter of which is typical of formal proofs required to address a hostile audience.

Instead of formal proof, the content of epideictic rhetoric in general and the *probatio* in particular is the amplification of topics and statements advanced as certain (Aristotle, *Rhet.* 1.9.1368a.38–40; 3.17.1417b.3; [*Rhet. Alex.*] 3; Cicero, *Part. Or.* 21.71; Quintilian, *Inst.* 3.7.6). Amplification is most suited to epideictic rhetoric (Aristotle, *Rhet.* 1.9.1368a.40; 2.18.1392a.5; [*Rhet. Alex.*] 3.1426b.17ff; 6.1428a.1ff.), and brief and frequent amplification is the norm when it is employed (Rhet. Her. 3.8.15). Contrasting topics are characteristic of epideictic rhetoric and include the noble–disgraceful, virtue–vice, and useful–expedient (Aristotle, *Rhet.* 1.9; 2.22.1396a.8; 3.17.1417b.3; Cicero, *De or.* 2.84–85; *Part. Or.* 21–23; Rhet. Her. 3.6–8). As epideictic rhetoric, all of these features are typical of 1 John.[36]

Exhortation is also typical of epideictic rhetoric, for only a slight change of wording distinguishes exhortation from praise and blame (Aristotle, *Rhet.* 1.9.1367b.35–1368a.37). Epideictic rhetoric assigns what is noble, virtuous, and useful and their opposites as characteristics of people, but can just as easily be the subject of exhortation about what those people should embrace or reject. Exhortation is a type of amplification (Cicero, *Part. Or.* 17.58) and is expected in the *probatio* of epideictic rhetoric. Antithesis is yet another feature of epideictic rhetoric (Cicero, *Or. Brut.* 12.38), and there are many antitheses in the *probatio* of 1 John.

The structure of the *probatio* of 1 John is elusive, partly because epideictic rhetoric has fewer conventions for arrangement than judicial or deliberative rhetoric. In epideictic rhetoric, the arrangement of elements and the development of topics are extremely diverse (Cicero, *Part. Or.* 4.12). This is compounded by the frequent use of amplification. The *probatio* of 1 John exhibits a creative and varied development of topics using amplification. Topics are introduced, then continually reintroduced in relation to other topics, creating a complex web of informative interrelationships.

---

[36] D. F. Watson, "Amplification Techniques in 1 John: The Interaction of Rhetorical Style and Invention," *JSNT* 51 (1993): 99–123.

1:5–5:12: An Overview of the Rhetoric of the Letter Body or Probatio

The *probatio* of 1 John confronts us immediately with refutation.[37] "The refutation is that part of an oration in which arguments are used to impair, disprove, or weaken the confirmation or proof in our opponents' speech" (Cicero, *Inv.* 1.42.78). Judicial rhetoric usually employs refutation, not epideictic rhetoric. However, refutation here is not of charges made against the Elder or his audience in any formal sense, as they would be in a judicial context, but of propositions of the secessionists that challenge the Johannine tradition. To elicit the churches' adherence to this tradition, the Elder is distinguishing which propositions of the secessionists do not deserve adherence and why. Increasing and decreasing adherence to values and loyalties is a key purpose of epideictic rhetoric.

After the *exordium* in deliberative rhetoric the propositions of the opposition are stated one at a time and subsequently disproven (Aristotle, [*Rhet. Alex.*] 34.1440a.5ff.). Beginning the *probatio* with refutation is particularly expedient when the opposition has convinced the audience that their propositions are probable (Aristotle, *Rhet.* 3.17.1418b.15; [*Rhet. Alex.*] 36.1443b.25ff.). In refutation, if the opponent has spoken first and the arguments are numerous, strong, and have met with some approval, the rhetor must refute them first in order "to destroy the impression made by the adversary" (Aristotle, *Rhet.* 3.17.1418b.13–15). The fact that the Elder places refutation at the beginning of his *probatio* implies that the propositions he refutes engender some conviction and approval in his audience. He first refutes the arguments of the secessionists so that a call to adhere to traditional values will be clearly heard.

Two approaches to refutation are to confront the arguments of the opposition as a group if they are weak and individually if they have a cumulative force (Quintilian, *Inst.* 5.13.11–15). Refutation point by point is the proper and safest method of refutation (Cicero, *Part. Or.* 12.44; Quintilian, *Inst.* 5.13.28). When refuting an opponent's arguments one by one, Quintilian advises, "In no circumstances must we repeat our opponent's remarks together with their Confirmation, or help him in developing any topic ..." (Quintilian, *Inst.* 5.13.27). The Elder lists the arguments of the opposition Individually, which indicates that these arguments have cumulative force and are too strong to quickly brush aside as a group. He does so without ever reiterating the accompanying proof of the

---

[37] For further discussion of refutation, see Aristotle, *Rhet.* 2.25–26; 3.17.1418b.13–15; [*Rhet. Alex.*] 13; 34.1440a.5–25; 36.1443b.25–1444b.8; Cicero, *Inv.* 1.42.78–51.96; Quintilian, *Inst.* 5.13.

arguments, which would only further strengthen them in the minds of his audience.

The Elder does not refute the claims of the secessionists with enthymemes, syllogisms, or more elaborate refutational schemes. One common method of refutation is the syllogism that a rhetor uses when the opponent's "arguments have met with approval" (Aristotle, *Rhet.* 3.117.1418b.15). The Elder does not take this approach, further indicating that his audience is not fully convinced by the secessionists (only 2:9 is a refutation by syllogism). Rather than using elaborate arguments, he rejects secessionist claims and asserts his own claims based on his authority as a bearer of the Johannine tradition rooted in eyewitness testimony to Jesus.

1:5–2:2: GOD AS LIGHT AND ITS IMPLICATIONS

> **1:5** This is the message we have heard from him and proclaim to you, that God is light and in him there is no darkness at all.
>
> **1:6** If we say that we have fellowship with him while we are walking in darkness, we lie and do not do what is true;
>
> **1:7** but if we walk in the light as he himself is in the light, we have fellowship with one another, and the blood of Jesus his Son cleanses us from all sin.
>
> **1:8** If we say that we have no sin, we deceive ourselves, and the truth is not in us.
>
> **1:9** If we confess our sins, he who is faithful and just will forgive us our sins and cleanse us from all unrighteousness.
>
> **1:10** If we say that we have not sinned, we make him a liar, and his word is not in us.
>
> **2:1** My little children, I am writing these things to you so that you may not sin. But if anyone does sin, we have an advocate with the Father, Jesus Christ the righteous,
>
> **2:2** and he is the atoning sacrifice for our sins, not for ours only but also for the sins of the whole world.

This opening of the letter body or *probatio* of 1 John is a proposition that God is light (1:5). This proposition is a theological anchor for the remainder of the letter. The revealed nature of God assesses the truth of any claim by the Elder and his churches or the secessionists. The proposition of 1:5 is followed in 1:6–2:2 by a purposeful construct of six conditional clauses in three pairs. The Elder introduces three claims of the secessionists and his refutation of them introduced by "if we say" (*ean eipōmen*, 1:6, 8, 10). He follows each of these with a counterclaim derived from the Johannine tradition that supports his refutation, each beginning with "if" (*ean*, 1:7, 9; 2:1). There is an ascending order of importance in both the secessionist claims and the Elder's refutation of them. The secessionist claims move from having fellowship with God (v. 6), having no sin (v. 8), and not having sinned (v. 10). The Elder's refutation moves from lying (v. 6), to self-deception (v. 8), to making God a liar (v. 10). The entire section is a thinly veiled vilification of the secessionists' theology and ethics.

By beginning with a refutation of secessionist claims and doing so individually, the Elder assumes that their teaching is making or could make some inroads with the faithful (Aristotle, *Rhet.* 3.17.1418b.13–15; [*Rhet. Alex.*] 36.1443b.25ff.). Refuting these claims individually rather than as a group is a strong method of refutation (Cicero, *Part. or.* 12.44; Quintilian, *Inst.* 5.13.28). He refutes each of their claims by objection of their reasoning (Aristotle, *Rhet.* 2.25.1402a.1–1402b.7; 2.26.1403a.3–4; 3.17.1418b.14; Quintilian, *Inst.* 5.13.16). By using this approach, the Elder appears to consider these claims – while somewhat persuasive to some – weak enough that denying them is all that is needed to refute them (Quintilian, *Inst.* 5.13.15–16). Rather than formally refuting secessionist claims, the Elder relies upon his authority and the tradition he represents to reject them and make counterclaims (Cicero, *Inv.* 1.42.79; *De or.* 2.53.215). His refutation is based on the common topic of the possible–impossible (Aristotle, [*Rhet. Alex.*] 13; 34, 1440.5ff.). Considering their behavior, what the secessionists are claiming for themselves is impossible by the nature of the spiritual life as alleged by the Elder and the tradition he represents.

1:5: The Governing Proposition

As the Elder models the Prologue of 1 John on the Prologue of the Gospel of John, there is also a resemblance between the shifts to the main bodies of these two texts. The opening of v. 5 ("this is the message") parallels the opening of John 1:19 ("this is the testimony"), and both begin the bodies of their texts after the Prologue.[38] In 1 John the opening formula "and this is" (*kai houtos estin*) and variants (1:5; 2:25; 3:8, 23; 4:9, 10, 17, 21; 5:4, 11, 14), and the related formulas translated "for this is" (*hoti houtos estin*, 3:11; 5:9;

---

[38] Brown, *Epistles of John*, 225.

houtos gar estin, 5:3), are used throughout the letter body to define or explain a topic that has been previously discussed. Here the Elder defines more specifically the message heard and proclaimed (1:1–4).[39] He introduces a proposition that is a major component of the revealed word of life that he wishes to proclaim in more detail to the faithful: "God is light and in him is no darkness at all" (cf. John 8:12). The proposition is based on the Old Testament portrayal of God as light (Pss 27:1; 36:9; 104:2; Isa 10:17; 60:19–20; Mic 7:8) and is related to the description in the Gospel of John of the coming of Jesus as light (John 1:4–9; 3:19–21; 12:46) and Jesus's own self-designation as the Light (John 8:12; 9:5; cf. 12:35–36, 46). Light is God's nature and holiness. It entered the world with the incarnation of God in Jesus Christ (John 1:9; 3:19). God as light determines, influences, guides, and shapes the Christian life. The life of the redeemed includes walking in the light (1:7) and abiding in the light and loving fellow Christians (2:10).

The proposition is highly emphatic. It employs rhetorical reduplication, saying the same thing twice – once positively and once negatively. The negative component uses a double negative (*ouk . . . oudemia*) for further emphasis: Darkness is *absolutely* not in the nature of God. The Elder's implicit ethical challenge is that all Christians must be walking and abiding in the light to be in fellowship with God who is light. All those walking and abiding in darkness are not in fellowship with God because there is no darkness in God.

The proposition's affirmation that in God there is no darkness is the first instance of the topic of interiority using the formula "to be in" (*einai en*). This formula occurs eighteen times in 1 John, and four times "in" (*en*) occurs with "to be" (*einai*) understood. The topic can be grouped into three broad categories: (1) indwelling of God and Jesus in the Christian and vice versa (2:5; 4:4; 5:20); (2) indwelling or lack thereof of other realities in the Christian such as love, truth, word of God, and sin (1:8, 10; 2:4, 10, 15; 3:5); and (3) miscellaneous uses (1:5, 7; 2:9, 11, 15–16; 4:3–4; 17–18; 5:11).[40]

The proposition of v. 5 was "heard from him" – that is, Jesus. It is not a saying of Jesus known from the written Gospels but is Jesus himself

---

[39] Brown, *Epistles of John*, 192; Bultmann, *Johannine Epistles*, 15, n. 1; Smalley, *1, 2, 3 John*, 19.

[40] E. Malatesta, Interiority and Covenant: A Study of *einai en* and *menein en* in the First Letter of Saint John, AnBib 69 (Rome: Biblical Institute Press, 1978), 27–34; Brown, *Epistles of John*, 195–96.

understood by the Johannine churches to be a revelation of light from God (John 1:4-5, 7-9; 3:19-21; 8:12; 9:5; 11:9-10; 12:35-36, 46). The ethos of the Johannine tradition-bearers bolsters the initial proposition, for the "we" is distinctive. It is the Johannine tradition-bearers that have heard the message from Jesus and proclaim it to the churches. The topics of hearing (*akouō*) and proclaiming (*anangellō*) recur from the introduction and link this first proposition of the body to the historical and eyewitness proclamation of the Johannine tradition-bearers.

The message that God is light is given more authority by the switch from the verb "testify" (*apangellō*; 1:2, 3) to "proclaim" (*anangellō*; 1:5). "Proclaim" is the verb used in Johannine tradition for Jesus's proclamation to the world of all that he heard from the Father (John 4:25; cf. 12:49-50) and for the Paraclete's declaration to the disciples of what the Paraclete receives from Jesus (16:13-15; cf. 14:26). The verb also connotes reporting the words of someone else,[41] and here the someone else is Jesus through the Apostle John and/or the Paraclete to the Johannine tradition-bearers and ultimately to the Johannine churches.[42] "The reworking of the Jesus tradition through the Paraclete which produced GJohn [Gospel of John] did not stop with that document; and 1 John's tradition 'from Christ' may represent a (Paraclete-inspired) reworking of sayings similar to those in GJohn about light and darkness . . ."[43]

1:6-7: First Secessionist Claim, Its Refutation, and Counterclaim

In 1:6 the Elder provides a secessionist claim and its refutation, writing, "If we say that we have fellowship with him while we are walking in darkness, we lie and do not do what is true." He would accept their claim to have fellowship with God provided Johannine tradition is followed (1:3). Apparently, they claim to have fellowship with God while their behavior does not conform to Johannine tradition. The Elder refutes their claim by objection based on fact: It is simply a lie. The refutation, "lie and do not do what is true" is strong. "Lie" (*pseudomai*) is not just lying, but purposeful

---

[41] P. Joüon, "Le verb anangello dans Saint Jean," *RSR* 28 (1938): 234-36.
[42] Brown, *Epistles of John*, 194, 226-27; cf. John 14:26; 16:13-15; cf. Bultmann, *Johannine Epistles*, 15-16. Marshall (*Epistles of John*, 108, n. 1) and Smalley (*1, 2, 3 John*, 19) see the reference as being to the historical Jesus giving the message proclaimed to the author firsthand (cf. John 1:18; 3:32).
[43] Brown, *Epistles of John*, 227. E.g., John 1:4-5, 9; 3:19; 8:12; 9:5; 12:35-36, 46.

and planned lying.[44] The figure of speech called refining is used of the type that repeats the idea in alternative form (Rhet. Her. 4.42.54), and it amplifies by repetition: lie = do not do what is true.

The Elder's refutation has a strong basis in tradition. First, the proposition of 1:5 affirms that there is absolutely no darkness in God, so those walking in darkness cannot have fellowship with God. Second, those doing evil do not come to the light – only those doing truth (John 3:20–21). Third, fellowship with God depends in part upon obedience to the proclamation of the Johannine tradition-bearers (1:1–3), and they teach that their proclamation has ethical implications. Fourth, the dualism of light and truth versus darkness and falsehood (John 8:12; 14:6) makes walking in darkness while claiming to walk in the light impossible.

The Elder gives his counterclaim in 1:7: "but if we walk in the light as he himself is in the light, we have fellowship with one another, and the blood of Jesus his Son cleanses us from all sin." In 1:5 God as light is the basis of Christian behavior, now being with God in the light where he dwells (Ps 104:2; Dan 2:2; Isa 2:5; 1 Tim 6:15–16) is the model for such behavior.[45] The verb "walk" (*peripateō*) is a traditional metaphor for a way or course of life (Ps 1:1; 15:2; Rom 6:4; 8:4; 14:15;1 John 2:6, 11; 2 John 4; 3 John 3–4), and in Johannine tradition following Jesus is not to walk in darkness but to have the light of life (John 8:12; 11:9–10; 12:35–36; 1 John 2:11). Walking in the light is defined in part as doing what is true (1:6) as revealed in Jesus Christ (John 1:17).

The Elder affirms that the behavior of the faithful must accord with the nature of God as light. They must be walking in the light to experience fellowship with other Johannine Christians and cleansing from sin. As the present tense of "cleanse" (*katharizō*) indicates, cleansing occurs repeatedly as needed. As the faithful walk in the light they will inevitably sin, and the Elder assures them that there is cleansing available for those sins. He insinuates that the secessionists who walk in darkness do not have fellowship with other Johannine Christians and are not being cleansed by the blood of Jesus.

The Elder personifies the blood of Jesus itself as doing the cleansing from sin. This feature of style may aim at refuting secessionist claims that the death of Jesus had no salvific value, but salvation was affected by the

---

[44] H. Conzelmann, "*pseudos* . . ." *TDNT* 9:595–96, 602.
[45] Brown, *Epistles of John*, 200–01; 237, n. 32. A similar relationship is established with God and love in 4:7 ("love is from God") and 4:8 ("God is love").

knowledge that Christ revealed through Jesus. The topic of Jesus's blood returns in a veiled form in the third counterclaim of 2:2 (Jesus Christ as atoning sacrifice), in 4:10 (Christ is the atoning sacrifice for sins), and more explicitly in 5:6 (Jesus Christ came by water and blood). The blood of Jesus Christ cleansing from sin is an example of synecdoche, a trope "enabling the hearer to understand many things from one, the whole from the part, the genus from the species, the consequences from the antecedents, and vice versa" (Quintilian, *Inst.* 8.6.19). The word "blood" connotes the Jewish sacrificial system and the crucifixion of Jesus and what both mean for atonement (Lev 17:11; Rom 3:25; Heb 9:22).[46]

1:8–9: Second Secessionist Claim, Its Refutation, and Counterclaim

Verse 8 presents the second claim of the secessionists and its refutation: "If we say that we have no sin, we deceive ourselves, and the truth is not in us." The secessionists claim, "we have no sin," could be either a perfectionist claim ("we have never sinned") or a libertine claim ("we have sinned" but without spiritual consequences). The usage of the phrase "to have sin" (*hamartian echein*) in the Gospel of John supports the latter possibility, for there it refers to being in a state of sin (9:41; 15:22, 24; 19:11).[47] Apparently the secessionists are claiming that sinning does not break fellowship with God (vv. 6–7). As the Elder refuted the previous claim, he also refutes this one by objection based on fact: It is simply deceptive and untrue. The Elder does assume that a state of sinlessness before God is possible (3:6, 9; 5:18), but it is an unrealizable ideal because there is always sin and the need to confess it (1:9; 2:1–2).

The emphatic phrase "we deceive ourselves" (*heautous planōmen*) suggests a deliberate rejection of the truth, as indicated by the following phrase: "the truth is not in us." The implicit accusation is that the secessionists purposefully deceive themselves in order to claim, "we have no sin." Deceit (*planaō, planē*) is a common topic in 1 John. The Elder warns the faithful that the secessionists would deceive them (*planaō*, 2:26; 3:7) and are subject to the spirit of error (*planē*, 4:6). They are deceivers (*planoi*, 2 John 7). Deceit (*planē, planaō*) is also a common topic in

---

[46] J. Behm, "*haima* ..." *TDNT* 1:174–76.
[47] Brown, *Epistles of John*, 205–06, 233–34. For a full discussion, see J. Bogart, *Orthodox and Heretical Perfectionism in the Johannine Community as Evident in the First Epistle of John*. SBLDS 33 (Missoula: Scholars, 1977).

Jewish–Christian writings describing deceivers in the last days.[48] The Elder later associates the secessionists with the anti-Christian forces that will try to undermine the truth in the last days (2:18; 4:1–3).

In the counterclaim of 1:9, the Elder asserts his understanding of sin in the Christian life: "If we confess our sins, he who is faithful and just will forgive our sins and cleanse us from all unrighteousness." He shifts from the singular of sin referring to a state of sin, as in the secessionist claim, to the plural referring to individual sins committed. In contrast to the secessionist claim that they "have no sin," the Elder does not simply reply that Christians have sin but moves the discussion to the proper response to sin: public confession and forgiveness. Johannine (John 1:20; 9:22; 12:42; 1 John 2:23; 4:2–3, 15; 2 John 7; Rev 3:5) and New Testament usage (Mark 1:5; Acts 19:18; Rom 10:9; Jas 5:16) affirm that the confession (*homologeō*) is public.[49]

The Elder describes God as faithful (*pistos*) and just (*dikaios*), classic qualities of God in Judeo-Christian tradition (Deut 32:4; Ps 145:17; 1 Cor 1:9; 10:13; 1 Clem. 27:1; 60:1). God is faithful to God's covenant promises (Exod 34:6–7; Deut 7:9; Ps 89:1–4; Rom 3:3–4; Heb 10:23; 11:11), which include forgiveness of those who break covenant and seek forgiveness (Ps 32:5; Jer 31:34; Mic 7:18–20). God is just as God lives up to his covenant promises, including the offer of forgiveness (Deut 32:4; Pss 33:5; 145:17) and dispensing judgment (2 Macc 12:6; 2 Tim 4:8). The descriptors for God as "faithful" and "just" are the antithesis of those describing the lives of believers with their sin (*hamartia*) and unrighteousness (*adikia*). Fortunately, God is ready to forgive sin and cleanse from unrighteousness as an expression of God's faithfulness and justice.

1:10–2:2: Third Secessionist Claim, Its Refutation, and Counterclaim

The Elder provides a third claim of the secessionists and its refutation: "If we say that we have not sinned, we make him a liar, and his word is not in us" (1:10). Since the previous claims of the secessionists refer to life after conversion and baptism (1:6, 8), is it likely that they are not claiming to never have sinned at all, but rather not to have sinned after baptism.[50] The Elder himself

---

[48] Matt 24:11, 24; 1 Tim 4:1; Rev 12:9; Did. 16:4; H. Braun, "*planao* ..." *TDNT* 6:246–49.
[49] That the confession is public is affirmed by J. P. Thornton-Duesbery, "1 John i.9," *ExpTim* 45 (1933/34): 183–84; Brown, *Epistles of John*, 207–08, 237. That the confession is private is affirmed by Bultmann, *Johannine Epistles*, 21, n. 28; Schnackenburg, *Johannine Epistles*, 81, n. 41; L. M. Rogers, "1 John i.9," *ExpTim* 45 (1933/34): 527.
[50] Brown, *Epistles of John*, 211–12, 234, 238–39; Smalley, *1, 2, 3 John*, 33.

1:5–2:2: God as Light and Its Implications

seems to make similar claims of sinlessness (3:6, 9; 5:18), but he is describing the ideal conduct of those born of and abiding in God. The reference to the availability of forgiveness that immediately follows in the counterclaim (2:1–2) indicates that the Elder does not claim that Christians do not sin after conversion and baptism, but that they ideally do not and can be forgiven when they do. He acknowledges the possibility of sin, and even its likelihood.

Like the two previous claims of the secessionists (1:6, 8), the Elder refutes this third claim by objection based on fact. It is the judgment (*kriseis*) of God as expressed in Jewish and Johannine tradition that all of humanity is guilty of sin (Gen 8:21; 1 Kgs 8:46; Job 15:14–16; Prov 20:9; Eccl 7:20; Isa 53:6; 64:6; John 16:8–9; Rom 3:22–24). Thus, a consequence of a claim not to have sinned is to make God a liar (5:10) and be excluded from God's word. It is to associate God with the devil, the father of lies (John 8:44), and be excluded from life (cf. 1:1) and truth (John 8:31–32), which come from the word.

Between the claim and refutation of 1:10 and his counterclaim in 2:1b–2, the Elder inserts a parenthesis in 2:1a: "My little children, I am writing these things to you so that you may not sin." Although he assumes that Christians sin (1:10), he does not want to encourage it. The diminutive "little children" (*teknia*), as well as "children" (*paidia*), refers specifically to the Christians of the Johannine churches, unlike "children" (*tekna*), which refers to Christians in general.[51] In antiquity, wisdom teachers often addressed their students as children, patterning the teacher–student relationship on the father's instruction of his sons (Ps 34:11; Prov 4:10; 5:1; 7:24; 8:32; Sir 2:1; 3:1; Tob 4:3, 12, 13). In this parenthesis the Elder temporarily switches from the first-person plural of the Johannine tradition-bearers with whom he is associating to the first-person singular to speak more personally. He assumes the traditional role of a father instructing his sons and a wisdom teacher informing his students. The Elder may also be imitating Jesus, for the only use of "children" (*teknia*) in the Gospel of John is at the beginning of the Farewell Discourse in Jesus's address to his disciples (13:33).[52] All of these associations work to increase the authority (ethos) of the Elder and the affection (pathos) of the faithful.

---

[51] Brown, *Epistles of John*, 213–14.
[52] Brown, *Epistles of John*, 214.

The Elder states that his purpose in writing is so that the faithful will not sin. He refers to the entire unit of refutation and counterclaim in 1:5–10 that bases behavior on the nature of God as light.[53] He insinuates that his interpretation of tradition keeps the faithful from sinning, whereas that of the secessionists does not. While acknowledging that sin occurs, the Elder assumes that there is a need to make every effort not to sin after conversion, as does Johannine tradition (John 5:14) and early Christianity in general (Rom 6).

The Elder continues in 2:1b–2 with his counterclaim to the claim and refutation of 1:10: "But if anyone does sin, we have an advocate with the Father, Jesus Christ the righteous; and he is the atoning sacrifice for our sins, and not for ours only but also for the sins of the whole world." The switch from "if we," which began the counterclaims in 1:7 and 1:9, to "if anyone" (*ean tis*) indicates that the Elder expects the faithful will look upon sin as the exception and not the norm. He does not expect the faithful to have a problem with sin, just an occasional "anyone."

As he did in the counterclaims of 1:7 and 1:9, the Elder affirms God's provision for atonement. Whereas he affirmed that the blood of Jesus cleanses from sin (1:7) and God forgives and cleanses from unrighteousness (1:9), now he affirms that Jesus is an advocate before the Father and an atoning sacrifice for sin. The term "advocate" or "paraclete" (*paraclētos*) describing Jesus's role is also used in John's Gospel in the Farewell Discourse to describe the intercessory role of the Holy Spirit (14:16), who teaches the church and reminds it of the teaching of Jesus (14:24–26), testifies to Jesus (15:26–27), and proves the world wrong about sin, righteousness, and judgment (16:5–15).

The Elder describes Jesus Christ the advocate (*paraclētos*) as "with the Father" (*pros ton patera*). He uses the same terminology in the *exordium* of eternal life being with the Father in the beginning (1:2; cf. John 1:1). Jesus Christ, who is eternal life, is now once more with the Father. The imagery is of an advocate in a courtroom working on behalf of a client (Rom 8:34; Heb 7:25). The Elder describes Jesus Christ the advocate as "the righteous" (*dikaios*; 2:29; 3:7), and this virtue qualifies him to be an advocate before

---

[53] C. Haas, M. De Jonge, and J. L. Swellengrebel, *A Translator's Handbook on the Letters of John* (London: United Bible Societies, 1972), 40.

1:5-2:2: God as Light and Its Implications

God, who is righteous in forgiving the sins of those who confess their sins (*dikaios*, 1:9).[54]

In v. 2 the Elder switches from describing Jesus as an advocate to describing Jesus as the atoning sacrifice (*hilasmos*) for the sins of the whole world.[55] He emphasizes the salvific significance of Jesus's sacrifice of his own life – a significance the secessionists minimize. His description is reminiscent of the Old Testament ritual of the Day of Atonement and the blood of the sacrificial ram (Lev 16). There is a debate as to whether the atoning sacrifice denotes expiation (cleansing of sins is at the instigation of God) or propitiation (God's judgment for sin is abated by sacrifices offered for the sinner) or both.[56] It is probably expiation. In the only other passage in Johannine literature in which atoning sacrifice (*hilasmos*) appears, God sends the Son as an atoning sacrifice out of love for the world (1 John 4:9–10; cf. Rom 3:25), and here it is Jesus's blood that cleanses the Christian from unrighteousness (1:7). In the New Testament the word group in which *hilasmos* is found relates to God showing mercy to sinners (Matt 16:22; Luke 18:13; Rom 3:21–26; Heb 2:17; 8:12).

The topics introduced in 1:5–2:2 reflect what we know of conversion, initiation, and baptismal language used by the Essenes and early Christians (1QS 1:18–2:25; 3:3–4, 11–12, 17–22; Acts 26:18; Eph 5:6–11; Col 1:13–14; Heb 10:19–23; 1 Pet 1:18–19; Did. 1–7). The Elder's stress upon his tradition being "from the beginning" of Jesus's self-revelation (1:1, 3, 5) and his assumption that the churches know this tradition (2:7, 21, 24, 27; 3:11; 5:18–20) indicate that the content of 1:5–2:2 is what the church members heard when they converted to Christianity. He utilizes tradition that convinced them to convert, a tradition coming from the tradition-bearers and ultimately from Jesus Christ. The Elder reiterates this tradition to demonstrate to the churches how the secessionist claims have veered from it.[57]

---

[54] J. Behm, "*paraklētos* ..." TDNT 5:800–14; R. E. Brown, *The Gospel According to John*, 2 vols., AB 29 (New York: Doubleday, 1966, 1970), 2.1135–44; G. Johnston, *The Spirit-Paraclete in the Gospel of John*, SNTSMS 12 (Cambridge: Cambridge University Press, 1970).

[55] N. H. Young, "C. H. Dodd, 'Hilaskesthai' and His Critics," *EvQ* 48 (1976): 67–78; Brown, *Epistles of John*, 218–22.

[56] Brown, *Epistles of John*, 217–22, 239–40; cf. Witherington, *Letters and Homilies for Hellenized Christians*, 1.461–65.

[57] Brown, *Epistles of John*, 242–45.

BRIDGING THE HORIZONS

The secessionists view their spiritual status in Christ as secure and unaffected by their behavior. They do not see their behavior impinging on their spiritual life or sin affecting their righteousness and fellowship with God. They are even so blind as to deny sin in their lives altogether. They believe only the part of the Christian message easily given intellectual assent but do not conform their behavior to the message, which is much more difficult.

The Elder believes the opposite. He understands that since God is light, fellowship with God requires constant vigilance. To sin is to walk in darkness and destroy fellowship with the God who is light. The faithful need to acknowledge sin and avail themselves of God's provision of atonement through the blood of Jesus Christ. They can return to the light with restored fellowship with God and other Christians who are in the light.

The mindset of the secessionists lives on today. It is to gaze at the cross on Sunday morning and affirm personal salvation and continue to live the rest of the week with marginal concerns for the lifestyle that salvation requires. Unlike the secessionists, it would be rare to find Christians who vocally deny that they sin. Sin is all too apparent to us. Still, sin can be denied when it is ignored or minimized or not confessed to God. Self-deception is so much more comfortable than confronting personal disobedience before God and others affected by it.

Concern for the ethical walk and an awareness of sin's disruption of fellowship with God and other Christians puts us back in league with the tradition that was declared from the beginning of the church. The Elder reminds us that the atoning sacrifice of Jesus is available. The death of Christ makes forgiveness possible when we stray from the ethical walk (1 John 1:7, 9; 2:1–2). We can leave the lies and self-deception and live in truth before God, our friends, and ourselves.

The Elder's rhetorical approach is to rely on the authority of his position as a Johannine tradition-bearer and the tradition of the Johannine churches. This approach raises the question of where Christian authority is rooted today. With growing relativism in society, declining denominations, and the rise of independent churches, it is hard to find common authoritative ground. One constant is the tradition found in the Scriptures that incorporates the Elder's traditions and many others. Even so, the Scriptures are subject to an ongoing and necessary interpretation, but they do provide a grounding for affirmation and refutation for theological dialog.

One key aspect of this section is hard to bridge to today: the shedding of blood to forgive sins. Christians understand that the blood of Jesus brings forgiveness of sin. However, to the modern mind in the "Age of the Human," such a sacrificial way of thinking seems savage and unnecessary. If we can forgive others without shedding blood, why can't God? For many, religious sacrifice is a residual of a more primitive time, and its image is hard to weave into an understanding of our place before God in a modern age. This aspect of the Christian proclamation is mocked in much current media. This is a case in which the created must accept what the Creator has established. The justice, righteousness, purity, and light of God require purification for sin in God's creation. God's own love for fellowship with creation motivated God's sacrifice of Christ as a gift of immeasurable value to provide that purification.

2:3–11: WHAT IT MEANS TO KNOW THE GOD WHO IS LIGHT

2:3 Now by this we may know that we have come to know him, if we obey his commandments.

2:4 Whoever says, "I have come to know him," but does not obey his commandments is a liar, and in such a person the truth does not exist;

2:5 but whoever obeys his word, truly in this person the love of God has reached perfection. By this we may know that we are in him:

2:6 whoever says, "I abide in him," ought to walk in the same way as he walked.

2:7 Beloved, I am writing you no new commandment, but an old commandment that you have had from the beginning; the old commandment is the word that you have heard.

2:8 Yet I am writing you a new commandment that is true in him and in you, because the darkness is passing away and the true light is already shining.

2:9 Whoever says, "I am in the light," while hating a brother or sister, is still in the darkness.

2:10 Whoever loves a brother or sister abides in the light, and in such a person there is no cause for stumbling.

2:11 But whoever hates a brother or sister is in the darkness, walks in the darkness, and does not know the way to go, because the darkness has brought on blindness.

First John 2:3–11 is the second and final section of secessionist claims, their refutation, and counterclaims. The Elder previously offered a general proposition that God is light (1:5) and drew out the theological and ethical implications of that proposition while refuting secessionist claims and offering counterclaims (1:6–2:2). He now focuses on what it means to know the God who is light, again while refuting secessionist claims and offering counterclaims. In doing so, he structures this section like the preceding one. Both begin with "and" (*kai*, 1:5, 2:3) and a form of the demonstrative pronoun "this" (*haute*, 1:5; *kai en touto*, 2:3). Both begin with a general proposition (1:5; 2:3), followed by three claims of the secessionists, their refutations, and counterclaims (1:6–2; 2:4–11). The secessionist claims of 1:5–2:2 each begin with "if we say" (*ean eipōmen*) and use the first-person plural, while those of 2:4–11 each begin with the formula "whoever says" (*ho legōn*) and use the third-person singular.

As in 1:5–2:2, here the Elder refutes the claims of the secessionists singly rather than as one group, which is a more pointed method of refutation (Cicero, *Part. or.* 12.44; Quintilian, *Inst.* 5.13.28). He refutes their claims by disapproving of their reasoning (Aristotle, *Rhet.* 2.25.1402a.1–1402b.7; 2.26.1403a.3–4; 3.17.1418b.14; Quintilian, *Inst.* 5.13.16). He considers their claims to be fragile enough to be refuted with a mere dismissal (Quintilian, *Inst.* 5.13.15–16). He relies upon his own authority and the authority of his tradition to refute the secessionist claims and make counterclaims (Cicero, *Inv.* 1.42.79; *De or.* 2.53.215). The common topic of the possible-impossible undergirds his refutation (Aristotle, [*Rhet. Alex.*] 13; 34.1440a.5ff.). The bad behavior of the secessionists makes their spiritual claims impossible.

2:3: The Governing Proposition

The Elder begins this section with a general proposition containing elements of the secessionist claims. It governs his refutation of those claims and his own counterclaim: "Now by this we know that we have come to know him,[58] if we obey his commandments." Obedience to God is how a

---

[58] The referent of "this" (*autos*) in both occurrences is generally accepted to be God, not Jesus Christ of 2:1: (1) forms of *autos* in 1:6, 7, 10 refer to God last mentioned in 1:5; (2)

Christian knows God.[59] The formula "by this we know" (*en touto ginōskomen*) occurs ten times in 1 John (2:3, 5, 18; 3:16, 19, 24; 4:2, 6, 13; 5:2) and refers to knowing spiritual realities. This proposition introduces the key topic of "knowing" (*ginōskō*). The verb *ginōskō* occurs twenty-five times in 1 John (2:3 [2×], 4, 5, 13 [2×], 14, 18, 29; 3:1 [2×], 6, 16, 19, 20, 24; 4:2, 6 [2×], 7, 8, 13, 16; 5:2, 20) and the verb *ginomai* once (2:18). God or Christ is often the object of knowing as it is here (2:3, 4, 13-14; 3:1, 6; 4:6, 7, 8; 5:20).[60]

The Old Testament assumes the possibility of knowing God (Jer 9:24) and hopes for a world filled with the knowledge of God (Jer 31:33-34; Hab 2:14). The New Testament teaches that Jesus came to reveal the Father so God could be known (Matt 11:27; Luke 10:22) and that knowing God is eternal life (John 17:3). The Elder assumes that knowing God is possible, but only by obeying God's commandments. Disobeying God's commandments is not to know God (Job 36:10-12; Isa 1:3-4; 5:11-13; Jer 9:6; Hos 4:1-2).

Against this background, the Elder can affirm that obeying the commandments known from the founding of the community (2:7, 24; 3:11) is evidence of knowing God and a means of further knowing God. We find the same sequence from action to knowledge in 4:7b-8: "Everyone who loves is born of God and knows God. Whoever does not love does not know God, for God is love." He states the opposite in 3:6b: "no one who sins has either seen him or known him." This proposition that Christians must obey God's commandments to know God is another way of expressing the thought of the preceding section that to have fellowship (*koinonia*) with God, Christians must walk in the light (1:6, 7).

The governing proposition of 2:3 interrelates the topics of knowledge (*ginōskō*) and obeying or keeping (*tereō*) the commandment(s) (*entolē*) of

---

all of the claims of the secessionists in 1:5-2:11 concern God; and (3) Jesus is referred to as "that one" (*ekeinos*) in 1 John, not "this one" (2:6; 3:3, 5, 7, 16; 4:17).

[59] The initial formula "now by this" (*kai en touto*) points to the content of the proposition that follows, not the first section of proposition, claim, refutation, and counterclaim (1:5-2:2). For a discussion of the referent of the formula *en touto*, see Brown, *Epistles of John*, 248-49.

[60] For more on the topic of "knowing," see M.-E. Boismard, "La connaissance de Dieu dans l'alliance nouvelle d'après la Première Lettre de Saint Jean," *RB* 56 (1949): 365-91; B. E. Gärtner, "The Pauline and Johannine Idea of 'to know God' against the Hellenistic Background," *NTS* 14 (1968): 209-31; Schnackenburg, *Johannine Epistles*, 90-95.

God (2:3-4; 3:22-24; 5:3).[61] Jesus received a commandment(s) from the Father that he preached (John 12:49-50) and which guided his conduct (John 15:10) and the direction of his ministry, especially his death and resurrection (John 10:18; 14:31). In turn, Jesus gave his disciples the commandment to love (1 John 4:21; John 13:34; 15:12), often expressed in the plural since love covers all of the commandments that Jesus was fulfilling for the Father (John 14:15, 21; 15:10) and were passed on to the churches by the Johannine tradition-bearers (1 John 2:7-8; 2 John 5-6). This governing proposition with its association of topics allows the Elder to insinuate in the refutation to follow that the secessionists do not know God because they do not obey his commandments (2:4-11). He does so using a necessary sign or something that is irrefutable (Aristotle, *Rhet.* 1.2.1357b.16-17; [*Rhet. Alex.*] 12; Quintilian, *Inst.* 5.9.2-7): Obedience to the commandments is a necessary sign of knowing God. A faithful Christian obeying the commandments surely knows God and vice versa.

2:4-5a: First Secessionist Claim, Its Refutation, and Counterclaim

The Elder begins with a secessionist proposition and its refutation: "Whoever says 'I have come to know him,'[62] but does not obey his commandments, is a liar, and in such a person the truth does not exist" (2:4). The Elder's refutation is an objection based upon the stasis or basis of fact. He states the fact in the initial proposition in the preceding verse: No one can make a claim to know God without obeying God's commandments. He does not refute the underlying premise of the secessionist claim that God can be known, for knowing God is eternal life (John 17:3). Rather, he refutes the understanding that God can be known without corresponding ethical behavior.

The Elder makes his initial refutation more rhetorically effective by using the figure of speech of refining of the type that repeats the idea in alternative form (Rhet. Her. 4.42.54). "Being a liar" and "in such a person the truth does not exist" mean the same thing and amplify by repetition the deceptive nature of the secessionists (Cicero, *Part. or.* 15.54). Also, with

---

[61] Cf. "obey [lit. 'do'] the commandments" (5:2) and "walk according to his commandments" (2 John 6). See U. C. von Wahlde, *The Johannine Commandments: 1 John and the Struggle for the Johannine Tradition* (New York: Paulist Press, 1990).

[62] The referent of "him" (*autos*) is generally agreed to be God, not Jesus. In the parallel clauses in 2:3 and 2:6 God is the referent, and God is always the origin of commandments in 1 John. Brown, *Epistles of John*, 253.

this repetition the Elder insinuates that the secessionists are not Christian, for truth, which the secessionists are said not to possess, is the spirit of truth given to Christians (4:6; John 14:17; cf. 2 John 2). The Elder also uses refining of the type that alters the idea by employing the contrary (Rhet. Her. 4.43.56). The secessionist claim and its refutation (2:4) is the contrary of the Elder's initial proposition (2:3).

The Elder's counterclaim follows in 2:5a: "but whoever obeys his word, truly in this person the love of God has reached perfection." The adverb "truly" (*alēthōs*) subtly amplifies and further discredits the previous secessionist claim that they can know God without accompanying obedience to God's commandments. The counterclaim gains rhetorical strength by forming antithetical parallelism with the claim and refutation of 2:4. "Not obey his commandments" is replaced by "obeys his word," while "in such a person the truth does not exist" is replaced by "in this person the love of God has reached perfection." Commandments (*entola*) and word (*logos*) are synonyms, as confirmed by 2:7, which affirms "the old commandment (*entolē*) is the word (*logos*)."[63] The ethos of the secessionists suffers, for since they do not obey the commandments or the word, they are liars unable to claim they know God, and the love of God has not reached perfection in them.

Several interrelated topics central to 1 John are introduced in this section of 2:3-5a: obey (*tereō*; usually the commandments or Jesus's word),[64] love (*agapē*),[65] and perfect (*teleioō*; always with love).[66] Obeying the commandments is a manifestation of the person's love of God (John 14:15, 21; 15:10). This love is *agapē* love, an undeserved, life-giving love that comes from God as a gift to Christians (1 John 4:7-11) and the world (John 3:16). The love of God[67] reaches perfection or completion in Christians when they in turn love others (4:19). The passive voice of the

---

[63] There is a similar switch from keeping the commandments to keeping the word in John 14:21-24.

[64] Commandments: 2:3-5; 3:22, 24; 5:3, 18. Jesus is the actor in 5:18.

[65] *Agapē*: 2:5, 15; 3:1, 16, 17; 4:7, 8, 9, 10, 12, 16 (thrice), 17, 18 (thrice); 5:3 (twice); *agapaō*: 2:10, 15 (twice); 3:10, 11, 14 (twice), 18, 23; 4:7, 8, 10 (twice), 11, 12, 19, 20 (thrice), 21 (twice); 5:1, 2 (twice); *agapētos*: 2:7; 3:2, 21; 4:1, 7, 11.

[66] *Teleioō*: 2:5; 4:12, 17, 18; *teleios*: 4:18. See P. J. De Plessis, *Teleios: The Idea of Perfection in the New Testament* (Kampen: Kok, 1959).

[67] The genitive "of God" (*tou theou*) is an objective genitive of the Christian's love for God (2:15; 4:20-21; 5:1-3), a subjective genitive of God's love for the Christian (3:17; 4:9-12, 16, 19), or a genitive of quality (God's kind of love). I understand it to be all of these (cf. 4:19). For full discussion, see Brown, *Epistles of John*, 255-57; Painter, *1, 2, 3 John*, 176-77.

verb "perfect" (*teleioō*) indicates that God is the one working in Christians to perfect love. God loves Christians, and they return this love to others, and in that exchange God perfects God's love in them. Perfection is a goal for Christians in the New Testament (Matt 5:48; 1 Cor 2:6; 14:20; Eph 4:13; Col 1:28), and they realize it by obeying God's commandments (Matt 19:21; Jas 1:25), especially the commandment to love (1 John 4:12).

This first claim of the secessionists and its refutation is virtually identical to the first secessionist claim and its refutation in the preceding section: "If we say that we have fellowship with him while we are walking in darkness, we lie (*pseudomai*) and do not do what is true (*alētheia*)" (1:6). To have fellowship with God is equivalent to knowing him, walking in darkness is equivalent to disobeying God's commandments, and lying (*pseudomai*) and not doing the truth (*alētheia*) is equivalent to being a liar (*pseustēs*) and the truth (*alētheia*) not residing within. There is also similarity between the refutation of 2:4 and that of 1:8 and 1:10: "We deceive (*planaō*) ourselves, and the truth (*alētheia*) is not in us" (1:8) and "we make him a liar (*pseustēs*), and his word (*logos*) is not in us" (1:10) is now "is a liar (*pseustēs*) and in such a person the truth (*alētheia*) does not exist" (2:4), followed by "obeys his word" (*logos*, 2:5). This repetition ties the topics of lying/deceit, truth, and word to the topics of knowing God and obeying the commandments. This reiteration is an elaborate use of amplification by repetition (Cicero, *Part. or.* 15.54), further interrelating and developing key topics.

2:5b–6: Second Secessionist Claim, Its Refutation, and Counterclaim

The Elder opens the second secessionist claim with a formula like that which opens the governing proposition of this unit (2:3), beginning with "by this" (*en toutō*) followed by the verb "to know" (*ginōskō*): "and by this we know that we are in him" (2:5b).[68] What follows in the next verse gives that knowledge of

---

[68] "In him" refers to God, as it does in the introductory formula in 2:3 and in the synonymous expression "abide in him" in 2:6 to which it is closely tied. Also, God is the focus of 1:5–2:11 (Parsenios, *First, Second, and Third John*, 70). Since this formula is not followed by a subordinate clause modifying "this" (as in 2:3), it can refer either to what precedes or what follows. If referring to what precedes, it forms an inclusion with 2:3–5a; if referring to what follows, it introduces the claim of 2:6. I am assuming that the formula refers to what follows because it does in 2:3; the first set of secessionist claims begins with an introductory formula (*ean eipōmen*) referring to what follows (1:6, 8, 10); and the topics of "are in him" (*en autō esmen*) in 2:5b and "abide in him" (*en autō menein*) in 2:6a to follow are virtually synonymous.

being in God. "Whoever says, 'I abide in him,'[69] ought to walk in the same way as he[70] walked." Rather than refute the secessionist claim with an absolute denial, as was the case with the first claim of this section (2:4) and the three claims in the first section of refutation (1:6, 8, 10), here the Elder weaves the claim into positive instruction that only backhandedly refutes the secessionists on the basis of their observable behavior. He insinuates that the secessionists claim to abide in God but do not walk as Christ walked in his earthly ministry. Thus, their claim is false, and they cannot know that they are in God. The Elder's refutation is based on the stasis or basis of quality. He does not deny the claim that Christians can abide in God, for that was part of the Johannine tradition (5:20; John 17:21).[71] Rather, he denies that while claiming to abide in God a Christian's ethical walk can diverge from that of Christ.

The Elder's instruction to "walk as Jesus walked" patterns the Christian ethical walk on that of Jesus using the comparative "just as" (*kathōs*), a pattern found throughout Johannine tradition (2:6; 3:3, 7; 4:17; John 13:15, 34; 15:12, 17).[72] This comparison is developed here with the topic of "ought" (*opheilō*): As Jesus walked, so Christians ought to walk. Jesus's ethical walk obligates Christians to a similar one. As the context indicates (2:5, 7-8), the Elder grounds abiding in God in walking as Jesus walked; that is, the kind of love epitomized by Jesus (1:1-3). Walking as Jesus walked is to love others with the love he demonstrated in laying down his life (3:16) and God demonstrated in sending the only Son as an atoning sacrifice (4:11). This divine love obligates Christians to similar action (cf. 3 John 7-8). Walking as Christ walked, especially in love, testifies to the reality of the claim to abide in God.

The Elder connects the refutation to its introduction using refining, in which the idea is repeated in another form (Rhet. Her. 4.42.54). "We are in him" (*en autō esmen*; v. 5b) is repeated in synonymous forms as "I abide in him" (*en autō menein*) and "walk in the same way as he walked" (v. 6).

---

[69] "Him" (*autos*) refers to God rather than Christ, as the references to God in v. 5a and to "him" (*ekeinos* or Christ) later in the verse make clear. God is also the referent of "him" in the secessionist claims of 1:6 and 2:4.

[70] "He" (lit. "that one," *ekeinos*) refers to Christ here as it does in all but one use of *ekeinos* in 1 John: 2:6; 3:3, 5, 7, 16; 4:17 (cf. 5:16). Also, as here, in comparisons using "just as" (*kathōs*), *ekeinos* always refers to Christ (2:6; 3:3, 7; 4:17). Cf. John 7:11; 9:12, 28; 19:21, where *ekeinos* refers to Jesus.

[71] For the Christian abiding in Jesus, see 2:24, 27-28; John 15:4-7 (*menein en*) and John 14:20; 15:2 (*einai en*).

[72] See O. de Dinechin, "Kathōs: La similitude dans l'Évangile selon Saint Jean," *RSR* 58 (1970): 195-236.

This refining introduces the important Johannine topic of abiding in God or Christ. It is akin to the topic of fellowship with the Father and Son (1:3, 6).[73]

2:7–8: A Parenthesis

Verses 7–8 are a parenthesis that undergirds the authority of the second refutation and counterclaim of this section (2:5b–6) and acts as a transition to the third (2:9–11). Whereas the earlier parenthesis of 2:1a anticipates the misconception derived from 1:10 that the Elder expects sin to be a regular part of the Christian life, this parenthesis affirms that the instruction in the preceding verse to walk as Christ walked comes from Johannine tradition. In both parentheses the Elder adopts the more authoritative "I"–"you" posture rather than the more collegial "we" posture of the two preceding refutations and counterclaims to speak more directly as an elder of the Johannine churches.

This parenthesis opens with the vocative "beloved" (*agapētoi*), which emphasizes that the faithful are beloved of God (2:7; 3:2, 21; 4:1, 7, 11; 3 John 2, 5, 11). The LXX uses "beloved" as an adjective derived from covenant relationship to describe Israel as God's beloved people (Jer 6:26, 31:20 [38:20 LXX]) and is similarly used of Christians in the New Testament. The Gospel of John describes the founder of the Johannine churches as "the disciple whom Jesus loved" (13:23; 19:26; 20:2; 21:7, 20). By addressing the faithful as "beloved," the Elder demonstrates that he, God, and Jesus love them, as well as providing an example of love in action to prepare them for the following discussion of their obligation to love one another (2:9–11; 4:7–12).

The shift from the plural of commandment (*entolē*, 2:3–4) to the singular here in vv. 7–8 indicates that Jesus's comprehensive commandment to love one another is specifically in mind. The change from the plural to the singular of commandment and vice versa is found in Johannine literature (3:22–24; 2 John 4–6; John 15:10–12), and the singular commandment refers to Jesus's love commandment throughout Johannine literature (3:23; 4:21; 2 John 5–6; John 13:34; 15:12). In conjunction with the vocative "beloved" (*agapetoi*), this commandment prepares the faithful for the following instruction about loving brothers and sisters (2:9–11).

---

[73] Brown, *Epistles of John*, 259–61, 283–84. Schnackenburg, *Johannine Epistles*, 99–103.

2:3–11: What It Means to Know the God Who Is Light

This parenthesis is rhetorically sophisticated. It is structured using the figure of speech known as *correctio*, which "retracts what has been said and replaces it with what seems more suitable" (Rhet. Her. 4.26.36). The Elder first asserts that the love commandment is old (v. 7) and then that it is new (v. 8). Also present is *reflexio*, a figure of thought where the same word is used with contrary meanings (Quintilian, *Inst.* 9.3.68; Rhet. Her. 4.14.21). In v. 7, "new" (*kainos*) means newness in the sense of time, whereas in v. 8, it is newness in the sense of realization. There is chiasm in the pattern of not new, old, old, and new. There is antithesis in the juxtaposition of new commandment/old commandment and darkness/light. Antonomasia is found in the use of "true light" (*to phōs to alethinon*) to designate Jesus Christ and his salvific work (cf. John 8:12). All of these features enable the Elder to make fine distinctions.

The Elder begins in v. 7 by asserting that the commandment is old. He uses refining that reiterates the same thing in different fashion: It is not new (*kainos*), but old (*palaios*). Why does the Elder make this claim considering that in John 13:34 Jesus calls the love commandment new (*kainos*)? There are several explanations for this emphasis that the love commandment is old.

First, the Elder may be anticipating a secessionist claim. Considering their dismissal of ethical behavior, they may be claiming that he is going beyond the bounds of Johannine tradition by imposing the obligation to walk the same way as Christ walked (2:6). The Elder would thus be countering such a claim by affirming that his instruction is not new but rooted in the love commandment that is central to the founding tradition of the Johannine churches. He stresses elsewhere that his message was held from the beginning of the community (1:1–3; 3:11).[74] If this is the scenario, the Elder is using the figure of thought called anticipation (*prolepsis*), in which a rhetor anticipates and forestalls the objections of opponents (Quintilian, *Inst.* 4.1.49; 9.2.16–18).

Second, the secessionists may be touting their doctrine as new in the sense of it being better or supplanting previous tradition. In this case the Elder's denial that his commandment is new may be intended to imply that the secessionist claim to new teaching is not better, but rather a divergence from tradition. Compare 2 John 9 where the secessionists are accused of going beyond the traditions of the community and the Elder's

---

[74] Brown, *Epistles of John*, 264–65; Marshall, *Epistles of John*, 128–29.

stress that the command to love one another was from the beginning of the community.[75]

Third, no explicit polemic may be involved here at all. The Elder may simply be stressing that the love commandment is not new to bolster the ethos of his previous exhortation. This particularly rings true in the light of the Johannine Community's (and antiquity's) love of older tradition.[76] As the phrase "from the beginning" indicates, the love commandment is not new because it derives from Jesus himself (1 John 3:23; 4:21; John 13:34; 15:12, 17) and the preaching that founded the community (1:1, 5) and has roots in the Jewish Torah (Lev 19.18).[77]

Fourth, the emphasis on the commandment being old may refer to it being part of the initial proclamation of the Johannine tradition-bearers to the faithful. The commandment would be the word heard from the beginning as mentioned in 1:1–3. Tradition from the "beginning" was an important anchor of authority in the Johannine churches (1:1; 2:24; 3:11; 2 John 5–6).[78] The Elder may be reminding the faithful to embrace tradition that they had already determined for themselves was worth embracing.

Verse 8 is an enthymeme; that is, a single premise and a conclusion. If proof is used in epideictic rhetoric, like 1 John, it is usually an enthymeme (Aristotle, *Rhet.* 3.17.1418a.11–1418b.12). The conclusion is stated first: "a new commandment that[79] is true in him and in you." The minor premise is stated as "because the darkness is passing away and the true light is already shining." The unstated major premise can be expressed as "where the darkness is passing away and the true light is already shining, the love commandment is truly being realized."[80]

The minor premise (*hoti* clause) provides either a reason for why the commandment is new (because the darkness is passing away and the true

---

[75] Bultmann, *Johannine Epistles*, 27; Brown, *Epistles of John*, 264; Schnackenburg, *Johannine Epistles*, 104.
[76] Cf. R. W. Wilken, *The Christians as the Romans Saw Them* (New Haven: Yale University Press, 1984), 94–125.
[77] Brown, *Epistles of John*, 265; Marshall, *Epistles of John*, 129; Smalley, *1, 2, 3 John*, 54.
[78] Bultmann, *Johannine Epistles*, 27, suggested by Brown, *Epistles of John*, 265.
[79] Whereas commandment (*entolē*) in 2:8a is feminine, the pronoun beginning 2:8b is neuter. Scholars usually take 2:8b to be a relative clause and explain the neuter as modifying the whole idea of a new commandment, not just the commandment itself (C. F. D. Moule, *An Idiom-Book of New Testament Greek*, 2nd edition [Cambridge: Cambridge University Press, 1959], 130–31).
[80] Strecker, *Johannine Letters*, 50.

light is already shining) or for why it is true in Christ and the faithful (because they are exercising love that spreads light and diminishes darkness). Probably both ideas are present: The love of Christ and the faithful makes the commandment new or realized, and this realization is evident in darkness passing away.[81] In the conclusion of the phrase "true in him and you," "true" (*alēthes*) means "realized, made true" rather than "right or correct," and "in" (*en*) is instrumental. This means that the commandment is new because it is realized every day by means of the mutual love of Christ and the faithful (John 13:34; 15:12).[82] In light of 1:5-7, this premise is another way of saying that the churches are walking in the light as God is in the light, having fellowship with one another, and being cleansed by the blood of Jesus. In his incarnation Jesus brought the light into the world (John 1:9), giving people a choice between walking in darkness or light (John 3:19-21). The Elder is saying that the faithful have chosen light.

As the faithful live according to the love commandment in the same fashion as Christ and their lives realize that love, it causes the darkness to "pass away" (*paragō*). This verb refers to the return of Christ (cf. 2:17-18). The Elder assumes that through their love, the faithful will hasten Christ's return. The assumption that the destruction of darkness to be completed at Christ's return impinges upon current behavior constrains the faithful from emulating the unloving and unethical behavior of the secessionists.

2:9-11: Third Secessionist Claim, Its Refutation, and Counterclaim

The third claim of the secessionists, its refutation, and the Elder's counterclaim is given in 2:9-11.

Whereas the substantive "whoever says" (*ho legōn*) marks the subsections of this larger unit of 2:3-11 (2:4a, 6a, 9a), this third subsection is subsequently divided by the substantives "whoever says" (*ho legōn*, v. 9a), "whoever loves" (*ho agapōn*, v. 10a), and "whoever hates" (*ho misōn*, v. 11a). These three substantives interweave topics to form an epicheireme, which consists of a major premise, a minor premise, and a conclusion. Unlike a syllogism, the premises of an epicheireme are not certain, only credible (Quintilian, *Inst.* 5.10.1-8; 5.14.5-24).

---

[81] Brown, *Epistles of John*, 268; Marshall, *Epistles of John*, 129-30; Malatesta, *Interiority and Covenant*, 150-51. Smalley (*1, 2, 3 John*, 57) limits the reference to the realization of love in Christ and the community.

[82] Brown, *Epistles of John*, 267.

Major premise (v. 11): "But whoever hates a brother or sister is in the darkness, walks in the darkness, and does not know the way to go, because the darkness has brought on blindness."

Minor premise (v. 10): "Whoever loves a brother or sister abides in the light, and in such a person there is no cause for stumbling."

Conclusion (v. 9): "Whoever says, 'I am in the light,' while hating a brother or sister, is still in the darkness."

The conclusion of 2:9 is a secessionist claim and its refutation by objection. It is likely that the secessionists were claiming to be in the light based on their faith, as would every Johannine Christian (cf. John 8:12; 9:5; 12:46). The Elder does not deny the possibility of being in the light, only that the secessionists' claim is bogus because they do not walk in the light. He objects using the stasis or basis of fact: You cannot claim to be in the light while being in darkness. This objection is grounded in the immediately preceding parenthesis, for true light is realized and darkness passes away only when the love commandment is being obeyed (vv. 7–8).

It is unlikely that the secessionists were explicitly teaching others to hate members of the Johannine churches, for that would be in stark contrast to Johannine tradition in which love of the Johannine Christians was central. Rather, their behavior was tantamount to hatred, for they did not support the needy (3:17), left the fellowship of the community (2:19), and urged others to do the same (2 John 10). This destroyed fellowship (*koinonia*) with fellow Johannine Christians when they were supposed to be loving them because they are begotten by God (5:1; cf. John 1:12–13).

The secessionists can counter the Elder's refutation with an objection based on the stasis of fact: They do love the brothers and sisters and thus are in the light. The Johannine understanding of a brother or sister (*adelphos*) is in the narrow sense of a member of the Johannine Community (5:16; 3 John 3, 5, 10).[83] Thus, to claim that the secessionists hate a brother or sister loyal to the Elder does not refute the secessionist claim to be in the light. The secessionists have formed another Johannine Community, and as long as they love its members, they are in the light as far as they are concerned.

The two premises of vv. 10–11 are set up as an extended antithesis of love–abiding (*menein en*)–light–and no stumbling versus hate–being in

---

[83] Brown, *Epistles of John*, 269–73. Some commentators see *adelphos* as a reference to non-Johannine Christians as well: Bultmann, *Johannine Epistles*, 28; Smalley, *1, 2, 3 John*, 60.

(*einai en*)–darkness–and walking in the darkness (stumbling). This antithesis stresses that love and light are exclusive of hate and darkness, thus supporting the conclusion of v. 9 that light and hatred are exclusive. In Johannine theology, a love for other Johannine Christians is evidence that a person has passed from death to life, so hating such Christians is to be in the darkness still (3:14–15).

The antithesis incorporates metaphor and personification. The metaphor of stumbling (*skandalos*, v. 10) refers primarily to situations leaving people vulnerable to sin, just as real obstacles can cause them to trip in the dark (Lev 19:14; cf. John 11:9–10).[84] These situations can be temptations created by others (Matt 16:23; 18:7; Rom 14:13; Rev 2:14) or something said or done that deeply upsets others like the Gospel message when first heard (1 Cor 1:23; Gal 5:11; 1 Pet 2:8). There is no cause for stumbling in the light; that is, in the nature of God and Christ expressed as love for others. This can mean either there is no temptation for moral stumbling for people who love others, or they do not cause others to stumble (like the secessionists do; cf. Rom 14:13), or both.[85]

The metaphor of blindness (*typhloō*, v. 11) refers to a persistent and long-term refusal to see the truth. This blindness is not merely because eyes cannot see in the dark, but the permanent blindness of eyes that remain in darkness for a long time (Matt 13:13–15 and par.; John 12:38–40; Acts 28:25–27; Rom 11:9).[86] Johannine tradition was fond of the metaphor of walking and stumbling in darkness for spiritual blindness (John 11:9–10; 12:35–36). Here darkness is personified as blinding the eyes of haters (like the secessionists) so that they do not know the way to go (v. 11). They wander in darkness and do not walk as Christ walked – in the light (2:6). Darkness blinding the eyes of the secessionists sharply contrasts with the Johannine tradition-bearers' perception of the truth with their own eyes (1:1–3). Personified darkness points forward to the topics of the evil one

---

[84] G. Stählin, "*skandalon* . . ." *TDNT* 7:356–57.
[85] This verse is literally "No cause for stumbling in it." "In it" (*en autō*) can either be translated as "in such a person" (a person living in the light), as does the NRSVue, or as "in it" (the light). The symbolism supports the latter, for light enables a person to see and not stumble over objects (Brown, *Epistles of John*, 274–75; Smalley, *1, 2, 3 John*, 61–62; Schnackenburg, *Johannine Epistles*, 108; cf. John 11:9). In support of the former, the formula *einai en* used here almost always has a personal subject or object (Bultmann, *Johannine Epistles*, 28, n. 24; Marshall, *Epistles of John*, 132, n. 38; Haas, De Jonge, and Swellengrebel, *Translator's Handbook*, 52).
[86] Brown, *Epistles of John*, 275–76. He takes the verb "blinding" (*etyphlōsen*) as a complexive or constative aorist describing the result of a long process (BDF §332).

(2:13-14) and the antichrist (2:18, 22) as forces of darkness at work in the world.

Along with 2:8, these verses continue the antithesis of the topics of light (*phōs*) and darkness (*skotia*) from 1:5-7. These topics are not found again in 1 John. Their initial appearance in 1:5-7 and their last appearance here form an *inclusio* and help define 1:5-2:11 as a rhetorical section of claim, refutation, and counterclaim governed by the proposition that God is light in whom there is no darkness (1:5).

> **A CLOSER LOOK: ABIDING**
>
> In Johannine thought, abiding (*menō*) often describes the indwelling of God and Christ in the Christian and vice versa (2:6, 24, 27, 28; 3:6, 24; 4:12-13, 15-16; John 6:56; 15:4-7). It can also describe other realities residing in the Christian like the truth (2 John 2), the spirit of truth (John 14:17; cf. 1 John 3:24; 4:13), the love of God (1 John 3:17), and the anointing from Christ (2:27). Mutual abiding with God begins with the proper confession of Jesus Christ (4:15). Not to believe in Jesus Christ is to abide in death (3:14) and not have life abiding within (cf. 3:15). Paul's understanding of being in Christ (1 Thess 1:1; 2:14; 4:16; 5:18; Gal 1:22; 3:28; 5:6) and Christ being in him and others (Rom 8:10; Gal 2:20; 2 Cor 11:10; 13:5) is a very similar understanding of this mutual abiding.
>
> The Holy Spirit testifies to Christians that they are abiding in God and God in them (1 John 3:24; 4:13). Abiding is a spiritual status requiring obedience to the commandments and walking as Jesus walked (3:24; cf. John 14:15-17), which requires continued effort on the part of the Christian (2:24, 27-28; 3:6; 4:13), involves abiding in the proclamation and teaching about Christ (2:24; 2 John 9), abiding in the light and God by loving others (2:10; 4:12-13, 16). It is made possible through the love of God expressed in the gift of his Son and is evident and expressed in love for others (4:13-21). Continued abiding in Christ results in confidence before him at the judgment of the parousia (4:17).[87]

---

[87] J. Heise, *Bleiben: Menein in der Johanneischen Schriften*, HUT 8 (Tübingen: Mohr, 1967); Malatesta, *Interiority and Covenant*.

A CLOSER LOOK: THE LOVE COMMANDMENT

Several passages in Johannine literature are concerned with the commandment to love (2:7–11; 4:7–21; 5:1–5; 2 John 4–6). In the Gospel of John, Jesus refers to God's instructions for his earthly mission as a commandment (John 10:18; 12:49–50; 14:31; 15:10). More often he refers to the commandment he gives to the disciples to love one another (13:34–35; 15:7, 12; cf. 1 John 4:21). Such love is a sign of a disciple's love of Jesus (14:15, 21; 15:10, 12, 17; 1 John 4:17) and a response to the love of God in sending Jesus Christ (1 John 4:19).

In Johannine literature the alternation between the singular and plural of commandment (John 15:10–12, 17; 1 John 2:3–4, 7–8; 3:22–24; 4:21–5:3; 2 John 4–6) indicates that the love commandment is the core commandment upon which all of the commandments of Jesus are grounded. Also, the love commandment can be described as new (John 13:34), not new (2 John 5–6), and both old and new (1 John 2:7–8). The commandment is new because Jesus focused the will of God in all of the commandments on love. It is old because the love commandment was part of the founding proclamation of the Johannine Churches (1 John 1:1; 2:7; 2 John 5).

BRIDGING THE HORIZONS

This passage emphasizes the role of obedience to the commandments of God, especially the commandment to love. It is in obedience that we come to know God. As we love others, like our spouse or children, we truly get to know them, their interests, foibles, hopes, dreams, and character. As we love God and others, we come to know God. That love of God for us reaches its perfection, its full purpose as we give it back to God and others. It is interrelational and reaches its potential in community. God is the one perfecting love in us. God loves us, we love others in return, and, in this exchange, God perfects God's love.

The ideal is God's love exercised continually as we walk as Jesus did; that is, loving others with the love he gave in laying down his life (3:16). This is abiding in God – consistently exercising the love of God in obedience to his commandments. Jesus gave his disciples the commandment to love (1 John 4:21; John 13:34; 15:12). It covers all of the commandments, for how can people sin against others if they love others with God's love? Lack of love for others leads to unloving action and sin, and this is no longer abiding in God.

With the coming of the light of Jesus Christ, the darkness of sin and death began their retreat. We leave the realm of darkness when we enter that light at conversion. Our obedient love for others is part of our role as ambassadors of light bringing light into the world and pushing against the darkness. A key feature of this march of light into darkness is the elimination of hate, which so defines the darkness. Hatred is darkness. It blinds the eyes to seeing others clearly, breeding misunderstanding, rumor, inuendo, suspicion, and walls of ignorance. Love is to come to know, understand, appreciate, and trust others, spreading the light of the kingdom of the God who is light (1:5). The light of the kingdom is furthered when love is exercised individually and corporately, when physical, social, economic, and personal barriers are removed.

Another bridge to the present is the rhetorical approach of the Elder. He upholds and interprets the tradition of his community. He does not flinch from evaluating the behavior of those claiming to be faithful to those traditions when they are not. At the same time, he reaffirms the tradition for those who may be tempted to accept the claim of those challenging that tradition. The Elder demonstrates leadership that holds a community to its traditions with a balance of decisive action and reaffirmation.

2:12–14: A DIGRESSION AFFIRMING THE POSITIVE SPIRITUAL STATE OF THE FAITHFUL

> 2:12 I am writing to you, little children, because your sins are forgiven on account of his name.
>
> 2:13 I am writing to you, fathers, because you know him who is from the beginning.[88]

---

[88] Since the last instance of "his" referred to Jesus Christ (2:8), most scholars understand "his" (v. 12) and "him" (v. 13) to refer to Jesus Christ, not the Father.

2:12-14: Digression Affirming the Positive Spiritual State

> I am writing to you, young people, because you have conquered the evil one.
>
> 2:14 I write to you, children, because you know the Father.[89]
>
> I write to you, fathers, because you know him who is from the beginning.
>
> I write to you, young people, because you are strong and the word of God abides in you, and you have overcome the evil one.

This section does not seem to fit in its context. It is written in polished parallelism while surrounding verses are regular prose. The topic of love is central to what proceeds (love of the brothers and sisters, 2:3–11) and to what follows (love of the world versus love of the Father, 2:15–17) but is not found here. This section is usually understood as a summation of earlier topics and the introduction of new ones to be developed; a contrast of positive lives of the faithful and negative ones of the secessionists described in 2:3–11, and the basis for the commandment not to love the things of the world in 2:15–17.[90]

Rhetorically, 2:12–14 functions as a *digressio* within the body of the rhetoric (the *probatio*).[91] Rhetors often used digressions after they had refuted the propositions of their opponents and established their own. Digressions are especially used in important matters and are of many varieties, performing a multitude of functions including praising or blaming people, appealing to emotion, enhancing style, and amplifying topics (Cicero, *Inv.* 1.51.97; *De or.* 2.19.80; 2.77.311–12; Quintilian, *Inst.* 4.3.12–17). Having just completed two sections of claim, refutation, and counterclaim (1:5–2:2; 2:3–11), the Elder provides a digression that functions in these various ways before continuing with further matters. The digression praises the faithful in glowing terms to elicit positive emotion. The Elder shifts from the impersonal third-person singular to the more personal first-person singular to address the faithful with the affectionate title "little children," and he assures them that all is well with their spiritual lives. He enhances the style with a parallel structure and a variety of figures (to be discussed below). He reiterates previous topics for amplification and shows them to be the experience of the faithful (forgiveness of sin, knowing

---

[89] I am following the versification of the critical editions of the Greek New Testament and the NRSVue, not the English versions that often put the first sentence of v. 14 with v. 13 (e.g., King James Version, Revised Standard Version).

[90] For detailed discussion of the many issues of interpretation in this section, see Brown, *The Epistles of John*, 294–301; Lieu, *I, II, & III John*, 85–87.

[91] For the rhetorical features of 2:12–14, see D. F. Watson, "1 John 2.12–14 as *Distributio, Conduplicatio*, and *Expolitio*: A Rhetorical Understanding," *JSNT* 35 (1989): 97–110.

God and Christ, and the internal abiding word), and he introduces topics for the first time (forgiveness in Christ's name and conquering the evil one). The Elder assures the faithful that they possess the spiritual blessings that he has been upholding while refuting the secessionists who do not.

The digression is carefully structured and contains numerous rhetorical devices. It is composed of six sentences. Each contains the verb "to write" (*graphō*) followed by the pronoun "to you" (*hymin*), an addressee in the vocative, and a subordinate clause introduced by the conjunction "because" (*hoti*). Both repetition and variation characterize the six subordinate clauses. These six sentences are grouped into two sets of three. The first set employs the present tense of "to write" and the second set employs the past tense (aorist). As the previous two sections indicate (1:5–2:2; 2:3–11), the Elder has a penchant for groupings of three, which is now evident in the triad of children, fathers, and young people in each of the two sets of three (vv. 12–13), as well as the three coordinating clauses after the final "to write" in the second set (v. 14).

There are at least three long-standing questions about this section. The first question is whether there are one, two, or three groups represented here, and just what is the nature of each? Is there one group referred to with three different terms? Are there three groups differing in physical age and/or spiritual maturity? Or are there two groups, children being inclusive of the Johannine Community with fathers and young people being subgroups of the community categorized by physical age and/or spiritual maturity? Since in 1 John the two terms for children are inclusive of all of the addressees (*paidia*, 2:14, 18; *teknia*, 2:1, 12, 28; 3:7, 18; 4:4; 5:21), and neither "fathers" (*pateres*) nor "young people" (*neaniskoi*) are inclusive in this section, I am assuming that two groups of "fathers" and "young people" are subcategories of the inclusive category of "children."[92]

The Elder is using a figure of thought called distribution (*distributio*). After mentioning a whole, its parts are enumerated (Rhet. Her. 4.35.47). The Elder has begun with the inclusive grouping of children and then distributed it into the two constituent groups of fathers and young people. Distribution is by no means foreign to biblical usage, particularly regarding age categories like here. In the Septuagint, the constituents of the community are given as young (*neaniskoi*) and old (*presbyteroi, presbytai*) (Exod 10:9; Josh 6:21; Isa 20:4; Ezek 9:6). In the New Testament, distribution is

---

[92] Painter, *1, 2, 3 John*, 185.

used to distinguish between older (*presbyteroi, presbytēs, presbytis*) and younger (*neos, neaniskoi*) groups within the larger community (Acts 2:17; 1 Tim 5:1–2; Titus 2:1–8; 1 Pet 5:1–5).

A second question for interpretation is why the Elder presents two sets of three parallel verses, the second of which is a repetition of the first? The Elder employs the figure of speech known as *conduplicatio* or reduplication, "the repetition of one or more words for the purpose of Amplification or Appeal to Pity" (Rhet. Her. 4.28.38; cf. Quintilian, *Inst.* 9.3.28). The second set of parallel verses is a stylistic variation of the first for emphasis and to lead into what follows. Repetition creates vividness, especially when using the past tense instead of the present (Demetrius, *Eloc.* 4.211–14) as in the second set of parallel verses in 2:14. The Elder vividly emphasizes that the fathers know Christ and the young people have conquered the evil one to give the faithful confidence as he prepares to warn them about the world and the antichrist to follow (2:15–28).

A third question for interpretation is determining why the Elder shifts from the present "I am writing" (*graphō*) in the first set of parallel verses to the aorist "I wrote" (*egrapsa*) in the second set.[93] Explanations coalesce around determining the referent of the two tenses, whether both to 1 John or the present to 1 John and the aorist to a previous letter. Both explanations understand the present tense "I write" as a natural reference to 1 John. The first explanation understands the past tense to refer to a previous work like the Gospel of John, 2 or 3 John, or a lost letter. In the New Testament letters, the authors often describe the process of writing their letters in the present tense (*graphō*) (1 Cor 4:14; 14:37; 2 Cor 13:10; Gal 1:20; 1 Tim 3:14; 2 Pet 3:1) and previous letters in the past tense (1 Cor 5:9; 2 Cor 2:3–4, 9; 7:12).[94] The second explanation understands the past tense "I wrote" to be an epistolary aorist; that is, the Elder recognizes that, from the perspective of the faithful hearing or reading his letter, the writing is indeed past (2:21, 26; 5:13), a perspective also found in other New Testament letters (Rom 5:15; 1 Cor 5:11; 9:15; Gal 6:11; Phlm 19, 21; 1 Pet 5:12).[95]

The second explanation finds support in rhetorical analysis. A shift in verb tense lends variety and liveliness to style (Longinus, *Subl.* 23.1). It was

---

[93] Unfortunately, the NRSVue mistranslates *egrapsa* as present.
[94] Brown, *Epistles of John*, 297; Strecker, *Johannine Letters*, 55–56.
[95] Bultmann, *Johannine Epistles*, 31; Painter, *1, 2, 3 John*, 185; Parsenios, *First, Second, and Third John*, 82; Schnackenburg, *Johannine Epistles*, 118.

advised that the past tense be used instead of the present or the future because it is more vivid: "There is something more striking in the suggestion that all is over, than in the intimation that it is about to happen or is still happening" (Demetrius, *Eloc.* 4.214). Also, while the Elder refers to writing the faithful in the present and aorist tenses, he enumerates their spiritual qualities in the perfect tense (sins forgiven, knowing Christ and the Father, and conquering the evil one). This shift to the perfect tense not only contributes to the vividness of style but also amplifies the Elder's emphasis that the faithful possess the spiritual qualities that he has been discussing in 1:5–2:11 – and continue to do so.

Accompanying the verb to write is the conjunction *hoti*, which can be translated causally as "because" or "since," explaining why the Elder writes, or declaratively as "that," telling what he has to say. If the former, he writes because he knows that the faithful are spiritually secure. If the latter, he writes to assure them of their spiritual status in light of the secessionist threat. Except for the obscure use of "I write because" (*graphō hoti*) in 2:21 that is clearly causal, "I write" (*graphō*) is always followed by a direct object in 1 John (1:4; 2:1, 7, 8, 26; 5:13), and this points to a declarative usage here. The Elder's purpose it to affirm the positive spiritual status of the faithful.[96]

The digression develops several topics. Regarding the faithful, the Elder affirms that "your sins are forgiven on account of his [Jesus's] name" (v. 12).[97] This affirmation implies that the faithful have confessed their sins and have the truth within as promised in 1:7–9. This affirmation may have a baptismal background, for "being baptized in the name of Jesus Christ" was an early Christian expression (cf. Phil 2:9–11) and indicates that baptism may have involved a confession of Jesus through whom forgiveness was available (cf. 3:23; 5:13; 3 John 7).[98]

The Elder twice affirms that the fathers "know (*ginoskō*) him [Christ] who is from the beginning," which is also to affirm that they obey the commandments (2:3–4). The Elder twice asserts that the young people "have conquered the evil one," introducing the topic of conquering (*nikaō*) that recurs throughout 1 John in relation to overcoming the evil one

---

[96] Brown, *Epistles of John*, 300–01, 318–19; Painter, *1, 2, 3 John*, 185–86. *Contra* Parsenios, *First, Second, and Third John*, 80. Unfortunately, the NRSVue is translated causally as "because."

[97] The referent to the name, whether God or Jesus, is not specified, but is Jesus in the other two references in 1 John to follow (3:23; 5:13)

[98] Acts 2:38; 8:16; cf. 1 Cor 1:13–15. Brown, *Epistles of John*, 303, 319–23. *Contra* Bultmann, *Johannine Epistles*, 31, n. 8; Schnackenburg, *Johannine Epistles*, 116.

(2:13–14), the secessionists and their teaching (that is, those who have the spirit of the antichrist, 4:4), and the world (5:4–5; cf. John 16:33), which lies in the power of the evil one (5:18–19; cf. 2:15–17). This verb can be metaphorical of forces of light and darkness doing battle (cf. Luke 11:22; Rom 12:21). It is used seventeen times in Revelation in the context of the final battle between Christ and Satan. Thus, the young people are portrayed as current victors in the ongoing war with the power that the evil one wields in the world. Their victory is twice portrayed in the past tense to imply that their conquest is past, secure, and enduring. In addition, to his second assertion that the young people have overcome the evil one, the Elder adds, "You are strong and the word of God abides in you," which implies that they, unlike the secessionists, acknowledge their sin and rely on the atoning sacrifice of Jesus Christ (1:10; cf. 1:8).

> **A CLOSER LOOK: THE EVIL ONE**
>
> The leader of the power of evil has a variety of names in the Johannine literature, including Satan (John 13:27), the devil (John 8:44; 13:2; 1 John 3:8, 10), the "evil one" (John 17:15; 1 John 2:13–14; 3:12; 5:18–19; cf. Matt 5:37; 6:13; 13:19, 38–39; Eph 6:16), and the ruler of this world (John 12:31; 14:30; 16:11). The whole world lies under the power of the evil one (John 12:31; 14:30; 16:11; 1 John 5:19). As long as Christians are in the world, they are vulnerable to the evil one and need the protection of God and Jesus Christ (John 17:15–16; 1 John 5:18). The devil is a liar and the father of lies (John 8:44). He is associated with a spirit of antichrist and error (1 John 4:3, 6). He has been sinning from the beginning, and those who sin are his children (1 John 3:8, 10). Being in the world and of the devil leads to murder (John 8:44) like it did for Cain (1 John 3:12). Satan put it into the heart of Judas to betray Jesus (John 13:2) and eventually motivates Judas to do so (John 13:27). On account of Judas's allegiance to Satan Jesus calls him a devil (John 6:70). Jesus accuses the Jewish hierarchy of being in league with the devil for their lies and desire to kill him (John 8:44)
>
> God revealed Jesus to destroy the works of the devil (1 John 3:8). Jesus's hour drives out the ruler of this world (John 12:31) and condemns him (16:11). Jesus has conquered the world (John 16:33), and, through faith, Christians have also conquered the world (1 John 4:4; 5:4–5), the evil one (1 John 2:13–14), and the secessionist antichrists (1

John 4:4). The evil one cannot harm Christians under the protection of God (1 John 5:18), and Christians conquer evil forces in the present (Rev 2:7, 10–11, 17, 26–28; 3:5, 12, 21; 12:11; 21:7). However, people resist the revelation of God in Christ and remain aligned with the devil (John 8:44). The secessionists are such people and belong to the world and Satan.

2:15–17: EXHORTATION NOT TO LOVE THE WORLD

2:15 Do not love the world or the things in the world. The love of the Father[99] is not in those who love the world;

2:16 for all that is in the world – the desire of the flesh, the desire of the eyes, the pride of riches – comes not from the Father but from the world.

2:17 And the world and its desire are passing away, but those who do the will of God abide forever.

Prior to this point in the letter the Elder has instructed (1:1–2:11) and praised (2:12–14) the churches. Now he turns to exhortation, which is common to epideictic rhetoric (Cicero, *Or. Brut.* 11.37). This is a natural move because wording alone distinguishes praise from exhortation (Aristotle, *Rhet.* 1.9.1368a.36–37). His digression of 2:12–14 affirms the churches of their spiritual health, preparing them for exhortation to elicit their continued adherence to the course of action they have already undertaken and constraining future behavior. The digression ends with the affirmation that the churches have overcome the evil one, and this section begins with an exhortation not to love the world that is under his control (5:19; John 12:31; 14:30; cf. 17:15–16).

Epideictic rhetoric needs proof if practical matters (like the proper object of one's love as in this context) are being discussed (Quintilian, *Inst.* 3.7.4–6). This section is a proof and is partially constructed according to a Greco-Roman standard elaboration pattern for argumentation. This

---

[99] The "love of the Father" (*tou patros*) can be an objective genitive ("love for the Father") or a subjective genitive ("love coming from the Father"). Being in contrast with the "love of the world," the former is indicated, but the latter cannot be ruled out since God's love is transforming and only found in those so transformed who should no longer love the world.

pattern underlies a variety of ancient forms, including the basic speech form, supporting arguments, the complete argument, the amplification of a theme, and the elaboration of a chreia.[100] Pertinent to this portion of 1 John, Pseudo-Cicero offers a pattern of argumentation for the complete argument composed of the proposition, reason, confirmation of the reason, embellishment, and conclusion or résumé (Rhet. Her. 2.18.28–29.46).

The argument of 1 John 2:15–17 is composed according to this pattern. The exhortation "Do not love the world or the things in the world" is really a proposition that the Elder wishes to develop, for phraseology alone distinguishes exhortation from a proposition. The proposition can be stated as "Christians should not love the world or the things in the world" (v. 15a). This proposition is followed by the reason that provides a basis for and establishes the truth of the proposition: "The love of the Father is not in those who love the world" (v. 15b). The reason in turn is followed by the confirmation, which uses additional arguments to corroborate the briefly presented reason. The confirmation begins with the conjunction "for" (*hoti*), indicating that it provides further support for the reason, and it is composed of two statements: "For all that is in the world – the desire of the flesh, the desire of the eyes, the pride in riches – comes not from the Father but from the world" (v. 16) and "And the world and its desire are passing away, but those who do the will of God abide forever" (v. 17). Antitheses, central to epideictic rhetoric (Cicero, *Or. Brut.* 12.38), pervade the argument: love of the world versus love of the Father (v. 15), coming from the world versus coming from the Father (v. 16), and the world and its desire passing away versus those who do the will of God living forever (v. 17). Antithesis and the juxtaposition of contraries make things clearer in argumentation (Aristotle, *Rhet.* 2.23.1400b.30; 3.17.1418b.13).

This argument has a strongly deliberative intent. Epideictic and deliberative rhetoric share the common topics of what is honorable and expedient (Aristotle, *Rhet.* 2.22.1396a.8). Here the Elder advises the churches not to love the world (v. 15) as expedient because it results in living forever as the honorable reward (v. 17). There is an implicit invective here that the secessionists love of the world because they indulge the desire of the flesh,

---

[100] This pattern is discussed in detail in R. F. Hock and E. N. O'Neil, *The Chreia in Ancient Rhetoric. Volume I: The Progymnasmata*. Texts and Translations 27; Graeco-Roman Religion Series 9 (Atlanta: Scholars Press, 1986); B. L. Mack, "Elaboration of the Chreia in the Hellenistic School," in B. L. Mack and V. K. Robbins, eds., *Patterns of Persuasion in the Gospels* (Sonoma: Polebridge, 1989), 31–67.

the desire of the eyes, and the pride in riches (cf. 3:17).[101] These verses are the only elaborate argument in 1 John. Few such units of structured proof would be expected in epideictic rhetoric. This argument's high degree of amplification indicates that the Elder believes that churches are vulnerable to the love of the world.

The argument contrasts the opposite and exclusive nature of the love of the Father and the love of the world. The love of the Father entails obedience to the word (2:5) and results in abiding with God forever. The love of the world entails disobedience and passing away along with the world. The disobedient nature of love of the world is described as "the desire of the flesh, the desire of the eyes, and the pride in riches." This triad represents the figure of speech called *definitio* or definition, which "in brief and clear-cut fashion grasps the characteristic qualities of a thing" (Rhet. Her. 4.25.35). This triad also amplifies by accumulation, giving a quick understanding of a topic (Quintilian, *Inst.* 8.4.26–27; cf. Longinus, *Subl.* 12.2). It was a widespread practice in antiquity to list three sources or species of evil.[102]

In the first part of the confirmation of the argument (v. 16), the desire of the flesh is more than sexual sin, although such sin is often its main referent. It is human nature in its mortal and vulnerable condition, trying to be self-sufficient without acknowledging God. The flesh is not inherently evil, but its desires can lead to sin. It cannot find God without being transformed by the Spirit (John 3:6; 6:63). The desire of the eyes is to see only the physical world and not the spiritual kingdom that God has introduced into the world through Jesus Christ. Sexual desire and desire for riches were often associated with the desire of the eyes. Pride in riches (lit. "of life") is contentment with physical life (*bios*), like possessions, social status, and power (cf. 1 John 3:17), without striving for the spiritual life God gives in Christ (*zōē*). Jesus warned of the dangers of riches shifting allegiance away from God (Mark 10:23–27 par.; Luke 6:24; 12:13–21, 32–34; 16:19–31). In summary, loving the world is to let fleshly desires direct life, to be content with temporary physical life and relying on earthly gains, and to be unwilling to receive the gifts of God.

---

[101] Painter, *1, 2, 3 John*, 190–91.
[102] For references, see Brown (*Epistles of John*, 307–08). Some scholars see the first element in the triad as inclusive of the other two (J. L. Houlden, *The Johannine Epistles*. HNTC [Peabody: Hendrickson, 1988], 74), but this ancient practice of listing three sources of evil does not support this assumption.

2:15–17: Exhortation Not to Love the World

In the second part of the confirmation of the argument (v. 17), the antithesis contrasts the world and its desire passing away with those doing God's will and abiding forever. The verb "passing away" (*paragō*) is reintroduced from 2:8, where it refers to the darkness passing away as the return of Christ approaches. As in 2:8, here the verb is a durative present tense stressing that, like the darkness, the world has already begun to pass away because Christ is returning (2:18, 28; cf. 1 Cor 7:31). In contrast, those doing the will (*thelēma*) of God live forever (Matt 7:21; John 8:51). The antithesis offers the constraint of not aligning with the world and passing away along with it, strongly implying that doing the will of God is the ultimate expedient and honorable choice.

A CLOSER LOOK: THE WORLD

In Johannine literature, the term "world" (*kosmos*) is richly nuanced. The world is God's good creation, but it is also the realm of sin, opposed to God, and in the power of the evil one (1 John 5:19; John 12:31; 14:30; 16:11; cf. 1 John 4:3–4). The love of the world with its fleshly desires and love of riches can usurp humankind's love of God even though the world and its desires will pass away (1 John 2:15–17). The world is the sphere of the antichrist, with whom the secessionists are identified (1 John 2:18, 22; 4:3; 2 John 7). False prophets with the spirit of the antichrist, like the secessionists, are in the world, and the world listens to them (1 John 4:1–6). The world does not know God, Christ, or Christians who are God's children (1 John 3:1; John 14:17). The world hates Jesus as well as Christians (1 John 3:13; John 7:7; 15:19; 16:2, 33; 17:14).

Regardless, God loves the world (1 John 4:9–10; John 3:16) and sends Jesus to the world as an atoning sacrifice (1 John 2:2; 3:16; 4:9–10; cf. 1:7; John 1:29), as Savior of the world (1 John 4:14; John 3:16–17; 4:42; 12:47). Jesus brought light (1 John 1:5; John 3:19; 8:12; 9:5; 12:46) and life (John 6:33, 51) into the world, which brought judgment to the world (John 9:39; 12:31). He came to drive out Satan, the ruler of this world, and conquer the world (John 12:31; 16:33).

The world is the workplace of the spirit of truth and the spirit of error. Christians who are of God and have the spirit of truth within them have conquered the spirit of error (4:1–6). Jesus sends Christians into the world to transform it (John 17:18), but they are not to be of the world (John 15:19; 17:14–19). They have conquered the world through faith in the Son of God (1 John 5:4–5) and can bring God's transforming love to the world (cf. Jas 4:4).

BRIDGING THE HORIZONS

The Elder's approach here is a teachable moment. He first affirms that the faithful experience key theological realities (2:12–14). Then, with that position of spiritual strength in the forefront of their minds, he exhorts them about a key threat to the experience of those realities (2:15–17). They are forgiven in the name of Christ, know God, and have conquered the evil one, and the word of God abides within them. While experiencing such a strong spiritual position, love of the world poses a great threat. The world offers many idolatrous distractions vying for attention, devotion, ambition, selfish goals, and more. Loving the world is to venture back to darkness and death. It is ultimately a foolish, regressive move because the world and all that it offers is already passing away, but the love of God and obedience to God are eternal life. This section puts before us the age-old struggle with holding to theological realities that are invisible and cannot be grasped and the lure of what is visible and graspable. It is the struggle between a promised long-term investment payout and immediate satisfaction.

2:18–27: BEWARE THE ANTICHRISTS AND AFFIRM JESUS AS THE CHRIST

> 2:18 Children, it is the last hour! As you have heard that antichrist is coming, so now many antichrists have come. From this we know that it is the last hour.
>
> 2:19 They went out from us, but they did not belong to us, for if they had belonged to us, they would have remained with us. But by going out, they made it plain that none of them belongs to us.
>
> 2:20 But you have been anointed by the Holy One, and all of you have knowledge.

> 2:21 I write to you, not because you do not know the truth, but because you know it, and you know that no lie comes from the truth.
>
> 2:22 Who is the liar but he who denies that Jesus is the Christ? This is the antichrist, the one who denies the Father and the Son.
>
> 2:23 No one who denies the Son has the Father; everyone who confesses the Son has the Father also.
>
> 2:24 Let what you heard from the beginning abide in you. If what you heard from the beginning abides in you, then you will abide in the Son and in the Father.
>
> 2:25 And this is what he has promised us, eternal life.
>
> 2:26 I write these things to you concerning those who would deceive you.
>
> 2:27 As for you, the anointing that you received from him abides in you, and so you do not need anyone to teach you. But as his anointing teaches you about all things and is true and is not a lie, and just as it has taught you, abide in him.

Although the Elder has been indirectly referring to the words and deeds of the secessionists from the beginning of his letter, now for the first time he specifically identifies them and the threat they pose to the faithful and their spiritual status (he will do so again in 4:1–6). He opens this section with the familiar address, "children" (*paidia*), and structures it with three negative characterizations of the secessionists and their message (vv. 18–19, 22–23, 26) juxtaposed with three positive affirmations of the faithful and their spiritual status (vv. 20–21, 24–25, 27). Each of the affirmations begins with the second-person plural "you" to help contrast the faithful with the secessionists, and each refers to a message or anointing received from Christ that protects the faithful from secessionist deceits.

The three negative characterizations of the secessionists are invectives based on their character and deeds; that is, artificial proofs of pathos (emotion) that are commonly employed in epideictic rhetoric to refute the opposition (Aristotle, [*Rhet. Alex.*] 34.1440a.20ff.). In epideictic rhetoric, the rhetor considers what the audience deems praiseworthy or condemnable as a basis upon which to construct praise or blame (Aristotle, *Rhet.* 1.9.1367b.30–31). The Elder does just this. He declares the secessionists to be former imposters in the Johannine churches (vv. 18–19), calls their denial of Jesus as the Christ a lie that makes them the antichrist (vv. 22–23), and denigrates their overall message as deceitful (v. 26). Clearly the above characteristics are condemnable in Johannine tradition.

As is common in epideictic rhetoric, this section is composed of facts to be taken on trust and amplification of topics (Aristotle, *Rhet.* 1.9.1368a.38–40; 3.17.1417b.3; [*Rhet. Alex.*] 3; Cicero, *Part. or.* 21.71; Rhet. Her. 3.8.15; Quintilian, *Inst.* 3.7.6). The facts taken on trust are judgments (*kriseis*); that is, commonly held beliefs and opinions (Cicero, *Inv.* 1.30.48; Quintilian, *Inst.* 5.11.36–44), here of the Johannine Community as interpreted by the Holy Spirit. Brief and frequent use of amplification enhances these facts.

2:18–19: First Negative Characterization of the Secessionists

This section begins with the bold proclamation, "Children, it is the last hour! As you have heard that antichrist is coming, so now many antichrists have come. From this we know that it is the last hour" (v. 18; cf. 4:3). This heralding of the last hour is made as an epicheireme, a syllogism in which the premises are not necessarily certain. "You have heard that antichrist is coming" can be expressed as the major premise "the antichrist will come in the last days." The minor premise is "Now many antichrists have come." The conclusion is "it is the last hour."

The Elder uses a sign to formulate the premises of his epicheireme. A sign is "a thing that normally precedes or accompanies or follows a thing" (Aristotle, [*Rhet. Alex.*] 12.1430b.30ff.). The sign of the last hour is the appearance of the secessionist antichrists. Their coming is a sign because, as the Elder assumes here and elsewhere (4:3; 2 John 7), Jesus's prophecies about an antichrist in the last days were preserved in Johannine tradition.[103] The phrase "the hour is coming" (*eschatē hora estin*) was used in a simpler form by Jesus in John's Gospel to herald crucial moments in salvation history (John 4:21, 23; 5:25, 28; 16:25). The coming of the antichrists indicates that it is the last hour within God's plan.

The topic of the antichrist introduced here is both singular and plural. It reappears twice in the singular and is defined as denying that Jesus is the Christ (2:22) and not confessing Jesus (4:3; cf. 2 John 7). It has a plural component when multiple people share an erroneous Christological confession. By switching the singular to the plural of antichrist, the Elder uses Johannine tradition to associate the plural secessionists and their teaching

---

[103] Cf. Jesus's warnings against false messiahs and false prophets in Mark 13:5–6, 22 and Matt 24:24.

with the ultimate single evil antichrist of tradition. Eschatological expectations could be molded to suit rhetorical and theological needs.[104]

In v. 18 the verb "hear" (*akouō*) is in the second-person plural ("you have heard") and the contrasting verb "know" (*ginoskō*) is in the third-person plural ("we know"). The Elder implies that the faithful ("you") have heard about the antichrist from the tradition-bearers of which he is a member ("we"; cf. 1:1–3; 2:7, 24; 3:11; 4:3), but he includes himself, the other tradition-bearers, and the faithful together as knowing that the antichrists have come and thus that it is the last hour. The entire community brings its previous knowledge of tradition and current eyewitness experience to conclude that the antichrists have come. This interplay acts as a constraint, making it harder to deny the Elder's conclusion.

The pronouncement that it is the last hour is highly amplified. It repeats "the world and its desire are passing away" from the preceding verse in more pointed form. The pronouncement both begins and ends v. 18, forming an inclusion, which is amplification by repetition (Cicero, *Part. or.* 15.54). In addition, there is asseveration or a firm assertion (Quintilian, *Inst.* 5.12.12), and an exclamation (Rhet. Her. 4.15.22; Quintilian, *Inst.* 9.2.26–27; 9.3.97), both of which are intended to arouse emotion. The Elder amplifies the urgent nature of the time in which he and the faithful find themselves, as the last hour calls for preparation so as not to be caught unaware by coming judgment.

The last hour is probably the final moment before the return of Jesus, not the last days that constitute the entire period between the first and second comings of Jesus.[105] In the preceding verse the world is already passing away (2:17), and the following section begins by assuming that the faithful will be present at the second coming of Jesus (2:28). While the "hour" in Johannine thought often refers to the climax of Jesus's ministry (John 2:4; 7:30; 8:20; 12:23, 27; 13:1; 17:1), it can also refer to the resurrection and judgment of the end of time (John 5:25–29). The similar phrase "the last day" (*eschatē hemera*) refers to the future resurrection (John 6:39–40, 44, 54; 11:24) and final judgment (John 12:48). By historicizing the antichrist and identifying the secessionists as antichrists, the Elder has made the Johannine churches players in the apocalypse.

---

[104] Brown, *Epistles of John*, 337; Bultmann, *Johannine Epistles*, 35–36; Smalley, *1, 2, 3 John*, 98–99.

[105] This understanding is akin to "the last days" in 2 Tim 3:1 and 2 Pet 3:3 and "the last time" in Jude 18.

In v. 19 the Elder makes every effort to completely dissociate the secessionists from the faithful of the Johannine Community. He presents an enthymeme (a premise and conclusion). The premise (also a sign) is "if they had belonged to us, they would have remained with us." The secessionists' departure from the community is a sign that they never truly belonged to the community. The conclusion is "They went out from us, but they did not belong to us." The unstated premise is "those who leave the community were never truly part of it." The enthymeme is amplified by a repetition of the premise: "But by going out,[106] they made it plain that none of them belongs to us."[107]

The dissociation of the faithful and the secessionists is carefully crafted using an interplay of verbs and prepositions. A component of this dissociation is the verb "going out" (*exerchomai*), which denotes both a positive and negative movement in the Johannine Epistles. It is positive if going out is for the name of Christ (3 John 7) and negative if it is to spread false prophecy (4:1) and deception (2 John 7). It describes Judas going out from the last supper to betray Jesus (John 13:30–31). Similar language of "going away" is used of disciples who chose to no longer follow Jesus (*aperchomai, hypagō*; John 6:66–67). Here in v. 19 the secessionists who once followed Jesus no longer do so, and they go out of the community to spread lies and false Christology as antichrists (2:19–23).

Another component creating dissociation of the faithful and the secessionists is the threefold use of the expression "being of" (*einai ek*); that is, being physically but never spiritually part of the community. In Johannine literature, the "being of" topic is used of being of God (1 John 3:10; 4:4, 6; 5:19; 3 John 11; John 8:47), the Father (1 John 2:16), and the truth (1 John 2:21; John 18:37). The only other option is not to be of God (1 John 3:10; 4:6; John 8:47) and Jesus's sheep (John 10:26) and to be of the devil (1 John 3:8) and the world (1 John 4:5). By "going out" of the community to spread lies and deceit, the secessionists were never of God and the truth, but reveal themselves as being of the devil and the world. The assumption is that only

---

[106] The Elder uses ellipsis here, so a phrase like "this happened" or "they went out" needs to be supplied.

[107] With most scholars, I am assuming that "not" (*ouk*) modifies the verb "are" (*eisin*) rather than the pronoun "all" (*pantes*); that is, as "all [antichrists] do not belong to us" rather than "not all [antichrists and followers] belong to us," the latter of which implies that some of the secessionists are still in the community. Leaving the community is a defining characteristic of an antichrist. *Contra* Bultmann, *Johannine Epistles*, 36–37; Dodd, *Johannine Epistles*, 52.

2:20-21: First Affirmation of the Faithful

After negatively characterizing the secessionists as antichrists (vv. 18-19), the Elder affirms the faithful: "But you have been anointed by the Holy One, and all of you have knowledge.[109] I write to you, not because you do not know the truth, but because you know it, and know that no lie comes from the truth" (vv. 20-21). The anointing by the Holy One refers to Christ spiritually anointing believers with the Holy Spirit at conversion and baptism (cf. John 6:69).[110] The anointing abides within the believer as a teacher of truth (2:27) and is probably to be equated with "God's seed abiding within" (3:9). It is not mere baptism, for the secessionists have also been baptized, but a divine gift requiring proper faith, which the secessionists lack. The Gospel of John uses this language of the Paraclete, a spirit of truth who abides in believers and witnesses about Jesus and guides them into the truth (John 14:16-17, 15:26; 16:12-15).[111] The Elder assures the faithful that they can rely on the anointing of the Holy Spirit for knowledge in the face of secessionist teaching and their exclusive claims to knowledge (cf. 2:12-14; 3:19-22).

This affirmation of the faithful is highly amplified. It is only after the Elder affirms that they know (v. 20) that the object of that knowledge is

---

[108] Brown, *Epistles of John*, 339; Smalley, *1, 2, 3 John*, 102-03.

[109] Readings vary between the masculine nominative *pantes* ("you all know") and the neuter accusative *panta* ("you know all"). With the NRSVue I choose the reading *pantes* because it is supported by older manuscripts and just occurred in the previous verse. The reading *panta* can be explained as scribes giving the verb "know" (*oidate*) an object and as assimilation to *panta* in the parallel passage of 2:27 (cf. John 14:26). Metzger, *Textual Commentary*, 710.

[110] The Holy One who anoints the faithful is either God, Christ, or the Holy Spirit. The Spirit is called "holy" (John 1:33; 14:26; 20:22) and a "spirit of truth" (1 John 4:6). Leading into truth is the role of the anointing here (vv. 21, 27) and of the Holy Spirit in the Gospel of John (14:17, 26; 16:13). However, the Holy Spirit anointing believers with itself is not Johannine thought. God is called "holy" (John 17:11) and Jesus is "the holy one of God" (John 6:69). Both the Father (John 14:16, 26) and the Son (John 15:26; 16:7) send the Holy Spirit. Later in this passage Christ sends the anointing (1 John 2:27), so it is likely he is the one anointing here (Painter, *1, 2, 3 John*, 198).

[111] For further discussion of the complexities of this passage, see Brown, *Epistles of John*, 342-48; Painter, *1, 2, 3 John*, 197-99; Strecker, *Johannine Letters*, 64-66.

revealed to be the truth (v. 21). The three consecutive clauses of v. 21, each introduced by "because" (*hoti*) and referring to the faithful knowing (*oidate*) the truth, represent amplification by reduplication, which strongly affirms that the faithful are in full possession of the knowledge of the truth (as in 2:7, 12–14). In light of Johannine tradition, to affirm that the faithful know the truth is also to affirm that they are children of God rather than of the devil, the father of lies (John 8:44), and are obedient to Christ (John 18:37). This affirmation constrains the faithful by bringing the authority of their anointing to confirm the Elder's preceding characterization of the secessionists as antichrists (vv. 18–19) and his negative assessment of their Christology that immediately follows (vv. 22–23). For the faithful to reject the Elder's assessment of the secessionists and their Christology is to deny their knowledge derived from the Holy Spirit. As a good rhetorician, the Elder has linked the praise of his audience to the advantage of his cause and his desired outcomes (Cicero, *Inv.* 1.16.22; Rhet. Her. 1.5.8; Quintilian, *Inst.* 4.1.16). Now to know (*oida*) the truth (*aletheia*) provided by the Holy Spirit enables the faithful to distinguish truth (*aletheia*) from falsehood (*pseudos*) and reject secessionist claims.

2:22–23: Second Negative Characterization of the Secessionists

The Elder now poses a rhetorical question (Aristotle, *Rhet.* 3.18; *Top.* 8; Rhet. Her. 4.15.22–16.24; 4.23.33–24.34; Quintilian, *Inst.* 9.2.6–16). Rhetorical questions posed in argumentation either do or do not receive an answer by the one posing them (Cicero, *Part. or.* 13.47; Quintilian, *Inst.* 5.11.5). Here the answer to the question is contained in the question itself: "Who is the liar but the one who denies that Jesus is the Christ?"[112] The confession that "Jesus is the Messiah, the Son of God" culminates the Gospel of John (20:31), and the confession Jesus is the Christ was central to the Johannine tradition (1 John 5:1) and not to be modified (2 John 9). The Elder follows his rhetorical question with a further identification of the liar who denies Jesus is the Christ: "This is the antichrist, the one who denies the Father and the Son" (cf. 4:2–3; 2 John 7).[113] The addition of the Father in this second identification is amplification by augmentation (Cicero, *Part. or.* 15.54; Quintilian, *Inst.* 8.4.3–9) based on Johannine tradition that the Father and Son are a unity and to deny the Son is to

---

[112] A similar rhetorical question with the answer subsumed in the question is found in 5:5.
[113] Compare 5:10, where the one denying that Jesus is the Son makes God a liar.

deny the Father (cf. 1:2–3; 5:5; John 5:23; 8:19; 10:30; 12:44–45; 14:6–11; 15:23; 16:3; 17:3).

The Elder has already identified the secessionists as the antichrists (2:18), and now he identified them as the liar. The word "liar" (*pseustēs*) is used seven times in Johannine literature (John 8:44, 55; 1 John 1:10; 2:4, 22; 4:20; 5:10). This is the only occurrence preceded by the definite article, which elsewhere generally indicates something distinct and known.[114] Here it refers to an anticipated opponent of the faithful of the last times known for deceit (CD 20:14–15; cf. Matt 24:4–5; 2 Thess 2:8–12). The Gospel of John applies *pseustēs* to the devil (8:44, 55). Second John 7 joins "the deceiver" (*ho planos*) with the antichrist.

The rhetoric is subtle. There is only insinuation here. The Elder does not explicitly identify the secessionists as the liar or the antichrist but has led the faithful to easily draw that conclusion for themselves. He has associated the secessionists with lying and deceit (1:6, 8, 10; 2:4) and identified them as antichrists for leaving the community (2:18–19), and the community knows what the secessionists teach about Christ. How can the faithful draw any other conclusion, especially since, as he has just said, they know the truth from their anointing by Jesus Christ!

Verse 23 draws out the full implication of denying the Son as mentioned in v. 22 – not having the Father either. It is a fine example of refining of the type in which the idea is altered by using the contrary (Rhet. Her. 4.43.56). Both sentences say the same thing, the only difference being the former is negative and the latter positive: "No one who denies the Son has the Father; everyone who confesses the Son has the Father also" (cf. Matt 10:32–33). Refining amplifies the inseparable connection between the Father and the Son in Johannine tradition. Confessing that Jesus is the Christ is necessary for mutual abiding of God and the believer and being born of God (4:15; 5:1; cf. 2 John 9).

2:24–25: Second Affirmation of the Faithful

In v. 24 the Elder makes an appeal to the faithful to adhere to the Christian tradition, a common move in early Christian polemic against false teaching (2 Tim 1:13; 2 Pet 3:2; Jude 3, 17, 20). He gives a positive exhortation with a supporting reason: "Let what you heard from the beginning abide in you. If what you heard from the beginning abides in you, then you will abide in

---

[114] BDF §§252.

the Son and in the Father." The exhortation begins emphatically with the pronoun "you" (*hymeis*), which emphasizes the subject of proclamation introduced later in the sentence (*casus pendens*). It includes three uses of the pronoun "you" (*hymeis*) with the verb "abide" (*menō*), the first two of which are part of a chiasm with the proclamation. The exhortation is amplified using repetition to make a strong distinction between the secessionist liar/antichrists and the faithful and to encourage the faithful to abide in the proclamation of the Johannine Community and thus in the Son and the Father. This is the proclamation that the faithful heard at the beginning of their Christian lives that came from the beginning of Jesus's self-revelation (1:1–3; 2:7; 3:11; 2 John 5–6).[115] The need to confess Jesus as the Christ is one of the most important features of this proclamation, something that the liar secessionists do not do (2:22).[116] This verse unites two related aspects of abiding: Jesus's commandment to abide in his word (John 8:31; 15:7) and the resulting mutual abiding and fellowship between God, Christ, and the believer (1:3; 2:5–6; John 15:1–10; 17:20–23).

In v. 25 the Elder adds that eternal life awaits those who abide by the initial proclamation that they heard: "And this is what he[117] has promised us,[118] eternal life." This is the first of three affirmations that the Johannine proclamation includes the promise of eternal life, each one introduced by the phrase "and this is" (*kai autē estin*; 2:25; 3:11–17, 5:11). Eternal life is not an endless heavenly bliss per se but a quality of life that transcends the world and its desires that are passing away (1:2; 2:17; 3:15; 5:11, 13, 20; John 3:36; 6:47; 10:10, 28; 17:3).

The Elder switches from addressing the faithful in the second-person plural "you" to include himself with them in the first-person plural "we." He does not include himself in the preceding exhortation to abide in what has been heard from the beginning (v. 24), the underlying assumption

---

[115] Some scholars extend the meaning of "from the beginning" to include the period of Jesus's own self-revelation (Brown, *Epistles of John*, 355; Smalley, *1, 2, 3 John*, 118) and even previous teaching about the Jewish Scriptures in the synagogue (Brooke, *Johannine Epistles*, 60). However, the former is what is being proclaimed and not the experience of the audience (1:1–3), and the latter would be an obscure referent.
[116] Bultmann, *Johannine Epistles*, 40.
[117] With most commentators, I assume that "he" (*autos*) refers to Jesus, not God. Although the closest referent is the Father in v. 24, *autos* is emphatic, and in the previous discussion the denial of Jesus is the focus (2:22–23).
[118] Some manuscripts read "to you" (*hymin*) instead of "to us" (*hēmin*). This reading is probably explained as a scribal change to conform v. 25 to the second person found four times in v. 24.

being that he is not in danger of doing so. However, he includes himself with the faithful as co-possessors of the promise of eternal life that all true believers already possess (3:14; 5:11–13; John 6:40; 17:3). This is a subtle way of maintaining his authority while relating to the faithful.

The phrase "and this is" (*kai houtos estin*) referring to what Jesus promised can refer back to the preceding verse on abiding in what had been heard leading to abiding in the Son and in the Father, or forward to eternal life, or both. While there is no explicit promise of Jesus corresponding to what precedes, the concept is found in Johannine tradition (cf. John 15:4, 7; 17:22–23). In contrast, Jesus's promise of eternal life in general (10:10, 28; 17:2–3) and for those who believe (John 3:16, 36; 5:24; 6:40, 47) is explicit. Even so, what Jesus promised probably refers both to what precedes and to what follows, for eternal life is a consequence of abiding in what has been heard and thus abiding in the Son and the Father.[119] This sudden reference to the promise of eternal life amplifies the need to abide because it pertains to heavenly matters, things advantageous to humankind, and the love of God (Cicero, *Part. or.* 16.55–56) and constrains behavior in those fearful of losing this blessing.

2:26: Third Negative Characterization of the Secessionists

The Elder begins closing this section in v. 26 with a reference to writing: "I write these things[120] to you concerning those who would deceive you." He shifts back from the first-person plural "we" that included himself with the faithful as recipients of the promise of eternal life (v. 25) to the first-person singular "I" to speak with the authority of the Johannine tradition-bearers. The present participle of "deceive" (*planōntōn*) denotes that the deception is in progress. Having identified the secessionists with the liar and antichrist (2:18, 22), the Elder now links the apocalyptic expectation of a great deception in the last days to them as well (cf. 2:18, 28; 2 John 7; Matt 24:11, 24; Mark 13:5–6, 22; 1 Tim 4:1; Rev 12:9; Did. 16:4). This is his first warning to beware of the activity of the secessionists, and it is in a strong apocalyptic context. The last hour calls for circumspection (2:18,

---

[119] Brown, *Epistles of John*, 356–57; Smalley, *1, 2, 3 John*, 120–21. Bultmann (*Johannine Epistles*, 40, n. 26) and Schnackenburg (*Johannine Epistles*, 148) restrict the referent of the promise to eternal life.

[120] The things being written are often identified as vv. 18–25.

28), for to be deceived is to be vulnerable to losing eternal life by not abiding in the life-giving proclamation of the community (2:25, 28).

2:27: Third Affirmation of the Faithful

This section ends with a highly rhetorical sentence: "As for you, the anointing that you received from him abides in you, and so you do not need anyone to teach you. But as his[121] anointing teaches you about all things, and is true and is not a lie, and just as it has taught you,[122] abide[123] in him."[124] The initial emphatic phrase "As for you" (*kai hymeis*) creates a strong contrast between the faithful and the deceitful secessionists (v. 26). The faithful do not need secessionist teaching because they have the anointing, the Paraclete, or the Holy Spirit as a teacher abiding within all believers (3:24; 4:13; John 14:17, 26; 15:26; 16:12–15). The Elder personifies the anointing as a teacher and underscores its veracity by using refining, in which the same thing is said using the contrary (Rhet. Her. 4.43.56): The anointing is true and not a lie. This antithetical refining is a subtle comparison between the true teaching of the Holy Spirit and the false teaching of the secessionists (2:21–22).[125] As 4:1 indicates, the underlying assumption is that the secessionists are the false teachers expected to appear in the last days with deceitful teaching (2 Tim 4:3; 2 Pet 2:1).

A CLOSER LOOK: THE ANTICHRIST

The antichrist in Christian tradition is a mysterious figure aligned with Satan who tries to depose Christ and God for the allegiance of humankind. He does so with false teaching supported by counterfeit signs and miracles and by persecuting Christians. He is a key player in the drama of the rise of evil in the last days to make a final attempt to overthrow

---

[121] I am assuming that "him" (*autos*) refers to Christ as it does in 2:25 and 28.
[122] The subject of "teach" (*edidaxen*) is either Christ or the anointing given by him. I am assuming the latter because the anointing is the subject of this verb earlier in the verse.
[123] "Abide" (*menete*) may be either imperative or indicative. I am assuming the former. It is indicative earlier in v. 27 because it is descriptive, but it is imperative elsewhere in the context (vv. 24, 28).
[124] The referent of "him" (*autos*) is either Christ or the anointing. I am assuming the former, for Christ is the referent of this pronoun earlier in the verse and in the phrase "abide in him" in v. 28 to follow.
[125] Cf. the antitheses between truth and falsehood in 1:6, 8; 2:4, 21, which contrast the teaching of the Johannine School and that of the secessionists (cf. 1:10).

God; a drama that culminates in Christ's victory over him in the battle that ends world history and inaugurates the new heavens and earth free of evil.

The antichrist has roots in ancient Near Eastern mythology of a primeval battle of a powerful creator god who subdues a chaos monster who opposes creation, Persian dualism which understands the world as a battleground between forces of good and evil, and adaptation of the two in messianic tradition and in Jewish apocalyptic tradition in the Second Temple period (third century BC to AD 70). The latter traditions shaped the mythology and dualism into prophecies explaining the suffering of God's people under political oppressors in terms of the struggle of God and God's people against Satan and the forces of evil. This adaptation of ideas by Jewish apocalyptic tradition was influenced by secular rulers who claimed to be divine and who persecuted God's people. The primary one was Anthochus IV Epiphanes of Syria (175–164 BC), whose very title "Epiphanes" means "God manifest" and who tried to destroy the Jewish religion to the point of rededicating the temple in Jerusalem to Zeus. The suffering of God's people and the cosmic struggle of which it is a part will end when the Messiah defeats all of God's enemies and establishes God's kingdom on earth (Dan 11:36; Ezek 28:2; 2 Bar. 36–40; T. Mos. 8).

Christianity continued to develop this tradition of focusing the struggle between good and evil on a historical figure working with Satan in opposition to God and God's people. The struggle between good and evil was now of God, Christ, and Christians against Satan, the antichrist, and the wicked. Paul is the first to describe the antichrist, using the title "man of lawlessness." He will place himself in the temple of God, demanding worship and performing signs and wonders empowered by Satan (2 Thess 2:1–12). In the Johannine Epistles, the antichrist is not an individual but the secessionists in the churches sharing the spirit of antichrist. They are false prophets not confessing that Jesus Christ is the Son of God come in the flesh (1 John 2:18, 22; 4:1–3; 2 John 7). Roman claims that the emperor was divine and their persecution of Christians greatly influenced the antichrist tradition. The emperors Nero (AD 54–68) and Domitian (AD 81–96) proclaimed themselves divine and persecuted Christians, both providing models for the portrayal of the antichrist in Revelation (Rev 13:1–10), so much

> so that the final battle between good and evil becomes in part a battle between God and Rome.[126]

BRIDGING THE HORIZONS

The Elder has a vital eschatological expectation, proclaiming that "it is the last hour" (2:18). This colors his interpretation and approach to the situation that he and the faithful face. He proclaims the secessionists to be antichrists and part of the great deception of the last hour. Obviously, it was not the last hour, since we are discussing the Elder's approach almost two millennia later. Many Christian communities have the same vital eschatology and interpret current events as signs of the second coming of Jesus Christ and the consummation of all things. They too may be calling the last hour long ahead of its time. Even so, one positive aspect of this dynamic expectation is that it invigorates the ethical walk and mission to the unrepentant. The accompanying fear of being caught unawares creates vigilance and a sense of urgency. Anticipating an impending full union with Jesus Christ and God and the coming judgment constrains ungodly behavior and motivates obedience. This is not some false hyper-Christianity, for it may very well be the last hour.

The Elder upholds the anointing of the Holy Spirit given to all Christians at conversion as a guide to help distinguish truth from falsehood (2:20, 27). Such a concept is mystical to us today. The Holy Spirit guides us, but how do we distinguish the voice of the Spirit from the voices of our own fears, prejudices, desires, and agendas? The Elder has given us the answer. The anointing of the Holy Spirit works alongside the tradition of our community, which in turn was created by the anointing of many Christians who have come before us and

---

[126] D. F. Watson, "Antichrist," in R. P. Martin and P. H. Davids, eds., *Dictionary of the Later New Testament and Its Developments* (Downers Grove: InterVarsity Press, 1997), 50–53; C. R. Koester, "The Antichrist Theme in the Johannine Epistles and Its Role in Christian Tradition," in Culpepper and Anderson, eds., *Communities in Dispute*, 187–96; L. J. Lietaert Peerbolte, *The Antecedents of Antichrist: A Traditio-Historical Study of the Earliest Christian Views on Eschatological Opponents*. SJSJ 49 (Leiden: E. J. Brill, 1996).

ultimately by the proclamation of Jesus Christ. That tradition is not comprehensive or perfect, but it is a dependable guide for listening for the internal guidance of the Spirit in prayer and fellowship with others in community.

Within some Christian circles there is too much emphasis placed upon the Elder's statement to the faithful that, because they have the anointing, "you do not need anyone to teach you" (2:27). There can be a rejection of the ecclesiastical and scholarly teaching of the Bible, theology, and ethics, with a naive emphasis placed upon listening only to what the "wee small voice" of the Holy Spirit has to say. The call of Martin Luther and others of *"sola scriptura"* or "Scripture alone" is taken out of context so that reading the Bible and waiting for the Holy Spirit to interpret it become private affairs requiring little external guidance. Without the voices from Scripture, tradition, and community there is a danger that what the "wee small voice" says is what is desired to be heard, is limited in perspective, or is just plain not true.

Confession of Jesus as the Christ coming from the tradition and the anointing of the Spirit facilitates and makes possible abiding in God and Jesus Christ. Confession guides us into truth and obedience rather than lies and disobedience, which sever the relationship with God and Christ. Confession is no guarantee of obedience and abiding. The need for the final exhortation of this section strongly implies such: "abide in him" (2:27). Once proper confession establishes the truth and the Holy Spirit guides us, there is continual and concerted work to be done to live by the truth and abide in the one confessed. In addition, having the Son and the Father further strengthens the confessor to continue toward the promised eternal life (2:25).

2:28–3:10: THE IDENTITY OF THE CHILDREN OF GOD

> 2:28 And now, little children, abide in him, so that when he is revealed we may have confidence and not be put to shame before him at his coming.
>
> 2:29 If you perceive that he is righteous, you also know that everyone who does right has been born of him.

3:1 See what love the Father has given us, that we should be called children of God, and that is what we are. The reason the world does not know us is that it did not know him.

3:2 Beloved, we are God's children now; what we will be has not yet been revealed. What we do know is this: when he is revealed, we will be like him, for we will see him as he is.

3:3 And all who have this hope in him purify themselves, just as he is pure.

3:4 Everyone who commits sin is guilty of lawlessness; sin is lawlessness.

3:5 You know that he was revealed to take away sins, and in him there is no sin.

3:6 No one who abides in him sins; no one who sins has either seen him or known him.

3:7 Little children, let no one deceive you. Everyone who does what is right is righteous, just as he is righteous.

3:8 Everyone who commits sin is of the devil; for the devil has been sinning from the beginning. The Son of God was revealed for this purpose: to destroy the works of the devil.

3:9 Those who have been born of God do not sin because God's seed abides in them; they cannot sin, because they have been born of God.

3:10 The children of God and the children of the devil are revealed in this way: all who do not do what is right are not from God, nor are those who do not love a brother or sister.

This section is very carefully crafted. It is framed by an elaborate *inclusio* of repeated topics in 2:28–29 and 3:9–10: children of God (*teknia*, 2:28; *tekna theou*, 3:1–2; *ta tekna tou theou*, 3:10), being born of God (*gennaō*, 2:29; 3:9; cf. *ek tou theo*, 3:10), doing right (*poiōn tēn dikaiosynēn*, 2:29; *ho mē poiōn dikaiosynēn*, 3:10), being revealed (*phanerothē*, 2:28; *phanera*, 3:10), and abiding in him (*menete en autō*, 2:28; *en autō menei*, 3:9). It begins like two preceding sections with the address "little children" (*teknia*, 2:28; *teknia*, 2:12; *paidia*, 2:18) and the preceding section with "and now" (*kai nyn*) followed by an eschatological reference serving as a rhetorical constraint (parousia, 2:28; antichrist, 2:18). It is composed of nine sentences with a participle preceded by a definite article (2:29b; 3:3a, 4a, 6a, 6b, 7b, 8a, 9a, 10b). Seven times this construction employs a form of "all" (*pas*, 2:29b; 3:3a, 4a, 6a, 6b, 9a, 10b). These sentences can be schematized as follows:[127]

---

[127] Brown, *Epistles of John*, 418.

2:29b Everyone who does right has been born of him.
3:3a All who have this hope in him purify themselves.
3:4a Everyone who commits sin is guilty of lawlessness.
3:6a No one who abides in him sins.
3:6b No one who sins has either seen him or known him.
3:7b Everyone who does what is right is righteous.
3:8a Everyone who commits sin is of the devil.
3:9a Those who have been born of God do not sin.
3:10b All who do not do what is right are not from God.

With the exception of v. 3a (which is part of a parenthesis), these sentences form four antithetical pairs. The first and third pair (2:29–3:4; 3:7–8) juxtapose doing right and sin, while the second and fourth pair (3:6; 3:9–10) juxtapose having or not having a relationship with the divine. In the second and fourth pair, the conclusion of the first part of the antithesis begins the second. These four antithetical pairs are in turn grouped into two units (2:28–3:6; 3:7–10), each beginning with the address "children" (*teknia*, 2:28; 3:7). Each of these two units has its own *inclusio*, for 2:28 and 3:6 both contain the topic of abiding in Christ (*menein en*), and 3:7 and 3:10 both contain the topic of doing what is right (*poiōn dikaiosynēn*). Intermediate verses that are not part of the antitheses further explicate the antitheses: 3:5 sets up the following antithesis of 3:6 and 3:8bcd further elaborates the preceding antithesis of 3:7b–8a.[128]

Regarding antithesis, Aristotle notes that "contraries are easily understood and even more so when placed side by side, and also because antithesis resembles a syllogism; for refutation is a bringing together of contraries" (Aristotle, [*Rhet. Alex.*] 3.9.1410a.8). Antithesis is integral to comparison (Rhet. Her. 4.45.58). Here antithesis aptly compares the desired ethical behavior and relationship with God of a true child of God with the immoral behavior and lack of a relationship with God of the secessionists.

This section continues the epideictic rhetorical strategy of amplifying topics and advancing statements as certain (Aristotle, *Rhet.* 1.9.1368a.38–40; 2.18.1392a.5; 3.17.1417b.3; [*Rhet. Alex.*] 3; 6.1428a.1ff; Cicero, *Part. or.* 21.71). Amplification techniques include refining, *reflexio* (a word used with two different meanings), repetition, and *comminatio* (a

---

[128] Brown, *Epistles of John*, 418–20.

warning). Standard features of epideictic rhetoric abound, including enthymemes (3:8, 9; Aristotle, *Rhet.* 3.17.1418a.11–1418b.12), exhortation (2:28; 3:7; Aristotle, *Rhet.* 1.9.1367b.35–1368a.37; Cicero, *Or. Brut.* 11.37), and antithesis (Cicero, *Or. Brut.* 12.38).

The vocative "little children" that opens this section in 2:28 introduces the father–child metaphor so prevalent in the Judeo-Christian tradition where it describes the relationship between God and God's people. This metaphor underlies this section in a subtle comparison that as Christ the Son of God demonstrates his family relationship by obeying God his Father and being righteous, so Christians as children of God demonstrate that family relationship by doing the same.[129]

In this section the Elder is subtly using several interrelated methods of refutation. The assumption that sin has a place in the life of a child of God is refuted by assuming that it is wholly incredible and false (Cicero, *Inv.* 1.42.79–43.80; 1.53.89–90; *Part. or.* 12.44; Quintilian, *Inst.* 5.13.15). The notion that sin is acceptable in the life of a child of God is refuted by denying the possibility based on the nature of being a child of God (Aristotle, [*Rhet. Alex.*] 13). One refutational strategy is to amplify your own points, disparage the points of the opposition, produce maxims and enthymemes, and recapitulate in a conclusion (Aristotle, [*Rhet. Alex.*] 34.1440a.21–25). In this unit, amplification occurs throughout, enthymemes comprise 3:8, 9, and paraenetic statements akin to maxims within the context of the Johannine Community are pervasive. The main point of distinguishing a child of God from a child of the devil introduced as the unit opens (2:29) is recapitulated in its conclusion (3:10).

2:28: Opening Exhortation

The Elder opens this section with an exhortation containing a supporting reason drawn from eschatological expectation: "And now, little children, abide in him, so that when[130] he is revealed we may have confidence and not be put to shame[131] before him at his coming" (cf. Mark 8:38). His

---

[129] For an extensive study of the family metaphor in 1 John, see D. G. Van Der Merwe, "Family Metaphorics: A Rhetorical Tool in the Epistle of 1 John," *Acta Patristica et Byzantina* 20 (2009): 89–108.

[130] *Ean* should be translated "when, whenever" rather than "if" (BDAG, 268, 2) because the Elder has no doubts about the coming of the parousia (cf. 2:18).

[131] *Aischynthōmen* can be either middle voice ("be ashamed"), emphasizing our psychological response to Christ's parousia, or passive voice ("be put to shame"), connoting being shamed by Christ's judgment at the parousia. It is better to see

exhortation is grounded in the tension between present salvation and its consummation at the parousia and the need for the faithful to prepare for the latter. As is his custom, the Elder introduces this new section with a topic found at the end of the preceding one. The exhortation to "abide in him" (*menete en autō*) is repeated from 2:27 and refers to obeying the teachings of Christ as preparation for the parousia.

The exhortation is rhetorically sophisticated, being an example of refining of the type in which the idea is altered by placing it in another form (Rhet. Her. 4.43.56) and fashioned in a chiasm: (A) "so that when he is revealed"; (B) "we may have confidence"; (B¹) "not be put to shame before him"; (A¹) "at his coming." Refining amplifies the exhortation through repetition (Cicero, *Part. or.* 15.54), allowing the Elder to exhort the same thing twice in succession without being obvious.

The Elder introduces the topic of boldness or confidence (*parrēsia*) before God or Christ. Here it is confidence in the judgment that accompanies the parousia of Christ; a confidence grounded in abiding (*menō*) in Christ and his teachings (cf. 2:27). A parousia denoted the arrival of a sovereign to visit his subjects to reward the faithful and judge the unfaithful. Early Christians adapted it to describe the return of Jesus Christ (Matt 24:3; 1 Cor 15:23; 1 Thess 2:19). Confidence is being able to bask in the presence of God with a free conscience and without fear, assured of salvation at the final judgment (4:17).[132] Confidence is also assurance that God will answer our prayers based on our obedience to his commandments (3:21-22; 5:14-15).

The Elder reintroduces the topic of appearing (*phanerō*). In the *exordium* appearing refers to Christ's incarnation and earthly career (1:2; John 1:31), as it also will again in this section (3:5, 8) and later (4:9). At the beginning of the preceding section in 2:19 it refers to the unveiling of the antichrists of the last hour and correspondingly refers to Christ's parousia here. The past earthly and future heavenly appearance of Christ are parts of a single revelation of Christ in the world. His first appearance revealed God's love and effected God's redemption, while his second appearance will reveal Christ as king and judge in all his glory.

The Elder skillfully works to build positive ethos and pathos. He begins with the affectionate vocative, "little children." He excludes himself from

---

aischynthōmen as middle voice ("be ashamed") as the opposite of the corresponding expression *schōmen parresian* ("we may have confidence").

[132] Strecker, *Johannine Letters*, 80-81.

the exhortation to abide in Christ, implying that he already does. After the exhortation he shifts from the second-person "you" to the first-person "we" in order to underscore the future confidence he hopes to share with the faithful at the parousia. He also attempts to arouse fear to constrain the faithful from adopting the deception of the secessionists (cf. Quintilian, *Inst.* 4.1.20–22). They are reminded that at any moment Christ might return in judgment and those who are not abiding in him will be put to shame. The Elder may be refuting secessionist claims that the judgment at the parousia was only for nonbelievers, something that could be surmised from Johannine tradition (John 3:17–21; 5:24).[133]

2:29–3:4: First Antithetical Pair

The Elder follows the opening exhortation with a proposition: "If you perceive that he[134] is righteous, you also know that everyone who does right has been born of him."[135] While it can be either, "know" (*ginōskete*) is not imperative exhorting the faithful to know, but indicative, making a statement that they already know. The Elder assumes that Christians possess spiritual knowledge here and now and often uses the verb "know" (*ginōskō*) in the indicative to convey this fact (2:3–5, 13–14, 18, 20, 21, 29; 3:16, 19, 24; 4:2, 6–7, 13, 16; 5:2).

As mentioned above, the vocative "little children" that opens this section (2:28) introduces the metaphor of the father–child relation describing the relationship between God and God's people. The related topics of being begotten of God (*gennaō*) and righteousness (*dikaiosynē*) are central to this metaphor, for the children of God must be righteous like their Father.[136] Both topics occur in this verse. The topic of being begotten of God (*gennaō*) is introduced and developed in this section, appears later in the body of the letter (4:7, 5:1–5), and is reiterated in the conclusion (5:18). The topic of righteousness receives its major development in this section as well. It was introduced earlier where being just (*dikaios*) is given as an

---

[133] Brown, *Epistles of John*, 420–21.
[134] Christ is also described as righteous in 2:1 and 3:7, so the pronoun here probably refers to Christ (cf. 1:9).
[135] "Him" (*autos*) refers to God. In Johannine usage, "born" (*gennaō*) in the passive voice followed by "of" (*ek*) never has Christ as a referent, but often has God as such (John 1:13; 1 John 3:9; 4:7; 5:1, 4, 18). Also, the next verse speaks of children of God, and later in the section 3:9 speaks of being born of God and of God's seed. Haas, De Jonge, and Swellengrebel, *Translator's Handbook*, 75.
[136] For references, see Brown, *Epistles of John*, 388–91.

2:28–3:10: The Identity of the Children of God

attribute of God (1:9) and Christ (2:1; 3:7). Now it again describes Christ, with the added point that righteousness (*dikaiosynē*) is a sign of being born of God who is righteous (2:29; 3:7, 10). Loving others and believing that Jesus is the Christ are additional signs of being born of God (4:7; 5:1). Although not explicit, one sign of righteousness is likely to be loving others (cf. 3:10).[137]

In 3:1–3 the Elder uses parenthesis, a figure of speech that interrupts the flow of language with a clarifying or related remark (Quintilian, *Inst.* 9.3.23).[138] The Elder has negatively characterized the secessionists and affirmed the faithful (2:18–27) and is now comparing the secessionists and the faithful as children of the devil and of God, respectively (2:29–3:10). He uses a parenthesis to reassure the faithful of their positive status before God (as he does in 2:12–14) and continues to place their status in a vibrant eschatological perspective. He employs the father–child metaphor inherent in the topic of being born of God in 2:29 to affirm that the faithful are children of God; a status to be revealed when Christ is revealed (cf. 2:28; 3:2).

The Elder begins the parenthesis with a figure of thought called an *exclamatio*, which stimulates and intensifies emotion (Cicero, *Or. Brut.* 39.135; Rhet. Her. 4.15.22; Quintilian, *Inst.* 9.2.26–27; 9.3.97): "See what love the Father has given us that we should be called children of God; and that is what we are!" (3:1a). The exclamation has considerable rhetorical power. In the Gospel of John, the verb "see" (*idete*), which begins this exclamation, is a revelatory formula that introduces a mystery about a person being presented or about something remarkable.[139] The faithful are exhorted to behold the gift of the mysterious love of the Father that made them children of God. The interrogative "what sort of" (*potapos*) underscores the vast quantity and quality of this love. The Elder further amplifies the exclamation and underscores the reality of the father–child relationship by ellipsis in the phrase "and that is what we are" (*kai esmen*), which requires the faithful to supply "children of God" as the predicate nominative and further confirms their status in their own minds. The emphatic position of "we are" at the end of the sentence contrasts the Elder and the faithful with the world in 3:1b to which the secessionists belong (cf. John

---

[137] Painter, *1, 2, 3 John*, 216–17.
[138] Brown (*Epistles of John*, 419) also considers 3:1–3 to be a parenthesis.
[139] Brown, *Epistles of John*, 387. John 1:29, 36, 47; 19:14, 26, 27.

3:16). The Elder appeals to emotion as he shifts from the second-person to the first-person plural to include himself as an object of God's love.

The topic of the benefits given (*didōmi*) to the believer by God is introduced here in conjunction with the gift of God's love. The giving topic will be augmented in the body of the letter by God's gift of the commandment to love (3:23; cf. John 13:34), the Spirit (3:24; 4:13; cf. John 3:34), and eternal life (5:11; cf. John 10:28), and in the conclusion by life (5:16) and understanding (5:20). Here God's gift is love that gives believers the status of the children of God (*tekna theou*). This topic always follows the topic of being born of God (*gennaō*, 2:29; 3:1; 5:1) as the new status that such birth creates for the believer. In Hebrew tradition the title "children of God" is one of sonship/childhood in a covenant relationship requiring obedience.[140] Thus, as expected, when this topic recurs the focus is on obedience in love as a distinguishing sign of a child of God (3:10; 5:2; cf. John 1:12; 11:52).

While the Elder exclaims that the faithful are children of God as a benefit of God's love, he understands that this status is not easily recognized in this life. He adds, "The reason the world does not know us is that it did not know him."[141] The world does not recognize the faithful because it does not recognize God whose children they are (John 15:18-21; 16:3; cf. 1 John 3:6; 4:8). The world refuses to accept God's truth (4:6) and love (4:7-8). The inability of the world, including the secessionists, to recognize the faithful as children of God and their inability to provide tangible proof of this status may have been discouraging to the faithful but actually provides them with a sign of their status as God's children.

In v. 2 the Elder continues to affirm the faithful in the spiritual status: "Beloved, we are God's children now; what we will be has not yet been revealed. What we do know is this: when he is revealed,[142] we will be like him, for we will see him as he is."[143] Both 3:1a and 3:2a constitute refining

---

[140] For a discussion of children, sons of God, see Brown, *Epistles of John*, 388-91; A. Culpepper, "The Pivot of John's Gospel," *NTS* 27·(1980): 1-31, esp. 25-26.

[141] The referent to "him" (*autos*) is probably to God as the context indicates (Father, 3:1; God, 3:2a). Also, Johannine tradition affirms that the world does not know God (John 5:18-21).

[142] The subject of "revealed" (*phaneraō*) can be "it" referring to "what we will be," as it is in the immediately preceding use of the verb. A personal referent "he" can also be supplied and refer to Christ revealed at the parousia as in 2:28 and 3:5 (Parsenios, *First, Second, and Third John*, 92-93; Painter, *1, 2, 3 John*, 218).

[143] God is the probable referent of "him" (*autos*) because in 3:1 the faithful are said to be God's children, and it is natural that in the future they will be like God their Father. Also, "he" (literally "that one," *ekeinos*) in 3:3 refers to Christ and would be appropriate grammatically only if Christ is not this prior referent. Brown, *Epistles of John*, 394-95.

of the type in which the thought is repeated in a different form (Rhet. Her. 4.43.56). In 3:1a the Elder affirms the love (*agapē*) of God for himself and the faithful as children of God (*tekna theou*) and reaffirms this reality (*kai esmen*). In 3:2a he addresses the faithful as beloved of God (*agapetoi*) and affirms that he and they are children of God (*tekna theou esmen*). This refining amplifies by repetition the status of the faithful before God. The Elder also reminds the faithful that they have the knowledge of their future status of being like God from their tradition ("they know" [*oida*]; cf. 3:5, 15; 5:15). The refining and amplification by repetition indicate that the faithful's assurance of their status as children of God may have been waning. There is concern that the world (secessionists included) does not recognize their status (3:1b), and even the nature of that status has yet to be revealed (3:2b). Perhaps the secessionists were denying that those whom they left behind in the Elder's community were true children of God.

The hope of the children of God is to be "like him" and to "see him as he is." The hope to be "like him" (*homoios*) is to share in God's nature, including God's glory and resurrected, eternal life with God (John 6:39-40, 44, 54). Here being like God is to experience being a child of God in all its fullness. The wording recalls Gen 1:26 where human beings were created in the image and likeness of God, and Gen 3:5 where the serpent promises that Eve will be "like God."

The Elder affirms that he and the faithful know that they will be like God, "for we will see him as he is." The causal "for" (*hoti*) may give the reason Christians will be like God in the sense that seeing God is transforming, as in Hellenistic religion in which deification comes through a vision of the gods. Or, more likely, it explains that Christians know that they are like him because they can see God as God is; that is, they have been transformed. The hope to "see him as he is" is to share the glory of God and Christ. No one can see the glory of God in the mortal state (1 John 4:12, 20; John 1:18; 5:37; 6:46; 14:8-9), except in Christ (John 12:45; 14:9). As Christ shares the glory of God (John 1:14; 2:11; 12:41; 17:5, 22, 24), so Christians will see and share the glory of Christ (John 17:22, 24). To see the glory of God is a hope shared by other early Christians (Matt 5:8; 1 Cor 13:12; 2 Cor 3:18; Rev 22:4; cf. Ps 11:7; 17:15).

The Elder continues in v. 3 with a moral maxim teaching what all who hope to see God must do: "And all who have this hope in him[144] purify

---

[144] The referent of "him" (*autos*) is probably God. At the end of the verse the Elder refers to Christ with the Johannine term "that one" (*ekeinos*) in distinction to "him" here. Also,

themselves, just as he is pure." The maxim is part of the Elder's use of comparison to uphold Christ as a moral example to be emulated (using *kathōs*; 2:6; 3:7, 16; 4:17). The Septuagint uses the verb "purify" (*hagnizō*) for ritual purification necessary before encountering or serving God (Exod 19:10–11; Num 8:21; 19:12). Jesus made atonement for the sins before the Father (1 John 2:1–2) and purified himself (*hagiazō*) in order that the world may be purified (John 17:17, 19; cf. John 6:69). The underlying assumption of the maxim is that Jesus made himself pure (cf. the topic of Jesus as righteous [*dikaios*] in 2:1, 29; 3:7; cf. 3:5) and can enter the divine presence, and if the faithful also want to enter God's presence, they must be made pure through him. They must be cleansed from sin by the blood of Christ and remain free from sin in accordance with that cleansing (1:7, 9; 2:1; 3:5; cf. John 17:19).[145]

After the parenthesis of 3:1–3 the Elder provides the other half of the antithesis begun in 2:29. There he stated, "everyone who does right has been born of him." Now in 3:4 he states, "everyone who commits sin is guilty of lawlessness; sin is the lawlessness" (cf. 2 Cor 6:14). Both 2:29 and 3:4 are united by the antithesis between "doing right" (*poiōn tēn dikaiosynēn*) and "doing sin" (*poiōn tēn hamartian*) or lawlessness (*anomia*).[146]

While sin (*hamatia*) and lawlessness (*anomia*) are synonyms (cf. Rom 4:7–8), the phrase "sin is lawlessness" is not merely a definition because the predicate nominative does not need an article as it has here.[147] Rather, it is a general truth or well-known fact.[148] With many interpreters I give the article before "lawlessness" (*anomia*) its full force, *the* lawlessness, and assume that it does not refer to lawlessness in general but to the apocalyptic expectation that lawlessness will accompany the climax of history.[149] The sin (*hamartia*) of the secessionists is part of the larger lawlessness

---

the hope is being like God and seeing him as he is, as mentioned in 3:1–2. Brown, *Epistles of John*, 396–97.

[145] Brown, *Epistles of John*, 397–98.

[146] *Anomia* and *dikaiosynē* are antithetical in Rom 6:19; 2 Cor 6:14; Heb 1:9; cf. 1 Tim 1:9; 2 Pet 2:8.

[147] Painter, *1, 2 ,3 John*, 222.

[148] BDF §273.1.

[149] T. Dan 5:4–6; 6:1–6; Matt 24:11–12; 2 Thess 2:3–8 (which identifies the antichrist as a man of lawlessness); Barn. 4:1; Did. 16:3–4; I. de la Potterie, "'Le péché, c'est l'iniquité' (1 Joh., III, 4)," *NRTh* 78 (1956): 785–97; revised in I. de la Potterie and S. Lyonnet, *The Christian Lives by the Spirit*, trans. John Morriss (Staten Island: Alba House, 1971), 37–55.

(*anomia*) of the end-times. The Elder has identified the secessionists as sinners (1:6, 8, 10; 2:4, 6, 9), antichrists (2:18-19, 22), and the liar (2:22) and will identify them shortly as children of the devil (3:8, 10). He assumes that the last days are imminent (2:18; 2:29-3:3). Now the sins of the secessionists are associated with the lawlessness of the last days in which the antichrist, the liar, and sinners play a large part. The secessionists are guilty of contributing to the increase of evil in the last days.[150]

Some interpreters see 3:4 as a general observation that is not specifically directed at the secessionists.[151] However, it is really functioning in both capacities. The contrast between the children of God and the children of the devil in the rest of the section (3:5-10) indicates that a general observation is being made that is pertinent to the faithful and the secessionists alike. The previous buildup of associations of the antichrist, the liar, and lawlessness with the secessionists is also a carefully planned rhetorical strategy of vilification by association, often by insinuation versus direct identification.

3:5-6: Second Antithetical Pair

As is his custom elsewhere (2:20-21, 27; 3:2; 4:2; 5:15, 18-20), in the second antithetical pair the Elder begins by affirming the faithful that they have knowledge of what he speaks: "You know that he was revealed to take away sins,[152] and in him there is no sin." To the interrelated topics of Christ as just/righteous (*dikaios*; 1:9, 2:1; 29; John 7:18) and pure (*hagnos*; 3:3) is now added the topic of Christ as sinless (*hamartia*). There is sacrificial language here of Jesus as the Lamb of God who takes away the sin of the world (1:7; 2:1-2; 3:8; 4:10; cf. John 1:29, 36; Isa 53:4, 11-12). The sins Christ takes away are plural to stress individual sins, and the sin not in Christ is singular to emphasize his purity from any sin whatsoever.

Verse 6 is a corollary of v. 5: "No one who abides in him sins; no one who sins has either seen him or known him" (cf. 1:8, 10; 2:1, 6; 3:9; 5:16-18; 3 John 11). This corollary is expressed in antithetical parallelism, for the opposite of abiding in Christ is having neither seen nor known him.

---

[150] Brown, *Epistles of John*, 399-400; Bultmann, *Johannine Epistles*, 49-50; Smalley, *1, 2, 3 John*, 154-55.
[151] Schnackenburg, *Johannine Epistles*, 170-71; Strecker, *Johannine Letters*, 93-95.
[152] I am adopting the reading "sins" (*hamartias*) as opposed to the reading "our sins" (*hamartias hēmōn*), the latter reading being influenced by 2:2 and 4:10 where sins are plural. Metzger, *Textual Commentary*, 712.

This is also another case of *distributio*, for the constituent elements of abiding (*menō*) in Christ are distributed as seeing (*horaō*) him (John 12:37–46; 20:29) and knowing (*ginōskō*) him (John 8:19; 14:7); that is, believing in Christ (John 6:36; 14:9). To abide in and know Christ is to obey his commandments and not sin (2:3–6). Surely all faithful Christians still do sin, but when abiding in Christ and obeying his commandments they do not sin.

In the *exordium* the Elder claims that the Johannine tradition-bearers have seen (*horaō*) the manifestation of the word of life in Christ (1:1, 3). In the Gospel of John, the Beloved Disciple "saw [*horaō*] these things" (John 19:35); that is, the things to which the gospel testifies. The insinuation here is that the secessionists' sinful behavior proves that they have not seen (*horaō*) Christ; that is, they have no authority from the Johannine tradition or its founder, the Beloved Disciple.

3:7–8: Third Antithetical Pair

The Elder prefaces the third antithesis with the figure of speech called *comminatio* (*apeilē*), a warning to be on guard about a threatening condition (Cicero, *Or. Brut.* 40.138): "Little children, let no one deceive you" (v. 7a). The topic of deceit (*planaō*) is reintroduced from 1:8 and 2:26–27 (cf. 2:22–23). In the former the Elder states that anyone claiming not to have sin is deceiving themselves, and in the latter he describes the secessionists as those who would deceive the faithful. In 2 John 7 the deceivers (*planoi*) – the secessionists – are those who deny that Jesus Christ has come in the flesh. Now deception can take the form of not recognizing that ethical behavior is indicative of spiritual allegiance, either to Christ or to the devil.

This warning against deception strengthens the ethos of the Elder. In Johannine tradition, the Paraclete's role is to prove the world wrong about sin, righteousness, and judgment (John 16:8–11). The topic of judgment occurs in 2:28, and righteousness and sin are topics in 2:29 and 3:4 and in this antithesis in 3:7b–8. As Brown so aptly states: "The epistolary author is playing the role of the Paraclete in proving the secessionists wrong about sin, justice, and judgment."[153]

The third antithesis occurs in 3:7b–8a: "Everyone who does what is right is righteous, just as he is righteous. Everyone who commits sin is of the

---

[153] *Epistles of John*, 428.

devil, for the devil has been sinning from the beginning." The first half of the antithesis uses the comparative (*kathōs*) to uphold Christ's righteousness as the grounds of Christian behavior (v. 7b). Christ's ethical walk (2:6) and his purity (3:3) have been upheld for emulation. Now, as In 2:29, it is his righteousness, for in him there is no sin (3:5; cf. 2:1). The second half of the antithesis, v. 8a, is an enthymeme. The premise is "the devil has been sinning from the beginning" and the conclusion is "everyone who commits sin is a child of the devil." The unstated premise is "those who behave like the devil are of the devil." Whereas 3:4a identifies sinners as participants in the diabolic lawlessness of the last days, here they are identified as children of the devil.

In v. 8a the Elder uses the "be of" (*einai ek*) topic of origin and allegiance to align sinners with the devil: "Everyone who commits sin is of (*einai ek*) the devil." This identification will be made more precise in the fourth antithesis to follow (3:9–10). In light of John 8:44, where Jesus tells those who would not hear his words that they are from their father the devil, the father of lies, the Elder insinuates that those who sin – that is, the secessionists – have the devil as a father. Thus, the initial warning of this antithesis is not to be deceived (v. 7a), for the devil's children are at play among the community.

This insinuation works on another level. The time reference "from the beginning" (*ap archē*) probably refers to the devil's work on earth from the beginning of human history. It is the work of the devil in Genesis 1–4, particularly the beginning of human hatred with Cain's murder of Abel. In John 8:44 the devil is called a murderer from the beginning, and here in 2:12 Cain is identified as being of the evil one.[154] Thus, the secessionists are linked intertextually with the work of the devil in the fall of humanity!

The antithesis of 3:7–8a is followed in 3:8b by the proposition "The Son of God was revealed for this purpose: to destroy the works of the devil." This proposition is another way to state 3:5 that Christ was revealed (*phaneroō*) to take away (*airō*) sins, a proposition from Johannine tradition tied to Jesus's baptism (John 1:29–31). Now the references to the lawlessness and sin in 3:4–5 are more specifically identified as referring to

---

[154] Brown, *Epistle of John*, 405–06; Schnackenburg, *Johannine Epistles*, 174; Strecker, *Johannine Letters*, 100–01; Parsenios, *First, Second, and Third John*, 93–94. Some interpreters understand "beginning" as the primordial beginning since the devil is the subject and has such a beginning. Bultmann, *Johannine Epistles*, 52, n. 35; Smalley, *1, 2, 3 John*, 168–69.

the devil and his works. As the Son of God came to destroy the works of the devil – that is, sin – those who sin and are children of the devil work against the very purpose of his mission.

3:9–10: Fourth Antithetical Pair

In the fourth antithetical pair the Elder juxtaposes the topics of doing right (*poiōn dikaiosynē*) and doing sin (*poiōn ten hamartian*) as in the first and third antitheses of this unit (2:29b; 3:4a, 7b, 8a). The first half of the antithesis, 3:9, is composed of two enthymemes (conclusion with one premise). In the first enthymene, v. 9a, the conclusion is "Those who have been born of God do not sin" and the supporting premise is "because God's seed abides in them." The unstated premise is "those in whom God's seed abides do not sin." In the second enthymeme, v. 9b, the conclusion is "they cannot sin" followed by the supporting premise "because they have been born of God" (cf. 3:6). The unstated premise is "those born of God cannot sin." Each enthymeme says virtually the same thing in reverse order, and together they constitute a chiasm as well as a refining of the type in which the thought is repeated in different form (Rhet. Her. 4.42.54). While repetitive, the second enthymeme is stronger than the first, for denying that Christians can sin is stronger than saying they do not sin. The content of this verse is reiterated in the conclusion: "We know that those who are born of God do not sin" (5:18a; cf. 5:4).

All of 3:9 is permeated by the metaphor of conception, with a strong father imagery (cf. 2:29–3:2). The Christian is begotten (*gennaō*) of God and God's seed (*sperma*) abides within. The referent of seed is debated. It has been defined as the internal abiding of Christ.[155] Seed is appropriate language to describe Jesus Christ as Son of God, as God's seed (1:3, 7; 3:8), and Christ is described as abiding in Christians (John 6:56; 15:1–11). Seed has been defined as God's word, which is described as abiding in Christians (1:10; 2:14, 24; John 15:7).[156] Seed is most often defined as the Holy Spirit, and that is our choice here.[157] The Spirit is the agent of rebirth (John 3:1–10), and the anointing of the Spirit abides within, instructs, and keeps

---

[155] Strecker, *Johannine Letters*, 102.
[156] Malatesta, *Interiority and Covenant*, 247–50. Cf. Luke 8:11; 1 Pet 1:23.
[157] Brown, *Epistles of John*, 410–11; Brooke, *Johannine Epistles*, 89; Schnackenburg, *Johannine Epistles*, 175. Smalley (*1, 2, 3 John*, 173–74) and Painter (*1, 2, 3 John*, 224, 229) define seed as the word and Spirit working together.

the Christian from sinning (2:20, 27; John 16:8–10). God's gift of the Spirit assures Christians that God abides within (3:24; 4:13).

This description of Christians as those who "do not sin" seems to stand in stark contrast to other passages that assume that Christians do sin (1:8, 10; 2:1–2; 3:4; 5:16, 18). The Elder is holding up the ideal to help the faithful further distinguish themselves from the secessionists and guide their behavior as children of God. Good conduct is integral in preparation for the parousia and becoming like Christ (3:2–3) and is aided by the guidance of the Holy Spirit (2:20, 27).

The second half of the antithesis of 3:9–10 consists of two interrelated signs that distinguish the children of God and the children of the devil: "The children of God and the children of the devil are revealed in this way:[158] all who do not do what is right are not from God, nor are those who do not love a brother or sister." This distinction could have had a positive component revealing the traits of the children of God but focuses on the negative components to highlight the behavior of the secessionists. The topic of "being from" God (*einai ek*) reappears to distinguish origin and allegiance. Whereas all that is in the world is not from the Father (2:16), now the absence of doing right and not loving the brothers and sisters are signs of not being from the Father (cf. 4:7–8).

BRIDGING THE HORIZONS

The greatest love to ever be given to us is the love of God that makes us God's own children through Jesus Christ. Our righteousness indicates our new status (2:29; 3:9), but even so we do not know the full extent of what it means to be children of God transformed to be like Jesus when he is revealed at his second coming. Our hope in this full revealing of our status before God obligates us to purify ourselves so as not to be shamed as disobedient children when all is consummated (3:3).

The world does not know our status as children of God because it does not know God (3:1). What knowledge it does have comes in part

---

[158] The formula *en touto* ("in this way") can refer to either what precedes (so that the presence or absence of sin is the distinction between the children of God and those of the devil), to what follows (so that doing or not doing right and loving a brother or sister is the distinction between the two types of children), or both. I understand the formula as introducing what follows. Haas, DeJonge, and Swellengrebel, *Translator's Handbook*, 86.

from observing us doing what is right. Hopefully that observation does not still leave the world in the dark about our status or about God! Ideally, as children of God we pattern our lives on the sinlessness and righteousness of Jesus Christ. This ideal is possible whenever we abide in Christ (3:6, 9). As long as we obey the commandments of God, especially the love commandment, and do what is right, sinlessness and righteousness characterize our lives. It is when we do not abide, disobey the commandments, and do what is wrong that we sin and are no longer righteous. The ideal is possible and to be striven after, but selfish human nature makes consistent sinlessness impossible.

When we sin, we are being lawless and doing the works of the devil. We are more akin to children of the devil than children of God (3:4, 8,10). Jesus came to destroy the works of the devil, and our sin and wrongdoing are evil, working against his purposes. Fortunately, there is forgiveness in the atoning blood of his sacrifice (1:7, 9; 2:1-2).

3:11-24: LOVE ONE ANOTHER

> 3:11 For this is the message you have heard from the beginning, that we should love one another.
>
> 3:12 We must not be like Cain, who was from the evil one and murdered his brother. And why did he murder him? Because his own deeds were evil and his brother's righteous.
>
> 3:13 Do not be astonished, brothers and sisters, that the world hates you.
>
> 3:14 We know that we have passed from death to life because we love one another. Whoever does not love abides in death.
>
> 3:15 All who hate a brother or sister are murderers, and you know that murderers do not have eternal life abiding in them.
>
> 3:16 We know love by this, that he laid down his life for us - and we ought to lay down our lives for the brothers and sisters.
>
> 3:17 How does God's love abide in anyone who has the world's goods and sees a brother or sister in need and yet refuses to help?
>
> 3:18 Little children, let us love not in word or speech but in deed and truth.
>
> 3:19 And by this we will know that we are from the truth and will reassure our hearts before him

> 3:20 whenever our hearts condemn us, for God is greater than our hearts, and he knows everything.
>
> 3:21 Beloved, if our hearts do not condemn us, we have boldness before God;
>
> 3:22 and we receive from him whatever we ask, because we obey his commandments and do what pleases him.
>
> 3:23 And this is his commandment, that we should believe in the name of his Son Jesus Christ and love one another, just as he has commanded us.
>
> 3:24 All who obey his commandments abide in him, and he abides in them. And by this we know that he abides in us, by the Spirit that he has given us.

The second half of the main body of the letter (the *probatio*) of 1 John is comprised by 3:11–5:12. As the first half of the letter body begins with the phrase "This is the message we have heard from him" (1:5), the second half begins with "For this is the message you have heard from the beginning" (3:11). The fact that these are the only two occurrences of these phrases outside the introduction (*exordium*; 1:1, 3) indicates that they mark substantial shifts in the letter body.[159]

The first rhetorical section of 3:11–5:12 is 3:11–24. This section elaborates what it means to do right and love one another, and their opposites, given in 3:10 as distinguishing characteristics of a child of God. *Inclusio* indicates that 3:11–24 is a section. As 3:11 begins with "This is the message" followed by an epexegetical (*hina*) clause that gives the partial content of that message as "that we should love one another," 3:23 begins with "this is his commandment" followed by an epexegetical (*hina*) clause that gives the partial content of the commandment as "love one another" (cf. 4:21). Within this unit there are two subunits introduced by direct address: 3:13–17 introduced by brothers and sisters (*adelphoi*) and 3:18–22 introduced by little children (*teknia*).[160]

Although this section does employ argument from logos (reason), the argumentation is mainly composed of artificial proofs from ethos (authority) and pathos (emotion). It concerns what is honorable and expedient and what ought to be done; that is, argument from ethos (Quintilian, *Inst.*

---

[159] Cf. 2:7, where a similar formula marks the introduction of a rhetorical subsection. Brown, *Epistles of John*, 467.
[160] Brown, *Epistles of John*, 467–68.

6.2.11). The faithful are reminded of the virtues of love, self-sacrifice, and helping the needy versus hate, evil, murder, and death. Signs are given to assure the faithful of their positive spiritual standing. Their mutual love indicates that they have passed from death to life (v. 14), their love in action assures their hearts that they are from the truth (vv. 18–19), and the Spirit of God assures them that God abides within (v. 24). It is implied that the secessionists lack virtue, do not look out for the goodwill of the faithful, and are unkind and disloyal (Aristotle, *Rhet.* 2.1.1377b.1–1378a.7; Cicero, *De or.* 2.43.182). They do not help the faithful when they are in need, which is hatred and murder as evil as Cain's murder of Abel (vv. 12, 15, 17). Calling someone a murderer was said to evince hatred (Quintilian, *Inst.* 6.2.21). Using the topic of murder is an example of deinosis, "language that adds force to facts which are disgraceful, cruel, or odious" (Quintilian, *Inst.* 6.2.24).

3:11: Proposition: Love One Another

The second half of the letter body (*probatio*) begins in v. 11 with a proposition: "For this is the message you have heard from the beginning, that we should love one another." As he did in the introduction to the first half of the body (1:5), the Elder reminds the faithful of what they heard from the tradition-bearers from the beginning of their lives as Johannine Christians, of which the love commandment was central (2:7, 24; 2 John 5–6). He refers to Jesus's commandment to love one another (3:23; 4:21; John 13:34–35; 15:12, 17). As such he introduces this section with a judgment (*kriseis*) of Jesus that lends authority to his development of this topic. Love (*agapē*) is the primary topic of the second half of the letter body (3:11, 23–24; 4:7, 11–12, 21; cf. 2 John 2:5–6). Love was first introduced in 2:3–11 as a quality perfected in the faithful who keep God's commandments and word and as a commandment possessed from the beginning guiding the love for other Christians. Love as a guide to behavior is further developed in this section.

3:12: Opposite by Example: Cain

The proposition that the Elder and the faithful should love one another is immediately followed by the negative example of Cain from Gen 4:1–16: "We must not be like Cain, who was from the evil one and murdered his brother" (v. 12a). The Elder employs litotes or understatement.

By negating the contrary, the positive is affirmed in an emphatic way (Rhet. Her. 4.38.50). The Elder wants the faithful to do far more than simply not be like Cain! They are to love one another. The Elder has portrayed the split within the Johannine Community as a matter of brother against brother (2:9–11; 3:10), thus the choice of the example of Cain and Abel. The inclusive language of "brothers and sisters" in the *New Revised Standard Version* partially conceals this rhetorical flourish.

The example of Cain is traditional.[161] The Genesis account implies that Cain's deed was sinful (4:7), and tradition developed this aspect along with Abel's deeds being righteous (Josephus, *Ant.* 1.52–59; Philo, *QG* 1.59; T. Benj. 7:3–5; Apoc. Ab. 24:5; Matt 23:35; Heb 11:4). Tradition also developed Cain as being under the influence of Satan (Apoc. Ab. 24:5).[162] In John 8:39–44 the Jewish authorities seek to kill Jesus and argue that they have Abraham as their father. Jesus counters that since they seek to murder him, their father is the devil who was a murderer from the beginning. He alludes to the devil being the father of Cain, the first murderer after creation.

Cain's example is amplified with the figure called *percontatio*, or a rhetorical question posed and answered by the rhetor (Cicero, *De or.* 3.53.203 = Quintilian, *Inst.* 9.1.29; *De or.* 3.54.207 = Quintilian, *Inst.* 9.1.35; Cicero, *Or. Brut.* 40.137; Quintilian, *Inst.* 9.2.14; 9.3.90): "And why did he murder him? Because his own deeds were evil and his brother's righteous" (v. 12b). A question emphasizes the rhetor's point (Quintilian, *Inst.* 9.2.7), which here is that murder and neglect are motivated by habitual evil deeds and jealousy. This emphasis artfully compares the faithful with Abel and the secessionists with Cain, which continues through v. 17. It insinuates that the secessionists are like Cain, being from the devil, hating their righteous brothers and sisters, and acting in a way akin to murder (v. 13, 15), especially in their refusal to help the faithful in need. They should have been willing to lay down their own lives as Christ did his own (vv. 16–17).

The wording of this example is highly emotive. The faithful can identify themselves with Abel as righteous and persecuted (murdered) by the secessionists motivated by the evil one. The verb for murder (*sphazō*) denotes violence and slaughter. It is found elsewhere in the New

---

[161] J. Byron, "Slaughter, Fratricide and Sacrilege: Cain and Abel Traditions in 1 John 3," *Bib* 88 (2007): 526–35.
[162] See Brown, *Epistles of John*, 442–43.

Testament only in Revelation, where it describes the fate of Jesus the slain Lamb and his followers (5:6, 9, 12; 6:9; 13:8; 18:24; cf. 6:4; 13:3). The secessionists' hatred of their brothers and sisters and dismissal of their physical needs is akin to the violent murder of Jesus and his faithful followers!

3:13: Exhortation: Do Not Be Astonished

The Elder continues with an exhortation: "Do not be astonished, brothers and sisters, that the world hates you." The exhortation is a corollary of the negative example of Cain, who epitomizes the evil world's treatment of the righteous. The address "brothers and sisters" (lit. "brothers," *adelphoi*) is deliberate, for this is the only use of *adelphoi* as an address within Johannine literature. It continues the previous topic of brother against brother, Cain against Abel. It is founded on Johannine tradition that Jesus warned his followers that the world will hate them like it hated him (John 15:18–25; 16:1–4a; 17:14–16) and that the world does not have the love of God (1 John 2:15; cf. 3:1).[163] The fact that the Elder exhorts the faithful not to be astonished implies that the hatred of the secessionists toward them – that is, not loving them and meeting their physical needs (cf. vv. 15, 17) – disturbed them.[164] They probably did not expect the persecution of the end-times associated with the antichrist (2:18) and the lawlessness of that time (3:4) to come from former members of their own community.

3:14: Syllogism: Love as a Sign of Life

The exhortation of v. 13 is followed by a proof from logos, an epicheireme, a syllogism with premises that are refutable. Such a structured, rational proof is indicative that the Elder was interested in proving to the faithful that they had indeed passed from death into life.

---

[163] Parsenios (*First, Second, and Third John*, 101) sees an allusion to Judas here as one who was faithful but showed he was of the world and the devil and contributed to Jesus's death. Thus, Judas provides a parallel to the secessionists who were faithful but showed they were of the world by leaving the community and now hate the faithful.

[164] The verb "be astonished" (*thaumazō*) being followed by the conjunction "if" (*ei*) indicates only the possibility of hatred, not the fact of it as when followed by "that" (*hoti*). However, *ei* can have the force of *hoti* (BDF 454.1), which means the hatred here may already be a reality.

Conclusion: "We know that we have passed from death to life"
Premise 1: "because we love the brothers and sisters"
Premise 2: "Whoever does not love abides in death"

The "because" (*hoti*) clause ("because we love the brothers and sisters") can be understood as causal (love is the cause of our passing from death to life) or as a sign (love is the reason we know we have passed from death to life). The causal interpretation is a minority opinion because it implies that we can obtain life through loving others, and that is not a Johannine concept. The transition from death to life is a gift of Christ (1:2; 2:25; 5:11, 13, 20; John 5:24; 6:50; 11:25–26), and love (*agapaō*) originates in God through those who have been born of God and know God (4:7).[165]

Most interpreters understand the *hoti* clause as offering a sign, and this understanding is supported by rhetoric. The premises of arguments from logos, like this epicheireme, are often signs (Aristotle, *Rhet.* 1.2.1357b.16–17; [*Rhet. Alex.*] 12; Quintilian, *Inst.* 5.9.3–7), and the Elder often uses signs of spiritual status in his argumentation (2:29; 3:9; 4:7; 5:1, 4, 18). Here the "because" (*hoti*) clause introduces mutual love between the Elder and the faithful as a sign giving them knowledge that they have passed from death to life.[166] The Elder stresses the shared nature of this knowledge by sign, for "we know" (*hemeis oidamen*) is emphatic. Even though the world hates the faithful, their mutual love gives the Elder and the faithful assurance that they have life and are quite distinguishable from the secessionists who hate them and abide in death (cf. 2:7–11).

3:15: Proposition: Hatred Is Murder

The Elder continues with a proposition: "All who hate a brother or sister are murderers, and you know that murderers do not have eternal life abiding in them" (cf. Rev 21:8). Verses 14b and 15 form another example of refining of the type in which the idea is repeated with slight alteration (Rhet. Her. 4.43.56–44.58). Not loving and abiding in death (v. 14b) is equivalent to hating and not having eternal life abiding within (v. 15). Refining amplifies the proposition by repetition that those who hate have not transitioned from death to life. The faithful can identify the

---

[165] Brown (*Epistles of John*, 446) understands *hoti* as causal. It is God's love expressed through Christians, not love they generate and for which they can take credit.
[166] Bultmann, *Johannine Epistles*, 55; Dodd, *Johannine Epistles*, 82; Painter, *1, 2, 3 John*, 234; Schnackenburg, *Johannine Epistles*, 180, Smalley, *1, 2, 3 John*, 189.

secessionists as children of the devil akin to Cain because they experience mistreatment from those who were supposedly their brothers and sisters (cf. 2:9, 11; 3:14, 17). The insinuation is that the hateful secessionists were never Christians in the first place.

3:16: Example and Exhortation: Christ's Love Obligates the Same

In contrast to the example of hatred of a brother provided by Cain, the Elder now provides Christ's sacrificial death as an example of love, as well as an exhortation based on that example to love others: "We know love by this, that he laid down his life for us – and we ought to lay down our lives for the brothers and sisters." Both "for us" (*hyper hēmōn*) and "we ought" (*hēmeis opheilomen*) are emphatic, stressing that what Christ has done for us ought to be repeated in the life of the faithful who are beneficiaries of his sacrifice. As elsewhere in the Johannine literature, the example of Christ is made an ethical obligation for Christians and a guide to their behavior using the topic of "ought" (*opheilō*; 1 John 2:6; 4:11; John 13:14). The example and the exhortation share the Johannine metaphor of the shepherd laying down his life for his sheep (John 10:11–18), which recalls the sacrificial death of Christ (1:7; 2:2; 4:10). It is an example of using a metaphor to create a vivid mental picture, magnify, and embellish a point (Demetrius, *Eloc.* 2.78; Longinus, *Subl.* 32.5; Cicero, *De or.* 3.40.60–61; Rhet. Her. 4.34.45; Quintilian, *Inst.* 8.6.6).

3:17: Rhetorical Question

The exhortation is followed by a rhetorical question: "How does God's love[167] abide in anyone who has the world's goods and sees a brother or sister in need and yet refuses help?" Since the question is posed without an answer provided, it is the figure of thought called *rogatio* or *interrogatio* used to amplify a message (Cicero, *De or.* 3.53.203 = Quintilian, *Inst.* 9.1.29; Cicero, *Or. Brut.* 40.137; Rhet. Her. 4.15.22; Quintilian, *Inst.* 9.2.7; 9.3.98). The rhetorical question is composed of three coordinate clauses followed by the main clause containing the main verb at the end. The

---

[167] It is debated whether "love of God" is a subjective genitive ("the love God has for others"), objective genitive ("our love for God"), or qualitative genitive ("divine love"). In light of 3:15, where eternal life from God abides within, and 3:16, where Christ loves us, the love God has for others is the most likely translation (so the NRSVue). Haas, De Jonge, and Swellengrebel, *Translator's Handbook*, 92.

faithful are left to ponder what is related to having resources and ignoring the needs of others, only to discover that such disregard is possible if a person does not have the love of God abiding within.

In v. 16 Christ's willingness to lay down his physical life (*psychē*) is an example obligating the faithful to lay down their physical lives for others. Now the love of God for us manifested in the sacrifice of Christ should at least manifest itself in laying down our resources to sustain the life (*bios*) of others. This verse expands the rare and unique occasion of giving of one's life for others to the common occasion of giving material goods to the needy (Matt 6:2-4; Mark 10:21; Luke 3:11; 12:33; Jas 2:15-17). God's love for us is a prerequisite of our love for others (4:19; cf. 4:21) and is demonstrated by our loving others by meeting their physical needs.

The rhetorical question is an obvious critique of the secessionists. Verse 13 refers to the world's hatred of the faithful (cf. John 15:18-19; 17:14). Now the world's lack of love is expressed as the withholding of necessary provisions. This verse reintroduces the interrelated topics of life (*bios*) and world (*kosmos*) from 2:15-17, where the world (*kosmos*) takes pride in riches (*bios*). The secessionists are in the world (4:5; 2 John 7), and it is insinuated that the secessionists are materially better off than the faithful and should be responding to their needs; needs that their secession may have caused or at least exacerbated.[168] The love of God does not abide in them.

3:18: Exhortation to Fully Love

The Elder begins the second half of 3:11-24 with an exhortation based upon the content of the preceding half: "Little children, let us love not in word or speech but in deed and truth" (cf. 3:14, 23; 4:7-8, 19; John 13:34-35; 15:12, 17; Jas 1:25; 2:15-17). He softens the exhortation by addressing the faithful as "little children" and by including himself in it as well. It has been argued that the exhortation is composed of an antithesis between two spheres: speech and truth. In each half of the antithesis, the second of the two nouns is the sphere from which the first emerges: Speech (lit. "tongue") is the source of words and truth is the source of deeds (lit. "works").[169] However, both words in each pair have similar meanings, and

---

[168] Brown, *Epistles of John*, 475-76.
[169] For detailed discussion of the relationship between the two nouns in each of this contrast, see I. de la Potterie, *La verité dans saint Jean*, 2 vols. AnBib 73-74 (Rome: Biblical Institute Press, 1977), 2.663-73; Brown, *Epistles of John*, 451-53.

the latter pair can simply mean "doing the truth." Also, speech is not being rejected for action as would be implied by an antithesis, but rather the point is that love must move beyond just speech to action. There is no antithesis here, but rather exhortation to love in word and speech, as well as deed and truth.[170] The exhortation insinuates that by neglecting to help meet the needs of others (v. 17), the secessionists love only in words or, more likely, not at all.

3:19–22: Love in Deed and Truth Brings Reassurance and Boldness Before God

Love in deed and truth (v. 18) provides the faithful with knowledge and reassurance of their spiritual status before God: "And by this we will know that we are from the truth and will reassure our hearts before him whenever our hearts condemn us, for God is greater than our hearts, and he knows everything" (vv. 19–20).[171] The heart (*kardia*) is the mind and spirit, the measure of morality (1 Sam 12:20; 24:5; Ps 24:4; Luke 16:15; Acts 2:37; Rom 8:27; 1 Thess 2:4; Rev 2:23), and is equivalent to the conscience (*syneidēsis*) in Paul (Rom 13:5; 1 Cor 8:7; 10:25). The heart may condemn (*kataginōskō*) the faithful like a judge's verdict in a courtroom,[172] eroding their confidence in their status before God. Perhaps they have not been attending to the needs of others (3:17), or, in line with their disregard for moral behavior, the secessionists may be claiming that if the faithful must concern themselves with moral behavior, they cannot be confident before God. In any case, the Elder affirms that moral behavior before God, who knows (*ginōskō*) everything, including the deeds of love performed by the Elder and the faithful (v. 18), is the basis for their knowledge (*ginōskō*) that they are of (*einai ek*) the truth and reassures them so that they can have confidence before God.[173] It is not the heart, which can be condemning

---

[170] Painter, *1, 2, 3 John*, 243.
[171] The formula *en toutō* ("by this") beginning v. 19 usually points ahead when followed by a *hoti* ("that") clause that offers explanation (2:3; 3:24). Although two *hoti* clauses follow the formula here in v. 20, *en toutō* should be viewed as pointing backward to v. 18 as the basis of knowledge and reassurance (cf. 4:6; 5:2).
[172] The pronoun *hēmōn* ("our") can be either an emphatic possessive ("our heart condemns") or the object of the verb *kataginōskō* ("the heart condemns us"). The word order with *hēmōn* following heart favors the latter.
[173] Brown, *Epistles of John*, 478–79. This reassurance is similar to the one in 2:3–5a in which obeying the commandments (love being primary as here) is to know God and disobeying the commandments is not to be indwelt with the truth (cf. 1:8).

without warrant in moral matters, but God who can render a correct verdict in the trial of judgment (cf. John 21:17; 1 Cor 4:3-5).

Whereas vv. 19-20 present a heart that condemns, vv. 21-22 present a heart that does not: "Beloved, if our hearts do not condemn us, we have boldness before God; and we receive from him whatever we ask, because we obey his commandments and do what pleases him." If their hearts do not condemn them, then the faithful have been obeying God's commandments and doing what pleases God. These actions are synonymous and constitute refining, in which an idea is repeated in an alternative form (Rhet. Her. 4.43.56). The refining amplifies the character of the moral life that undergirds confidence before God and receipt for what is asked of God.

Confidence before God is an aspect of a broader topic of the faithful being "before the Father" that runs throughout 3:19-22. The topic uses a variety of synonyms for "before": *emprosthen* (3:19), *pros* (3:21; 5:14), and *enōpion* (3:22). The topic is closely connected with those of confidence (*parrēsia*), loving (*agapaō*), abiding in (*menein en*), and asking (*aiteō*). Confidence (*parrēsia*) before Christ in judgment is based on abiding in (*menein en*) Christ (2:28-29). Abiding in (*menein en*) God perfects love (*agapē*) in the faithful and gives them confidence (*parrēsia*) in judgment (4:16-17). Confidence (*parrēsia*) before (*pros*) God for whatever we ask (*aiteō*) is reaffirmed in 5:14.[174]

Here in 3:19-22 abiding in (*menein en*) God and loving (*agapaō*) one another give confidence (*parrēsia*) before God and assurance of receipt of whatever is asked (*aiteō*) in prayer. In Johannine tradition, Jesus assured his disciples that they would receive what they ask for if they ask in his name, keep his commandments, abide in him, and bear fruit (John 14:13-14; 15:7, 16-17; 16:23-26; cf. Matt 18:19; 21:22). Jesus himself did what was pleasing to God (John 8:28-29). This tradition once more makes Jesus the model for imitation in the moral walk (1 John 1:7; 2:6; 3:3, 16; 4:11).

---

[174] In light of the positive and reassuring use of the topic of boldness or confidence (*parrēsia*) before God throughout 1 John (2:28; 3:21; 4:17; 5:14), I reject an alternative interpretation of these verses that assumes that the severity, not the mercy of God is primary here. The focus is reassurance before God based on God's knowledge of our loving deeds, not motivation to good deeds based on fear of God's knowledge of our deeds or lack thereof (cf. 1 Cor 4:3-5). Brown, *Epistles of John*, 459-60; Bultmann, *Johannine Epistles*, 58; Painter, *1, 2 and 3 John*, 248-49.

It may seem that obeying the commandments and doing what pleases God is a precondition for asking and receiving, as if God will not hear the prayers of those who are in any way disobedient. However, the Elder encourages the faithful to love in deed and truth. He reassures them that in spite of their condemning hearts, God knows everything, including their efforts to obey and please God. Confidence before God and receiving what is asked for are parts of an ongoing and maturing relationship with God in which one strives to please God through obedience as one lives out God's love in community. It may also seem that obedience is just a way to get what we want in prayer from God the heavenly Santa Claus. However, obedience motivated by love of others excludes the selfish prayer.

3:23–24: Definition of the Commandment and Benefit of Obeying It

The Elder concludes this section with a definition of the commandment (v. 23) and an assurance that obedience to the commandment results in abiding in Christ (v. 24). In the previous verse he mentions that obedience to the commandments provides boldness before God and answered prayer. Now he defines the commandment: "And this is his commandment, that we should believe in the name of his Son Jesus Christ and love one another, just as he has commanded us" (cf. John 13:34; 15:12; 2 John 4–6).[175] The commandment is twofold, involving both belief and love. Whereas the Elder has previously discussed the need to obey the commandment of love (2:3–11), he now introduces the topic of belief (*pisteuō*) as an aspect of the commandment. Belief is in Jesus as the Christ (2:22; 5:1), as Son of God (4:15; 5:5, 13), and as incarnate (4:2; 2 John 7). These two topics of belief and love are the twin topics of 4:1–5:13 that follows.

Belief is in the "name of his Son Jesus Christ." The name of a person reflected the essence of their being (Gen 32:29; Exod 33:19; 1 Sam 25:25). Here to believe in the name of Jesus is to commit to what he is and has done and to accept his claims upon us and obey his teachings. It is to be forgiven (2:12), have eternal life (5:13), not be condemned (John 3:18), and love one another (John 13:34; 15:12, 17). Belief is the prerequisite to love (cf. Gal 5:6).

---

[175] The shift from the plural to the singular of commandment and back again in vv. 22–24 is a stylistic variation common to 1 John (cf. 2:3–4, 7–8).

3:11–24: Love One Another

God gives the commandment to believe and love. The topic of "giving" (*didōmi*) refers to heavenly realities that God gives Christians, including the love commandment (John 13:34; 15:12, 17), and the Spirit who confirms the abiding of God in those who obey God's commandments (v. 24). In 3:1 the topic was introduced as God giving us love, which is the content of the commandment. The reference to the commandment at both the beginning (3:11) and ending (3:23–24) of this section forms an *inclusio* and emphasizes the topic.

The commandment to believe and love confronts the secessionists, who can do neither. They can believe in "his Son, Christ," but not "his Son, Jesus Christ" (cf. 2:22–23). The secessionists could not obey the commandment to love the brothers and sisters (2:3, 11; 3:18), as proven by their departure from the Johannine Community (cf. 2:19) and denial of the physical needs of its members (3:15, 17).

In v. 24 the Elder provides a corollary of obeying the commandment to believe and love: "All who obey his commandments abide in him, and he abides in them. And by this we know that he abides in us, by the Spirit that he has given us" (cf. 4:13). The topics of abiding (*menō*) and keeping/obeying (*tereō*) the commandments have been previously developed separately. It has only been implied that Christians abide in God if they obey the commandments (2:5b–6). Now that connection is made explicit. The mutual abiding of God and the Christian mentioned here is developed further in 4:12–16.

The formula "by this we know" (*en toutō ginōskomen*) presents the third test of knowledge based on divine realities using this formula to be found in this section (3:16, 19). In all three cases, and elsewhere in 1 John where this formula is found (2:3, 5; 4:13; 5:2), the test of knowledge follows the formula. In 2:20 and 2:27, the anointing with the Spirit grants true knowledge, and here the Spirit provides knowledge of mutual abiding to those who obey the commandments (4:13).[176] Jesus promised his disciples that the Spirit would abide with them (John 14:15–17). This reference to the Spirit ends this section and introduces the next section dealing with the Spirit in more detail (4:1–6).

---

[176] Painter (*1, 2, 3 John*, 252) and Brown (*Epistles of John*, 466) see the source of knowledge of mutual abiding to be the Spirit-inspired confession of faith in 4:2, but the vocative in 4:1 introduces a new section and makes this association unlikely.

BRIDGING THE HORIZONS

Love is the central commandment in Johannine tradition. Loving others is a sign that the faithful have moved from death to life, while hating others is to remain in death (v. 14). In fact, hating others is to murder them, analogous to how Cain murdered Abel (vv. 12, 15). We are reminded of Jesus's teaching that being angry with others long term and dismissing them as irrelevant or worthless is also to murder them (Matt 5:21–22).

Jesus is the model for how we should love, most notably in his laying down his life for us (v. 16). We cannot grasp just how loving Jesus's sacrifice was. How can we comprehend how the Son of God, creator of the universe, loves us enough to be shamed and humiliated and painfully crucified by beings he created that are so vastly inferior in every way. His love is beyond words. It may be a rare situation that we have to lay down our lives to save others, but at least we can lay down our resources to sustain those without the necessities for life, especially our fellow Christians (v. 17). This is the tangible self-sacrifice of love.

Such modeling of Jesus is to move from mere words about love to actively demonstrating that love as he did (v. 18). Such love in action is a sign to ourselves that we are in the truth, even when we doubt our spiritual status (vv. 19–20). So many things can move us to doubt that we are in the truth, like addictions, mental health issues, struggles with difficult relationships, comparing ourselves with the more spiritually mature – the list goes on. The ultimate assurance of our spiritual health is the realization that God knows everything, including our transfer from death to life and the truth by our confession of Jesus Christ as Lord (v. 20).

If we obey God's commandments and do what pleases God and our consciences do not condemn us, we can come to God with confidence in prayer. In such a state we are likely to ask for things that are pleasing to God and not selfish, things that God is happy to bless as part of his love for us and the world. We know that we will not always receive what we pray for, but the chances are much greater when the prayer is spoken while we are obedient to and abiding in God (vv. 21–22).

God commands that we believe in the name of Jesus Christ and love one another, which creates a mutual abiding of God in us and us in God. The reality of this mystical union is confirmed by the internal witness of

> the Holy Spirit (vv. 23-24) as well as living others in word and action (vv. 18-20).
>
> The instruction in this section originates in the internal struggles of the Johannine Community. We need to be cautious that this love of others is not just directed to fellow Christians who agree with us or to our specific community as is evident here, but as seen in Johannine tradition more broadly where love is directed to the whole world – even our enemies (cf. 2:2; 4:14; John 3:16).

4:1-6: DISTINGUISHING THE SPIRIT OF GOD FROM THE SPIRIT OF THE ANTICHRIST

> **4:1** Beloved, do not believe every spirit, but test the spirits to see whether they are from God, for many false prophets have gone out into the world.
>
> **4:2** By this you know the Spirit of God: every spirit that confesses that Jesus Christ has come in the flesh is from God,
>
> **4:3** and every spirit that does not confess Jesus is not from God. And this is the spirit of the antichrist, of which you have heard that it is coming, and now it is already in the world.
>
> **4:4** Little children, you are from God and have conquered them, for the one who is in you is greater than the one who is in the world.
>
> **4:5** They are from the world; therefore what they say is from the world, and the world listens to them.
>
> **4:6** We are from God. Whoever knows God listens to us, and whoever is not from God does not listen to us. From this we know the spirit of truth and the spirit of error.

Whereas 3:23 gives the twofold commandment to believe in the name of God's Son Jesus Christ and to love one another, 4:1-6 develops the former (cf. vv. 13-16) and 4:7-5:4a develops the latter. Whereas 3:24 introduces the topic of the Spirit, 4:1-6 develops it. This section provides two tests of the spirits at work in the world and in the church: the confession one makes (vv. 1-3) and to whom one listens (vv. 4-6).

The topic of "from, belonging to" (*einai ek*) structures this section. It is introduced in the opening exhortation to test where the spirits are from (v. 1), and the test that follows contrasts the origin of the spirits and their followers as either "from God" (vv. 2, 4, 6) or "not from God" (vv. 3, 6) and "from the world" (v. 5). Many of the topics of 2:18–27 on true and false teaching recur, including the going out of the antichrists (2:18–19), truth versus lying and deceit (*alētheia/pseustēs* and *planaō*; 2:21–22, 26), confession (*homologeō*; 2:23), and the Spirit (2:20, 27). The contrast and recurrence of previous topics solidifies the identity of the faithful in opposition to the secessionists. Chiastic arrangement allows for amplification by repetition and aids memory in an oral culture.

This section is divided into two units, each beginning with a vocative address: "beloved" (*agapētoi*, 4:1) and *teknia* (4:4), respectively. The first unit is chiastic in structure with an abc/c'b'a' arrangement:[177]

    a. v. 1: false prophets have gone out into the world
      b. v. 2: the Spirit of God
        c. v. 2: Every spirit that confesses that Jesus ... is from God
        c.' v. 3: Every spirit that does not confess Jesus is not from God
      b.' v. 3: the spirit of the antichrist
    a.' v. 3: antichrist is ... already in the world

4:1–3: First Test of the Spirits: Confession as Sign

The early church advised believers to test the prophets who came to them because false prophets motivated by greed and bearing false teaching were prevalent (1 Clem. 42:4; Did. 11:6–8; Herm. Mand. 11:7). The Elder begins this section with such an exhortation and supporting reason: "Beloved, do not believe every spirit, but test the spirits to see whether they are from God, for many false prophets have gone out into the world." The exhortation is rooted in many rich traditions: One is that a divine spirit and a diabolic spirit influence humankind (cf. John 16:11; Eph 2:1–2; 1QS 3:18–21; T. Jud. 20:1–2). Another is the Old Testament instruction to test prophets to see if they teach the worship of other gods (Deut 13:1–5), speak in the name of another god, or presume to speak in God's name and their words do not come true (Deut 18:15–22; cf. Jer 14:13–16). A third tradition is that prophets are motivated by God's Spirit or an evil spirit (God's Spirit: 2 Chron 15:1; Isa 61:1–2; Ezek 2:2; Micah 3:8; Zech 7:12; 2 Pet 1:21; Ign. Phld. 7:1–2; evil spirit: 1 Kgs 22:22–23; Rev 13:11–18; 16:13; 19:20). A fourth is Christian eschatological expectation of the appearance of false

---

[177] Brown, *Epistles of John*, 502.

prophets (Matt 7:15–23), especially as a sign of the last days (Matt 24:11, 24; Mark 13:21–22; 2 Pet 2:1–3; Rev 16:13–14; 19:20; 20:10; Did. 16:3).

The exhortation and its associations in tradition lessen the ethos of the secessionists by insinuating that they are false prophets inspired by an evil spirit and allied with diabolic forces to appear in the last days who do not speak truthfully about God. The need to test the spirits implies that the secessionists are deceitful and that their true nature must be revealed (2:19–22). The exhortation does not ascertain that the secessionists were claiming to be prophets whose teachings are inspired. The Elder associates them with the false prophets of the last days but is more concerned with the spirit that motivates them and the content of their teaching than in actual prophesying.[178]

The phraseology of "have gone out into the world" brings the faithful back to the affirmation that the secessionists once left them (2:19; 2 John 7) and facilitates them identifying the secessionists with the false prophets. The secessionists are a parody of Jesus, the truth, who went out from the Father and came into the world (John 16:28), and of the disciples, whom Jesus sent into the world but, like him, were not of the world (John 17:14, 18). The world is not of God (1 John 2:16) and, unlike Jesus and the disciples, the secessionists are of the world (4:5).[179]

The present imperative "do not believe (*mē pisteuete*) every spirit" may have an iterative force meaning "do not go on believing," which would imply that the faithful have a tendency to accept the secessionists as prophets of the Spirit and they need to stop doing so.[180] The present imperative "test (*dokimazō*) the spirits" may have an iterative force meaning "keep on testing," which would imply that the faithful are already reacting appropriately for a Christian community living in the last days. Epideictic rhetoric strives to increase audience adherence to values and understandings it already holds and decrease the same for the opposite. That seems to be the Elder's strategy here.

In 4:2–3a the Elder provides another reassurance of spiritual knowledge (cf. 2:29; 3:16, 18–19, 24) using two signs in antithetical parallelism: "By

---

[178] Brown, *Epistles of John*, 489–90; Parsenios, *1, 2, 3 John*, 110. Schnackenburg (*Johannine Epistles*, 199) does not associate these secessionists with the false prophets of the last days because there is no indication that they perform signs and wonders.
[179] Brown, *Epistles of John*, 490–91.
[180] Brown, *Epistles of John*, 485–86.

this you know[181] the Spirit of God: every spirit that confesses that Jesus Christ has come in the flesh[182] is from God, and every spirit that does not confess Jesus is not from God" (cf. 1 Cor 12:3). The confession topic (*homologeō*) was introduced in 2:23 in the related unit of 2:18–27, where everyone who confesses the Son has (*echō*) the Father. Now confession is tied to the topic of "being from" (*einai ek*), for confessing Jesus Christ come in the flesh demonstrates being from God. This confession fully embraces Jesus Christ as incarnate and all this means for salvation (John 1:14; 6:51). Confession (*homologeō*) in 1 John has different forms, including "Jesus is the Christ" (2:22; 5:1; cf. 5:6–7), "Jesus is the Son of God" (4:15; 5:5; cf. 5:20), and "Jesus Christ has come in the flesh" (4:2; cf. 2 John 7).

In v. 3b the Elder further identifies the nature of the ungodly spirits that do not confess Jesus Christ has come in the flesh: "And this is the spirit[183] of the antichrist, of which you have heard that it is coming, and now it is already in the world." The secessionists were previously identified as the antichrists of eschatological expectation by their denial that Jesus is the Christ (2:18–19, 22–23). The apocalyptic expectation of the antichrist has been historicized in terms of the appearance of the secessionists and their confession. The shift from the plural antichrists in v. 3a to the singular antichrist in v. 3b implies that all of the individual secessionists are influenced by the one evil spirit.

4:4–6: Second Test of the Spirits: Listening to the World versus Listening to God

The vocative "little children" transitions from discussing the two spirits to those who live by those spirits. The test of the spirits now shifts from confession (vv. 1–3) to listening (vv. 4–6), from belief held about Jesus Christ to the source being credited with speaking with authority about Jesus Christ. The second test of the spirits more specifically contrasts the faithful and the secessionists based on the sign of who listens to the faithful

---

[181] "Know" (*ginoskete*) is probably indicative rather than imperative. The Elder is affirming the knowledge of the faithful (as in 2:27, 29, 4:6), not commanding them to know.

[182] With most commentators, I am assuming that "Jesus Christ come in the flesh" is a descriptive unit rather than assuming that the verb "confess" (*homologeō*) has two objects as in the translations "Jesus Christ, come in the flesh" or "Jesus, Christ come in the flesh."

[183] Ellipsis requires supplying the word "spirit" here.

4:1–6: The Spirit of God and the Spirit of Antichrist

and the Elder and who does not (vv. 4–6): "Little children, you are from God and have conquered them, for the one who is in you is greater than the one who is in the world. They are from the world; therefore what they say is from the world, and the world listens to them. We are from God. Whoever knows God listens to us, and whoever is not from God does not listen to us. From this we know the spirit of truth and the spirit of error." These verses are connected by antithetical parallelism in their emphatic beginnings: "you (*hymeis*) are from God" (v. 4), "they (*autoi*) are from the world" (v. 5), and "we (*hēmeis*) are from God" (v. 6). This construction distinguishes the faithful and the Elder from false prophets and others from the world.[184]

The contrast is formally argued with two enthymemes. In the first half of the contrast, 4:4, the stated premise is "the one who is in you is greater than the one who is in the world" and the conclusion is "Little children, you are from God and have conquered them." The unstated premise is "those having in them the one who is greater than the one in the world have conquered those having in them the one who is in the world." This enthymeme employs the common topic of degree and the specific topic of "being of or from" (*einai ek*) in relation to supernatural forces. It compares the status of the faithful as greater than that of the secessionists. In the stated premise, we expect the Elder to write "greater than the one who is in them," referring to the secessionist false prophets (v. 1), rather than "greater than the one who is in the world," referring to the evil one (2:13–14; 5:18–19; John 12:31; 14:30; 16:11). The more general reference emphasizes the secessionists' association with the evil one and the world in opposition to God (2:15–17; 3:1, 13).[185]

This enthymeme of v. 4 employs the imagery of victory in battle in the metaphorical verb "conquer" (*nikaō*). Johannine literature typically uses this verb with Satan, the antichrist, and the world as objects. The perfect

---

[184] "You" (*hymeis*) also emphatically introduces a contrast in 2:20, 24, 27 in another rhetorical section distinguishing those anointed by the Holy One and those from the antichrist(s).

[185] "The one who is in you" and "the one who is in the world" do not represent a contrast between God or Christ versus the devil or antichrist. Rather, they continue the contrast between the Spirit of God and the spirit of the antichrist in the world from vv. 2–3 (cf. John 14:16–17; 16:7–11) and anticipate the contrast between the spirit of truth and the spirit of error in v. 6. Brown, *Epistles of John*, 497–98, 507, n. 14. *Contra* Bultmann, *Johannine Epistles*, 63; Smalley, *1, 2, 3 John*, 227; Haas, De Jonge, and Swellengrebel, *Translator's Handbook*, 104; Brooke, *Johannine Epistles*, 114–15; Painter, *1, 2, 3 John*, 255.

tense of the verb indicates a past victory with continuing effect. This topic was introduced in 2:13 in the initial discussion of the antichrist where the young people have conquered the evil one. Now the source of that victory is given as the Spirit of God in the faithful. They have conquered those who have the spirit of the antichrist that is in the world; that is, the secessionists. This conquering probably refers to not being deceived by the teachings of the world promulgated by the secessionists. The conquering topic will be developed further in 5:4–5, where the faithful are said to have conquered the world by maintaining the confession that Jesus is the Son of God (cf. John 16:33).

In the second enthymeme of the contrast, v. 5, the stated premise is "they are from the world" and the conclusion is "therefore what they say is from the world, and the world listens to them." The unstated premise is "those who belong to the world have the world's attention" (cf. John 3:31). In the preceding section also devoted to the relationship between the secessionists and the antichrist, it is stated that the secessionists do not belong to the Johannine Community (2:19). Now the contrast of vv. 4–5 makes it explicit that they belong to the world and share the spirit of the antichrist that has come into the world (4:3). This is the only mention in 1 John of the secessionists have a "hearing" (*akouō*) and have success in attracting followers (cf. 4:1; 2 John 7).

The contrast in vv. 4–5 is followed by another in vv. 5–6. Whereas those of the world listen to the secessionists (v. 5), those from God listen to the Elder and the faithful (v. 6). Like the preceding contrast in vv. 4–5, this one begins with an emphatic pronoun, but it changes from "you" to "we" (*hēmeis*) as the Elder joins himself to the faithful as being from God.[186] This second test of the spirits involves hearing/listening. The topic of hearing/listening (*akouō*) grounds the Elder's message in the revelation of Jesus Christ as heard by the Johannine tradition-bearers (1:1, 3, 5) and the proclamation of that message by the Elder and the tradition-bearers to the faithful who heard it (2:7, 18, 24; 3:11; 4:3, 6). Now listening to this message is made the test of knowing God or not knowing the spirit of truth (cf. John 8:26–27, 47; 18:37).

There is also a contrast within v. 6, although inexact. The contrast is between "whoever knows God" and "whoever is not from God" rather than

---

[186] With the majority of commentators, I am assuming that this is the nondistinctive use of the pronoun *hēmeis*. The Elder groups himself with the faithful to build positive pathos, not with the Johannine tradition-bearers in opposition to the secessionist leadership.

"whoever does not know God." This an example of refining, in which the same thing is said by the contrary and in an altered form (Rhet. Her. 4.42.54). The refining reintroduces the "being from" topic (*einai ek*) to make the point that knowledge of God is equated with "being from" God. Knowledge of God brings a person into the sphere of God's being (2:3–6, 13–14) and experience of the spirit of truth (4:6).

The Elder opened this section with the exhortation to "test the spirits to see whether they are of God" (v. 1). Having provided two tests of the spirits, he concludes with one final contrast: "from this we know the spirit of truth and the spirit of error." This reintroduces the topics of truth (*alētheia, alēthēs*) and deceit/error (*planē*). Truth dwells in Christians who are obedient (1:6, 8; 2:4, 27; 3:19). Now the spirit of God, the spirit that confesses Jesus Christ come in the flesh, is identified as the spirit of truth (John 14:17; 15:26; 16:13). Deceit/error is a distinguishing mark of the secessionists (1:8, 3:7; 2 John 7) and characterizes their activities as the antichrists (2:26). Now the spirit behind such activity is explicitly identified as the spirit of deceit/error, of the antichrist (4:3), which makes the secessionists false prophets (4:1). This contrast is traditional, for the spirits of truth and deceit/error are contrasted in earlier Jewish literature as wrestling for the allegiance of humankind (T. Jud. 14:8; 19:4; 20:1; 23:1; 25:3; T. Sim. 3:1; 1 QS 3:13–4:26).

> **BRIDGING THE HORIZONS**
>
> The full confession that Jesus is the Christ come in the flesh is spoken by those sharing the Holy Spirit who motivates the confession. These confessors are for Christ. Those not making this confession are still of the world that does not know God and they share the spirit that is anti-Christ. Those that know God acknowledge the confession and its truth, while those in the world that do not know God listen to those from the world and their error. The Elder has a strongly dualistic way of thinking, which might leave the impression that our proclamation should only be directed to Christians because the world will not listen. The Spirit of God works through our proclamation to open the ears of those in the world that are open to hearing the truth and make the confession that Jesus is the Christ come in the flesh. In our increasingly secular age, I have noticed that the Church is often reluctant to proclaim its message or all too ready to accommodate the message to the world's

expectations. There is hesitation to offend a particular group or a lowering of the gospel to mere promises of health and affluence. This is the time to unapologetically proclaim the full message of sin, redemption, abiding in God, and expectantly awaiting the return of our Lord Jesus Christ. It is also a time to be sure that our proclamation conforms to the truths of our traditions.

4:7–5:5: OBLIGATIONS INCURRED AND BLESSINGS OF GOD'S LOVE FOR US

4:7 Beloved, let us love one another, because love is from God; everyone who loves is born of God and knows God.

4:8 Whoever does not love does not know God, for God is love.

4:9 God's love was revealed among us in this way: God sent his only Son into the world so that we might live through him.

4:10 In this is love, not that we loved God but that he loved us and sent his Son to be the atoning sacrifice for our sins.

4:11 Beloved, since God loved us so much, we also ought to love one another.

4:12 No one has ever seen God; if we love one another, God abides in us, and his love is perfected in us.

4:13 By this we know that we abide in him and he in us, because he has given us of his Spirit.

4:14 And we have seen and do testify that the Father has sent his Son as the Savior of the world.

4:15 God abides in those who confess that Jesus is the Son of God, and they abide in God.

4:16 So we have known and believe the love that God has for us.

4:17 Love has been perfected among us in this: that we may have boldness on the day of judgment, because as he is, so are we in this world.

4:18 There is no fear in love, but perfect love casts out fear; for fear has to do with punishment, and whoever fears has not reached perfection in love.

4:19 We love because he first loved us.

> 4:20 Those who say, "I love God," and hate a brother or sister are liars, for those who do not love a brother or sister, whom they have seen, cannot love God, whom they have not seen.
>
> 4:21 The commandment we have from him is this: those who love God must love their brothers and sisters also.
>
> 5:1 Everyone who believes that Jesus is the Christ has been born of God, and everyone who loves the parent loves the child.
>
> 5:2 By this we know that we love the children of God, when we love God and obey his commandments.
>
> 5:3 For the love of God is this, that we obey his commandments. And his commandments are not burdensome,
>
> 5:4 for whatever is born of God conquers the world. And this is the victory that conquers the world, our faith.
>
> 5:5 Who is it who conquers the world but the one who believes that Jesus is the Son of God?

The next rhetorical section is 4:7–5:5. It is the development of the second part of the commandment given in 3:23 that functions as a proposition for all of 4:1–5:5: "And this is his commandment, that we should believe in the name of his Son Jesus Christ and love one another, just as he has commanded us." Whereas 4:1–6 develops the first portion of the commandment pertaining to belief in the name of Jesus, 4:7–5:5 develops the second portion pertaining to love. Both sections begin with the vocative "beloved" (*agapētoi*) indicating this division. This section ends with the topics of love and commandments (5:2–3) and thus reiterates the proposition of 3:23 to form an *inclusio*.[187]

Of this section and the next, Bultmann writes, "It cannot be denied that in 4:7–5:12 there is no unified sequence of thought ... One is inclined to the view that we have to do here with the work of a school. One could almost say that in 4:7–5:12 there is reflected something like the discussion of a theological 'seminar' of the Johannine 'school'."[188] Bultmann is not far from the mark. What the Elder does in this section is develop and amplify topics, a practice central to school exercises. He develops the topic of love for the third time (2:3–11; 3:10–24), infusing this development with the tradition of the Johannine school.

---

[187] For a discussion of the debate about where this section concludes, see Brown, *Epistles of Johns*, 542–47.
[188] *Johannine Epistles*, 69.

4:7–10: God's Love as the Source and Imperative of Our Love of One Another

The Elder continues in 4:7–10 with a commentary on God's love for the world as also found in John 3:16–17. The opening vocative "beloved" (*agapētoi*) marks the beginning of a new section and is especially appropriate because this section pertains to love. The vocative demonstrates that the Elder himself obeys the commandment to love by loving the faithful and implies that God also loves them.

The Elder continues with an exhortation with supporting reason (v. 7a): "Beloved, let us love one another, because love is from God." This is not an exhortation to start loving as if he and the faithful have strayed from obeying the love commandment. The present imperative "let us love" (*agapōmen*) may have a durative sense of "keep on loving,"[189] in which case the Elder would be assuming that both he and the faithful have been properly loving one another and need to keep doing so.

Whereas earlier the love commandment is traced to Jesus (3:11, 23), here it is grounded in the nature of God using the topic of "being of or from" (*einai ek*): "because love is from God" (cf. 4:16). How God's love has been demonstrated will be immediately defined as the sending of the Son for the salvation of the world (vv. 9–10, 12, 14). God's love for us obligates us to love others (4:11, 19; 5:1) and is analogous to Jesus's exhortation to the disciples to love based upon his love for them (John 13:34–35; 15:12, 17).

The exhortation and its supporting reason are followed by an inexact antithesis and supporting reason (4:7b–8): "everyone who loves is born of God and knows God. Whoever does not love does not know God, for God is love." The antithesis uses the present articular participle "loving" (*agapaō*) to distinguish the faithful (and other Christians) from the secessionists (and others of the world) as the articular participle does elsewhere in the letter (2:4, 6, 9; 3:7, 8, 24).

The positive half of the antithesis (v. 7b) contains two topics central to the letter: birth from God (*gennaō*; 2:29; 3:9; 4:7; 5:1, 4, 18) and knowing God (*ginōskō*; 2:3–5, 13–14; 3:1, 6; 4:6–8; 5:20), but here is the only place in the letter where the Elder develops them together in relation to love. It is not that loving results in being born of God and knowing God, but loving is a sign of being born of God, knowing God, and sharing his loving nature.

---

[189] BDF §318.2.

The negative half of the antithesis is an enthymeme. The premise is "God is love," the unstated premise is "those who love know God," and the conclusion is "Whoever does not love does not know God" (cf. 3:10). The Elder may be refuting a secessionist claim to know God by insinuating that their lack of love of the faithful negates that claim (cf. 2:3-6; 3:1, 13, 15). He has already insinuated that the secessionists are of the world (3:1; 4:5) and that the world does not love the faithful (3:13; cf. 3:17; John 15:18-19; 17:14). The secessionists' lack of love is a clear indication that they have neither been born of God nor know God, for God is love.

The Elder's supports his premise of v. 8 that God is love with an example in vv. 9-10 revealing God's love: "God's love was revealed among us in this way: God sent his only Son into the world so that we might live through him. In this is love, not that we loved God but that he loved us and sent his Son to be the atoning sacrifice for our sins." God's supreme gift of the Son as an atoning sacrifice for sin (2:2; 3:5, 8, 16; 5:6; John 3:16-17) to bring life to the world (1:1-2; 2:25; 5:11-13; John 6:57-58; 11:25; 14:19) reveals (*phanerō*) that God is love. The description of the Son as God's "only-begotten" (*monogenēs*) amplifies God's love in sending the solitary Son as a sacrifice (John 1:14, 18; 3:16, 18).[190] This example of God's love is given in two versions for emphasis: God's love is revealed to give life (v. 9) and as an atoning sacrifice for sin (v. 10). The duplication is refining of the type in which the idea is altered in the repetition to further develop the topic based on what has already been said (Rhet. Her. 4.42.54). Life is given by means of the atoning sacrifice.

The example introduces the topic of "sending," which occurs only in this section, to describe the nature of God's salvific purpose in sending Jesus as an atoning sacrifice to give life. The tense shift of "sending" (*apostellō*) from the perfect (v. 9) to the aorist (vv. 10, 14) contrasts the continued effect of God's love revealed in sending the Son as an atoning sacrifice (v. 9) with the historical fact of the sacrifice of the Son God sent (v. 10). God's sending of the Son has continued efficacy. As described here, the sending of the Son is another way of stating that the Son appeared to take away sins and to destroy the works of the devil (3:5, 8), and he is the atonement (*hilasmos*) for the sins of the faithful and for the whole world (2:1-2; cf. 1:7). The secessionists may have claimed that the death of Jesus was outside the plan of God in sending him. Thus, the Elder asserts that

---

[190] Knowing the nature of love was previously rooted in the example of Christ laying down his life for humanity (3:16).

the atoning sacrifice of the Son was an integral part of God's loving plan in sending his Son.[191]

4:11–16a: Loving Others and Confessing the Son as Assurance of Abiding in God

The next section of 4:7–5:5 comprises 4:11–16a. As did the preceding section of 4:7–10, this section begins with the direct address "beloved" (*agapetoi*) and appeals to God's love as the source and imperative for the love of others. Whereas the preceding section describes God as love and the origin of love, now the love of others indicates that God and God's love abide within. Whereas in the preceding section the love of God was demonstrated in the incarnation and atoning sacrifice of Christ, now those God loves are to embody that love in loving others. The Elder begins in v. 11 with the exhortation: "Beloved, since God loved us so much, we also ought to love one another." The exhortation repeats that of 4:7a and is based upon the description in 4:9–10 of God's love as expressed in giving the Son as an atoning sacrifice. The "we" (*hēmeis*) of "we ought" is emphatic and forms a strong contrast between God's love and the love that should likewise characterize the faithful as a response to that love. As he did in 4:7, the Elder also directs the exhortation to himself as one of the faithful. The topic of "ought" (*opheilō*) recurs from 2:6 and 3:16, where Christ provided the model for ethical exhortation. In 3:16 it was the love of Christ in laying down his life that grounds the exhortation to lay down one's life, whereas now it is God's love in sending the Son that grounds the exhortation to love.

The Elder continues in v. 12 with two related propositions: "No one has ever seen God; if we love one another, God abides in us and his love[192] is perfected in us" (cf. vv. 16, 20). Johannine tradition assumes the spiritual rather than actual perception of God in this life, with God only made known through the Son (1 John 1:1–3; 4:20; John 1:18; 5:37; 6:46; 12:45; 14:8–9; 17:24) and with the ultimate vision of God reserved for the return of Christ (1 John 3:2). God becomes visible to us and others as we love one another. God's love is perfected (*teleioō*) when we love one another with

---

[191] Brown, *Epistles of John*, 518–19, 552.
[192] "His love" (*agapē autou*) can be either an objective, subjective, or qualitative genitive. Since the context of vv. 7–12 speaks of God's love for us and a love revealed in us, the subjective genitive is indicated. It is God's love for us, not our love for God, that is perfected in us.

4:7–5:5: Obligations Incurred and Blessings of God's Love for Us

the love with which God loves us. Such love builds a community in which God is visible among those obeying the love commandment (2:5; 4:17–18).

The Elder may be refuting the secessionists. They may have been claiming to have had a vision of God, perhaps akin to the heavenly journey of the soul in Jewish apocalyptic literature[193] or ecstasy in Hellenistic religion,[194] or through ascension to heaven (John 3:13). Whether aimed at any particular secessionist claim or not, an antisecessionist polemic is insinuated in v. 12b. Mutual love is the evidence that God lives in the faithful and the means of perfecting God's indwelling love. Since the secessionists do not love the faithful (3:13, 15, 17), the clear implication is that the love of God is not living in them or being perfected in them.

The Elder teaches that the anointing by the Holy One that abides within (*menein en*) provides the faithful with knowledge and teaches them to abide in God (2:20, 27). In 3:24, the proposition governing this section of 4:7–5:4a, the Elder employs the Spirit as a guarantor of the mutual abiding (*menein en*) of God and the faithful who obey the commandments (the love commandment being primary). Now in v. 13 he again provides the Spirit as a sign of the mutual abiding of God and the faithful who love one another: "By this we know that we abide in him and he in us, because he has given us of his Spirit" (cf. Rom 8:16–17). In both contexts the proper confession of Jesus Christ (3:23; 4:14–15) and the need to obey the love commandment (3:24; 4:7–12, 16) are central to abiding.

The Elder continues with a reaffirmation of the eyewitness testimony of the Johannine Community: "And we have seen and do testify that the Father has sent his Son as the Savior of the world" (cf. 1:2; 4:9–10; John 3:17; 4:42; 12:47). The initial "we" (*hēmeis*) is emphatic, not distinctive. It refers to the Johannine Community as a whole, not just to the Johannine tradition-bearers. It is the Elder and the faithful versus the secessionists and the world.[195] That raises the question: How can the Elder and the faithful have seen (*theoreō*) and testified (*martyreō*) that God sent his Son as Savior? Even with the earliest proposed date for the letter in the late first century, they are unlikely to be eyewitnesses. The answer: The members of the Johannine Community understood the testimony that they had

---

[193] 1 En. 71; T. Levi 2–5; 2 Bar.; Gk. Apoc. Ezra.
[194] A. Oepke, "*ekstasis, existēmi* . . ." *TDNT* 2:449–60.
[195] Brown, *Epistles of John*, 522–23, 557, n. 44; Smalley, *1, 2, 3 John*, 251. Schnackenburg (*Johannine Epistles*, 219) and Painter (*1, 2, 3 John*, 275) understand the pronoun to be distinctive of the original eyewitnesses.

received from the Johannine tradition-bearers to be based on eyewitness testimony to the revelation of the word of life (1:1–4). Whereas no one has seen the Father (4:12), the Son has been seen and his appearance is the basis of Johannine tradition. Being receptive to this testimony made the faithful eyewitnesses to the revelation as well through the inner eyes of faith (John 9:39). They are as much eyewitnesses in the second and third generation as those who received the testimony originally.

How is Jesus the Savior? In this epistle salvation is from sin (2:2) and from the futility of the world (2:15–17); from death to life (1:1–2; 3:14; 5:11–12, 24; cf. John 1:4; 3:14–16, 36; 4:14). How does this verse fit within this context? Primarily it provides a footing in tradition for the affirmation that God's sending of the Son as an atoning sacrifice for salvation was an act of love (4:9–10, 16; cf. John 3:16–17). It also demonstrates that only those who possess the Spirit of God can confess the Son as Savior of the world (4:1–3, 13). This confession is probably aimed at the secessionists who would reject the atoning role of Jesus's death.[196]

The Elder continues in v. 15 by assuring the faithful that correct Christology is a tangible way to ascertain their status with God: "God abides in those who confess that Jesus is the Son of God, and they abide in God." He has previously affirmed that confession of Jesus come in the flesh is inspired by the Spirit (4:2–3), and that God gave the faithful his Spirit, which assures them of their abiding in God and God in them (4:13). Now proper confession of Jesus is an assurance of mutual abiding. The definite article before the predicate indicates that "the Son of God" is a familiar, distinguished, or unique designation[197] and thus "[t]he issue is not who Jesus is, but whether the well-known Son of God is Jesus."[198] The secessionists cannot experience mutual abiding with God because they cannot make this confession (2:22–23; 4:2–3; cf. 5:1, 5–6, 9–13, 20; cf. 2 John 7).

As the Elder opened this section of 4:11–16a, so he closes it with a reference to God's love based on the experience of the faithful and himself: "So we have known and believe the love that God has for us." Like v. 14, v. 16 begins with the emphatic "we" (*hēmeis*), which distinguishes the Elder and the faithful from the secessionists. Like v. 14, the emphatic opening is followed by two verbs affirming the experience of the faithful. In v. 14 it was seeing (*theoreō*) and testifying (*martyreō*) and now it is

---

[196] Brown, *Epistles of John*, 558.
[197] MGNTG 3.183; BDF §273.
[198] Brown, *Epistles of John*, 524. Also, Smalley, *1, 2, 3 John*, 254.

knowing (*ginōskō*) and believing (*pisteuō*) God's love as experienced from conversion. Since the love of God is manifest in the giving of his Son as an atoning sacrifice that gives life (vv. 9-10), confessing Jesus as the Son of God and Savior (vv. 14-15) is to know and believe the love of God (v. 16a). The perfect tense of both verbs indicates that the knowledge and belief continue in the Christian life once the confession is made. The confession empowers God's love to make Christians God's children (3:1). The verbs knowing (*ginōskō*) and believing (*pisteuō*) are often used together to describe a single action in Johannine tradition, for to know is to believe and to believe is to know (4:1-2; John 6:69; 8:31-32; 10:38; 14:7-10; 17:8).

4:16b-21: Perfect Love Casts Out Fear

The Elder opens this section with the proposition that "God is love, and those who abide in love abide in God, and God abides in them." The mutual abiding (*menō*) of God and the Christian is the result of the Christian's abiding in love. This love would include loving others as a perfecting of the love of God demonstrated in the giving of his Son as an atoning sacrifice (3:16-17; 4:11-12). Previously, the Elder stated that God is love, love is from God, and mutual love in community indicates a person is born of God and knows God (4:7-8). Also, those confessing Jesus as the Son of God abide in God and God in them (vv. 15-16a). Here those abiding in love experience mutual abiding in the God of love. God's love, love of God, love of one another, confession, and mutual abiding with God are now all shown to be interrelated experiences. This is one of the more intricate interlacements of topics by the Elder.

The Elder continues in v. 17 with a proposition related to that of v. 16b: "Love has been perfected among us in this: that we may have boldness on the day of judgment, because as he[199] is, so we are in this world." The love being perfected here is probably God's love. God's love is perfected in us (v. 12), God is defined as love (v. 16b), and in this verse the stated goal is to be as God is. The love perfected here is not the mutual love between Christians, but God's love that reaches perfection in Christian mutual love.[200] Even so, it is hard to separate God's love from Christian mutual love since the former is the source of the latter (cf. 2:5).[201]

---

[199] "He" (literally "that one") refers back to the Christ mentioned prior to God in vv. 14-15.
[200] Brown, *Epistles of John*, 527; Bultmann, *Johannine Epistles*, 72; Haas, De Jonge, and Swellengrebel, *Translator's Handbook*, 111-12; Painter, *1, 2, 3 John*, 277-78, 280-81. *Contra* Schnackenburg, *Johannine Epistles*, 222.
[201] Smalley, *1, 2, 3 John*, 257; Strecker, *Johannine Letters*, 165, n. 22.

The phrase "in this" (*en touto*) that begins the verse refers backward (as in 3:19) to v. 16b. It is in the mutual abiding of God and Christians in love that love is perfected. The following is a result clause. We have boldness on the day of judgment because (*hina*) love has been perfected among us. This grammatical understanding agrees with v. 12 that mutual abiding in love leads to the perfection of God's love in and among believers.[202]

Since elsewhere in 1 John when a demonstrative pronoun is followed by a *hina* clause the latter is explanatory (1:4; 3:8, 11, 23; 4:21; 5:3), some interpreters argue that "in this" (*en touto*) refers to what follows and is explained by the *hina* clause so that v. 17b explains v. 17a: Our love is perfected because we have boldness on the day of judgment. Boldness on the day of judgment is the perfection of love.[203] However, how can love already be perfected by something that is in the future?[204]

The topic of perfection (*teleioō, teleios*) is used in three places in 1 John and always in connection with love (*agapē*). In 2:5 our love for God and God's love for us are perfected through obedience to God's word, and in 4:12 God's love is perfected by loving one another. Now in vv. 16b-17 God's love has been perfected among the community as the members love one another and abide in God and God in them. The verb "to perfect" (*teleioō*) is always passive in 1 John: God's love is perfected as it is operative in the community (3:11, 23; 4:7, 12; 2 John 5).

The eschatological expectation heightened by the appearance of the antichrists and the liar (2:18-19, 23; 4:1-6) is again apparent in the need to establish confidence or boldness before the Judge on the day of judgment rather than fear (2:28). The concept of the day of judgment is rooted in that of the day of Yahweh in the Old Testament (Joel 3:4 LXX; cf. Acts 2:20). In Jewish tradition it is the day of the revelation of the judgment on sinners (1 En. 22.4, 13; 45.6; 98.8; 100.4; 4 Ezra 7.112-15; Pss. Sol. 15.12). In Christianity it is the day of Christ, Jesus Christ, the Lord, or God (Acts 2:20; 1 Cor 5:5; Phil 1:6, 10; 2:16; 1 Thess 5:2; 2 Pet 3:10, 12), a day of judgment (Matt 10:15; 11:22, 24; 12:36-37; 13:36-43; 2 Pet 2:9; 3:7; Jude 6; Barn. 19:10; 21:6; 2 Clem. 16:3).

---

[202] Brown, *Epistles of John*, 526-27; B. F. Westcott, *The Epistles of St. John* (Grand Rapids: Eerdmans, 1966), 157; Strecker, *Johannine Letters*, 162.

[203] Brooke, *Johannine Epistles*, 123-24; Bultmann, *Johannine Epistles*, 72, Haas, De Jonge, and Swellengrebel, *Translator's Handbook*, 111; Schnackenburg, *Johannine Epistles*, 222-23.

[204] Brown, *Epistles of John*, 526.

Confidence or boldness (*parrēsia*) is once again tied to eschatological judgment. Confidence in the love of God enables the faithful to be called God's children (2:28) and the heart's lack of condemnation about sin (3:21). Here confidence is derived from the faithful loving and experiencing mutual abiding in God and perfecting God's love. Mutual love indicates that Christians have passed from death to life (3:14). This confidence in judgment is amazing because this perfected love is not in the future, but now "in this world" among consistently loving Christians who thus mutually abide in God. This is another use of Christ as a model using the "just as" (*kathōs*) topic (2:6; 3:3, 7). However, here modeling Christ is not so much the focus as the need to reassure the faithful of their spiritual status in light of the teaching and influence of the secessionists.

In v. 18 the Elder uses refining to amplify the thought of v. 17 that perfect love casts out fear of judgment. The first half of the verse is refining, repeating the idea in similar form (Rhet. Her. 4.43.56): "There is no fear in love, but perfect love casts out fear." Both halves are virtually identical, with the repetition adding that the love the casts out fear is perfect love personified; that is, the God's love for us expressed in our love for others and for God.[205] The second half of this verse refines v. 17 using the type that repeats the idea using the contrary (Rhet. Her. 4.43.56): "for fear has to do with punishment, and whoever fears has not reached perfection in love." The eschatological tone continues, for fear is of judgment, the lack of boldness on the day of the judgment (v. 17). Punishment (*kolasis*) is the punishment accompanying divine judgment in its only other New Testament occurrence (Matt 25:46) and in other early Christian literature (1 Clem. 11:1; 2 Clem. 6.7; Herm. Sim. 9.18.1; Diogn. 9.2).

The Elder adds an emphatic proposition in v. 19: "We love because he first loved us."[206] The proposition begins with the emphatic "we" (*hēmeis*) contrasting the emphatic "he" (*autos*) or God to emphasize the priority and empowering nature of God's love. It also contrasts the faithful as loving with those not loving to be mentioned in the next verse. Verse

---

[205] Brown, *Epistles of John*, 530; Smalley, *1, 2, 3 John*, 260; Strecker, *Johannine Letters*, 166–67. Bultmann (*Johannine Epistles*, 73) limits love to God's love.

[206] The first verb for love (*agapōmen*) can be either indicative ("we love") or hortatory subjunctive ("let us love"). The emphatic "we" (*hēmeis*) used with the indicative in 4:14 and 16 as well as the Elder's expressed confidence in the faithful in this section support the indicative here. *Contra* those who point to *agapōmen* as hortatory subjunctive in 4:7 (Strecker, *Johannine Letters*, 169–70; Schnackenburg, *Johannine Epistles*, 225).

19 reiterates the content of v. 10, but rather than defining love by pointing to God's loving gift of his Son as an atoning sacrifice for sin, the priority of God's love is the focus here (cf. John 15:16). Thus, the object of our love is God and then, as vv. 20–21 to follow indicate, our brothers and sisters that God also loves (3:16; 4:11).[207] In light of the previous verse that perfect love casts out fear, we are drawn to God's love because God first loved us, not because we are afraid of God and want to avoid judgment.

Verse 20 begins with the formula "those who say" (*ean tis eipē*). This formula introduces a false secessionist claim as it does in 1:6, 8, and 10. It is akin to the formula "whoever says" (*ho legōn*) that introduces other secessionist claims in 2:4, 6, and 9. Apparently the secessionists claimed to love God, but their behavior toward the faithful was hateful. This claim is refuted by an enthymeme:

Stated premise: "Those who do not love a brother or sister, whom they have seen, cannot love God, whom they have not seen."
Conclusion: "Those who say, 'I love God,' and hate a brother or sister are liars."
Unstated premise: "One cannot love God while hating a brother or sister."

The enthymeme is based on the common topic of the possible–impossible. Verse 19 makes it clear that God's love is the source of Christian love of brothers and sisters. Therefore, anyone who hates brothers or sisters has not experienced God's love and is not able to love others. Previously the Elder made the point that God's love does not abide in unloving people (3:17), and it is only by abiding in love that people abide in God (4:16b). Now he adds that unloving people cannot love God, and claiming to do so makes them liars. To the secessionists being liars for claiming to have fellowship with God while walking in darkness (1:6) and to know God while disobeying his commandments (2:4) is added the claim to love God while failing to love others.

Verse 21 is a judgment or authoritative statement (*kriseis*) drawn from the Johannine tradition, Jesus, and ultimately from God, who is the source

---

[207] Haas, De Jonge, and Swellengrebel, *Translator's Handbook*, 114; Smalley, *1, 2, 3 John*, 262; Strecker, *Johannine Letters*, 169. Houlden (*Johannine Epistles*, 120) gives God as the primary object, while Bultmann (*Johannine Epistles*, 75–76) and Schnackenburg (*Johannine Epistles*, 225) assume it is the faithful (cf. 4:20–21). Brown (*Epistles of John*, 532) aptly describes the object as "all love that deserves the designation *agape*."

of the love commandment in the Johannine Epistles (2:3-4; 3:22-24; 2 John 4-6). The judgment is closely linked to the preceding verse by a conjunction and supplies further proof as to why hating the brothers and sisters while claiming to love God is a lie: "The commandment we have from him is this: those who love God must love their brothers and sisters also" (cf. John 13:34). The judgment continues the topic of loving one another according to the commandment (3:10-12; 4:7, 11, 19), sometimes explicitly defined as the love commandment (2:3-11; 3:23-24; John 15:12, 17). This Johannine tradition aligns with Synoptic tradition of the double commandment of Jesus to love God and neighbor (Matt 22:34-40; Mark 12:28-34; Luke 10:25-28) and adds this dual emphasis to the development of the love commandment as so far developed in this epistle. This commandment weakens the ethos of the secessionists because the Elder's portrayal of them as not loving their brothers and sisters and their observable actions show them to be in direct violation of the love commandment.

BRIDGING THE HORIZONS

A chief characteristic and obligation of being born of God and knowing God is to love others for the simple yet profound reason that God is love (vv. 7-8). God's love is all too apparent in sending God's only Son as an atoning sacrifice to bring us life (vv. 9-10). This loving act of God obligates us to love one another in return. If God loves us so deeply and broadly, so should we do the same for others. In this way the love of God who has never been seen lives in us and is perfected in us so that others can see that love (vv. 11-12).

The Holy Spirit witnesses to us that we abide in God. We also know that we abide in God and God in us by our ability to confess that Jesus is the Son of God sent by the Father as Savior of the world. By this confession we open ourselves up to God's love and know the love God has for us as we experience mutual abiding (vv. 14-16a).

Since God is love, when we love others we are abiding in God and God in us. This mutual love perfects love in us (v. 16b-17). Being perfected in love gives us confidence on the day of Christ's return and the judgment that accompanies it. We need not fear judgment because we are perfected in the love of God (v. 18). We love because God first loved us. God is the source of our love (v. 19). To claim to love God and

> hate others whom God loves is not to participate in the mutual love of God and to be a liar. If we cannot love others that are visible to us, then we cannot truly love God who is not visible (v. 20). Ultimately, it is a commandment from God that we love others (v. 21).

5:1–5: Conquering the World through Faith

Whereas in 4:21 the Elder exhorts the faithful that because they love God they must love their brothers and sisters in the faith, in 5:1 he defines just what is a brother or sister and then reiterates his exhortation in another form: "Everyone who believes that Jesus is the Christ has been born of God, and everyone who loves the parent loves the child" (cf. John 1:12–13). This reiteration is refining of the type in which the thought is repeated in different words (Rhet. Her. 4.42.54). Verses 4:21 and 5:1 are both structured with "whoever loves ... loves" (*ho agapōn ... agapa*) and say the same thing: "those who love God must love their brothers and sisters also" (4:21b) has become "everyone who loves the parent loves the child" (5:1b). The refining makes explicit that belief in Jesus Christ is the source of being born of God, of having God as parent and other Christians as siblings. Confession is the source of transformation, familial unity, and ties of love between parent and child and between children. This verse ties together true belief (*pisteuō*) about Jesus Christ and love of fellow Christians who share that belief, as does the proposition of 3:23 that governs this entire unit, thus beginning to form an *inclusio* as the unit draws to a close in 5:5.

There is debate about the scope of 5:1b as whether it is (1) a general statement pertaining to all parents that to love the parents is to love their children,[208] (2) a more specific statement that if you love your parents you will also love your siblings,[209] or (3) a statement that everyone who loves God the parent loves fellow Christians who are God's children.[210] If 5:1b is a maxim, option (1) is most likely, but options (2) and (3) are the conclusions that a maxim would likely lead the faithful to make in their

---

[208] Brown, *Epistles of John*, 536.
[209] Brooke, *Johannine Epistles*, 129; Haas, De Jonge, and Swellengrebel, *Translator's Handbook*, 115.
[210] Bultmann, *Johannine Epistles*, 76–77; Strecker, *Johannine Letters*, 175.

own contexts.[211] Ultimately, the Elder makes his point that confession and love of other confessors are to be presumed.

In conjunction with 5:5, this verse provides the full Johannine confession that "Jesus is the Christ, the Son of God" (John 20:31); the confession needed to be born of God. Previously, the topic of birth (*gennaō*) related being born of God to Christian behavior of doing right, not sinning, and loving (2:29; 3:9; 4:7; cf. 3:1; 5:4, 18). Now believing is added to the scope of the birth topic, with love recurring. This illustrates that belief and behavior define the faithful in opposition to the secessionists.[212] This description of the belief and behavior defines children of God in comparison with the secessionists, who cannot affirm that Jesus is the Christ (2:22) and cannot be expected to love the children with whom they are not siblings sharing God as parent.

In 5:2 the Elder offers a sign to determine whether or not the faithful love other children of God: "By this we know that we love the children of God, when we love God and obey his commandments." Commentators are divided as to whether the introductory "by this" (*en toutō*) points forward or backward. If it points forward, the following "when" (*hotan*) clause is a subordinate clause with the meaning that we know we love the children of God because we love God and obey his commandments. If it points backward to 5:1, the "when" (*hotan*) clause is an independent clause and the meaning is that we know we love the children of God when we believe Jesus is the Christ, have been born of God, and love the parent and the child. Unfortunately, the direction that "by this" (*en toutō*) points is unclear in its other three instances in 1 John (2:5; 3:10, 19).[213] In spite of modern preference for a backward reference here, I choose the forward reference because it best explains 5:1–2 as a continuation of a rhetorical strategy of refining, amplification, and dual presentation of Christology and ethics as explained below.

Regarding refining and amplification, in light of 5:1 that to love the parent is to love the child, the Elder now states that to love God (the parent) and to obey his commandments is to love the children. The primary commandment of God is to love the brothers and sisters (3:11, 23; 4:21; cf. 4:7). Thus, to love God and obey his commandments is to de facto love the children of God. Much of 5:1 is repeated in 5:2 and

---

[211] Smalley (*1, 2, 3 John*, 267) argues for all three options.
[212] Brown, *Epistles of John*, 535.
[213] For discussion, see Brown, *Epistles of John*, 536–38; Painter, *1, 2, 3 John*, 290–91, 293–94.

constitutes yet another example of refining. Also, 5:2 amplifies that the love of others is rooted in the prior love of God (3:16; 4:7-12, 16, 19) and presents the reverse of 4:20, where the love of the brothers and sisters is the indication of the love of God (3:10-18; 4:7-12, 20). Divine love is mutual and multidirectional. It is a love that is God to us and us to God and us to others. In 5:1 Christology provides the grounds for loving the brothers and sisters. Now it is ethics that does the same thing.

The Elder gave the love of God and obedience to God's commandments as a sign that the faithful love other Christians (5:2). Now he refines that sign: "For the love of God is this, that we obey his commandments" (cf. 2:4-5; John 14:15, 21, 23-24, 31; 15:10). Obedience to God's commandments is not just a sign of the love for God, but the very definition of it. Our love of God becomes a reality when the commandments of God are obeyed. Formerly, love was defined as God sending his Son as an atoning sacrifice (4:10), and now it is defined as obedience to God (cf. 2 John 6). Again, the secessionists are excluded, for they do not keep God's commandments and thus do not love God. The topic of obeying the commandments (*tas entolas tēpōn*) recurs and illustrates the Elder's penchant for developing facets of a topic individually. Obeying the commandments guarantees knowing God (2:3-4), being perfected in God's love (2:5), obtaining answers to prayer (3:22), and mutual abiding with God (3:24). Now it demonstrates love of God.

Having refined the sign that the faithful are loving the children of God, the Elder continues with an enthymeme in 5:3b-4a. The conclusion is "And his commandments are not burdensome" (cf. Matt 11:30), the stated premise is "for whatever is born of God conquers the world" (cf. John 16:33), and the unstated premise is "those who conquer the world by being born of God find the commandments light." The topic of being born of God has been connected with doing right (2:29), not sinning (3:9; 5:18), loving and knowing God (4:7), and believing that Jesus is the Christ (5:1). The topic of conquering (*nikaō*) previously described God's children overcoming the evil one (2:12-14) and those with the spirit of the antichrist (4:4). Now the two topics are linked: To be born of God is to conquer the world.

The Elder continues by defining the source of the conquest: "And this is the victory that conquers the world, our faith." This is another example of the figure of *definitio*. The conquering victory is defined as faith, a faith that always includes a proper confession of Jesus Christ (3:23; 4:2, 15; 5:1, 5-6). Faith is not so much beliefs or traditions, although it always includes such. Rather, faith is active confession of Jesus as the Christ, Son of God come in the flesh by water and blood. This confession transforms confessors into children of God who abide in God and God in them; who experience God's love and share that love with one another. This is an important definition because it is the only place in Johannine literature where the noun faith (*pistis*) appears.

The definition of faith as the source of conquest of the world is followed in 5:5 by a rhetorical question provided with an answer, a type of question often used in argumentation (Cicero, *Part. or.* 13.47; Quintilian, *Inst.* 5.11.3–5): "Who is it who conquers the world but the one who believes that Jesus is the Son of God?" (cf. 2:22–23; 3:23; 4:2–3, 15; 5:1, 10, 13). Verse 5 restates v. 4 in question form and is an example of refining, in which the idea is restated in a different way (Rhet. Her. 4.42.54). Refining amplifies by repetition the conquest of the world of those who properly confess Jesus Christ and have been born of God. The question implies that only those making this confession of Jesus, who has himself overcome the world (John 12:31; 14:30; 16:33; Rev 3:21; 5:5), have overcome the world through him (4:4). It is left to the faithful to draw the conclusion that the secessionists have not overcome the world because they do not make this confession.

The greatest threat to obeying the love commandment is the world. It is a realm in need of redemption (2:2; 4:9, 14), and it tempts people to indulge in its desires (2:15–17). Even so, those born of God can resist and be victorious. This victory over the world is obtained at baptism by the confession of faith (5:5–6; cf. 5:1). The play on the tense of the verb "conquer" (*nikaō*) is important here. Those born of God conquer (present tense) the world daily (vv. 4–5) through their confession of faith with which they conquered (aorist tense) the world once and for all (v. 4). We benefit from the once-for-all conquest of the lamb (perfect: John 16:33; aorist: Rev 3:21; 5:5) that allows us to conquer daily (present tense: Rev 2:7, 11, 17, 26; 3:5, 12, 21).

BRIDGING THE HORIZONS

There is power in the confession that Jesus is the Christ, the Son of God (vv. 1, 5). It is to be reborn as a child of God to join siblings in the family of God. That family is characterized by love. The love of God for all the children should extend from those children to God and to all other siblings in the family, like the love of a parent should extend to all their children. We know the latter can be difficult because not all the children of God are loveable, nor might we love ourselves enough to be capable of loving others. But realizing that we share the mutual love of God for us and us for God gives us perspective that if God loves our siblings, so should we even if it takes some work.

Our love for God is demonstrated when we obey God's commandments, chief of which is the love for others (vv. 2–3). The commandments of God are not burdensome. Those of us born of God have conquered the world through our faith. That conquest gives us the power and perspective to not let the lure of the world's selfishness, greed, and lust pull us back into its darkness and death.

Sometimes this truth seems too simplistic. Like any conquest, there needs to be vigilance to the loss of territory to the old enemy. Prayer and worship, fellowship with other Christians, and purposeful work for the kingdom using our spiritual gifts keep us in the position of a conqueror. But there are times when territory is lost to the forces of the world that lure us back. Thus, there is the need to remain on guard.

Often neglected in the discussion of this section is its implicit call to mission. The world poses a threat to the spiritual life of the community (2:15–17), persecutes the community (3:13), listens to false prophets and the spirit of the antichrist (4:1–6), and lies under the power of the evil one (5:19; John 12:31; 16:11). Christ came to bring life to the world as its Savior (4:9, 14). Our conquering of the world is not just in our escape from its sin, but also in being agents of God's love to bring the world to salvation.

5:6–12: DIVINE TESTIMONY THAT JESUS CHRIST CAME IN WATER AND BLOOD AS A GIFT OF LIFE FROM GOD

> 5:6 This is the one who came by water and blood, Jesus Christ, not with the water only but with the water and the blood. And the Spirit is the one that testifies, for the Spirit is the truth.
>
> 5:7 There are three that testify:
>
> 5:8 the Spirit and the water and the blood, and these three agree.
>
> 5:9 If we receive human testimony, the testimony of God is greater, for this is the testimony of God that he has testified to his Son.

> **5:10** Those who believe in the Son of God have the testimony in their hearts. Those who do not believe in God have made him a liar by not believing in the testimony that God has given concerning his Son.
>
> **5:11** And this is the testimony: God gave us eternal life, and this life is in his Son.
>
> **5:12** Whoever has the Son has life; whoever does not have the Son of God does not have life.

5:6–8: The Testimony of the Johannine Tradition, Water, Blood, and the Spirit

Having established that faith in Jesus Christ conquers the world, the Elder defines the testimony that gives that faith veracity. The topics of testimony (*martyreō, martyria*), life (*zōē*), and believe/have faith (*pisteuō*) are central to this section. Testimony and life are primary topics in the introduction (*exordium*) of 1:1–4, and thus the Elder ends the body of the letter (*probatio*) with the same topics with which he began it, reinforcing them and forming an *inclusio*.

The Elder opens by identifying Jesus the Son of God from the previous verse: "This is the one who came by water and blood,[214] Jesus Christ, not with the water only but with the water and the blood" (5:6a). This identification is a confession, for "this is" (*houtos estin*) is a standard formula for Christological confession in the Gospel of John (1:34; 4:42; 6:50, 58; 7:40, 41) and is akin to another formula in that gospel, "you are" (*su ei*), which introduces the confession of Jesus by others (1:49; 4:19; 6:69; 11:27).[215] As indicated by its kinship with the Johannine title "the one who is coming" (John 1:15, 27; 12:13) and "blood and water" of the crucifixion in John 19:34, this confession originates in Johannine tradition. It has the authority of a *krisis* or judgment, a proof by example expressing an authoritative opinion (Cicero, *Inv.* 1.30.48; Quintilian, *Inst.* 5.11.37, 42–44), here of those faithful of the tradition of the Johannine Community.

---

[214] A textual variant adds spirit (*pneumatos*) to water and blood. This triad would seem logical to scribes because it is found in vv. 6–8 and listed in v. 8, and water and spirit are mentioned together in Jesus's conversation with Nicodemus in John 3:5. Metzger, *Textual Commentary*, 715–16.

[215] Brown, *Epistles of John*, 572–73.

There are numerous interpretations of this verse and the referent(s) of water and blood.[216] These include baptism and eucharist, baptism and death of Jesus, Jesus's death, Jesus's birth, and Jesus's birth and death. These are outlined and evaluated in A Closer Look: Water and Blood in 1 John 5:6. These explanations are not totally satisfying, partly because they typically assume that water and blood each have single referents. Rhetoric of the period indicates that water and blood are each likely to have more than one referent, and this acknowledgment opens up new avenues for interpretation that are faithful to the text as understood in its own time.[217]

By positioning the title "Jesus Christ" at the end of the first clause, the Elder emphasizes that Jesus Christ is the one who came by water and blood. The twofold title affirms the unity of the human Jesus and the divine Christ. Using refining (Rhet. Her. 4.42.54), the Elder amplifies by repetition the nature of Jesus's coming: "by water and blood" becomes "not with the water only but with the water and the blood." This amplification by repetition incorporates a mix of rhetorical figures. One is paronomasia, a figure of speech with many forms (Rhet. Her. 4.21.29–23.32; Quintilian, *Inst.* 9.3.66–75), and here it is a word used with different nuances (Quintilian, *Inst.* 9.3.69).[218] As discussed below, the referent of water is not quite the same in all three instances. Also employed is reduplication (anadiplosis, *conduplicatio*), a figure of speech repeating words for amplification (Rhet. Her. 4.28.38; cf. Quintilian, *Inst.* 9.3.28–29).[219] Water is used three times in short order. Paronomasia and reduplication often work in tandem (Quintilian, *Inst.* 9.3.67).

This paronomasia and reduplication are part of the use of the figure of speech called distinction (*paradiastolē*, *distinctio*), which differentiates between similar things (Quintilian, *Inst.* 9.3.65, 82).[220] Verse 6 differentiates how Jesus Christ came: "not with the water only but with the water and the

---

[216] For a full discussion of the various interpretations of this passage, see Brown, *Epistles of John*, 572–85, 595–99; H.-J. Klauck, *Der Erste Johannesbrief*, EKKNT 23/1 (Benziger: Zurich and Braunschweig/Neukirchen-Vluyn: Neukirchener, 1991), 291–304; Lieu, *I, II, & III John*, 208–15; Smalley, *1 ,2, 3 John*, 277–83; Schnackenburg, *The Johannine Epistles*, 232–38; Strecker, *Johannine Letters*, 182–92; Painter, *1, 2, 3 John*, 300–01, 302–09.

[217] For a full discussion of the rhetoric of this section, see D. F. Watson, "Water, Blood, and Spirit in 1 John 5:6–8 Once More," in T. D. Still and J. A. Myers, eds., *Rhetoric, History, and Theology: Interpreting the New Testament* (Lanham: Lexington Books/Fortress Academic, 2022), 243–55.

[218] Lausberg, *Handbook*, 285–87, §637–39; Martin, *Antike Rhetorik*, 304–05.

[219] Lausberg, *Handbook*, 277–79, §619–22; Martin, *Antike Rhetorik*, 301–03.

[220] Lausberg, *Handbook*, 296–97, §660–62; 334, §749; Martin, *Antike Rhetorik*, 306, 315.

blood." As discussed below, a distinction is being made between two meanings of water. Dissociation is also employed, which separates what appears to be a whole into two parts and gives them a hierarchy of value and truth.[221] Water is not a unified concept. There is a coming in water and a coming in water and blood, the latter of which is dissociated from the former and designated as a differently nuanced and more complete description of the coming of Jesus Christ.

In conjunction with these four interrelated rhetorical figures, the Elder is also using the figure of thought called ambiguity (*amphibolia, ambiguitas*). Ambiguity is a desirable element of style[222] and is frequently used in dissociation to resolve a theoretical incompatibility.[223] Water and blood can have both different and overlapping referents. There is no need to restrict the referent of water and blood to specific referents separately or in combination as found in the interpretations outlined in A Closer Look: Water and Blood in 1 John 5:6.

The Elder's careful use of these five rhetorical figures to uncover fine nuances is quite useless unless he is countering a claim that coming in water alone identifies Jesus Christ as the Son of God (v. 5). In such a claim the referent of water would likely be the water of his birth, death, or baptism. To claim that the water of birth identifies Jesus Christ as the Son of God is unlikely. The same is true of a claim that the water of his death identifies him (John 19:34). For both claims, blood would also be needed. The water of Jesus's baptism is a more viable option for a claim that water identifies Jesus Christ as the Son of God. John the Baptist testified that Jesus was the Son of God at his baptism (John 1:29–34). Our passage agrees that the water of baptism does have a bearing on Jesus's identity but is not adequate in itself.

In v. 6 the preposition *dia* precedes the first occurrence of water and blood, which both lack definite articles. This construction indicates that water and blood are a unity describing how Jesus came.[224] Thus the aorist

---

[221] K. M. Olson, "Dissociation," in T. Enos, ed., *Encyclopedia of Rhetoric and Composition* (New York and London: Garland, 1996), 196–97; Perelman and Olbrechts-Tyteca, *New Rhetoric*, 411–15.

[222] The Greco-Roman rhetorical tradition often discussed ambiguity in the context of legal issues (Cicero, *Inv.* 1.13.17; 2.40.116–41.121; Rhet. Her. 1.11.19; 1.12.20; 2.11; Quintilian, *Inst.* 3.6.43–46, 88; 7.9; Lausberg, *Handbook*, 96–97, §222–23; Martin, *Antike Rhetorik*, 44, 50–51). In such issues ambiguity was a problem to be deciphered, not a boon to style and meaning.

[223] Olson, "Dissociation," 196.

[224] BDAG, 223–24.

participle, "the one who came" (*ho elthōn*), is "a historical reference designed to attach 'Son of God' and 'Christ' to Jesus in specific circumstances of his earthly career."[225] Only one historical reference makes this connection: the birth of Jesus in water and blood. The Elder's emphasis on "coming by water and blood" refutes a claim that the water baptism rather than his birth adequately identifies Jesus Christ as the Son of God.

The Hebrew Scriptures and Jewish tradition contemporary with 1 John associate water with physical birth.[226] In John 3:5, Jesus associates water with birth (although spiritual birth). In our passage water is often understood to refer to physical birth.[227] However, blood is also associated with birth, for Leviticus 12 refers to the flow of blood from a woman who has given birth. This understanding of water and blood in our passage as describing Jesus's birth finds support in 1 John at 4:2, where "Jesus Christ has come in the flesh," at 4:9, where Jesus is the only begotten (*monogenēs*) of God sent into the world, and at 5:18, where Jesus is the one who was born of God (*gennaō*). This understanding makes sense of the change here of word order from blood and water in the tradition of the crucifixion (John 19:34) to water and blood, since in childbirth the water breaks first and the blood comes second. It also allows water and blood to refer to that which came from Jesus's side at the crucifixion as also identifying him as the Son of God. Water and blood can only flow from someone with a human body; that is, who has come by water and blood. Ambiguity within distinction and dissociation allows water and blood to refer to Jesus's birth and death simultaneously.

In summary, in v. 6a the preposition *dia* (agency – through or by) precedes the first pairing of water and blood without definite articles. This indicates the coming of Jesus Christ in the singular event of birth through the agency of the womb. The preposition *en* (instrumentality – in) and the definite article precede the following singular reference to water, and the same occurs for both water and blood in the second pairing of the two. The change of preposition to *en* allows the singular occurrence of water to refer to baptism in water, which is being rejected as an adequate description of the coming of Jesus Christ, and the second pairing of water

---

[225] Brown, *Epistles of John*, 573.
[226] B. Witherington III, "The Waters of Birth: John 3.5 and 1 John 5.6-8," *NTS* (1989): 155-60.
[227] Witherington, "Waters of Birth," 158-60.

and blood to amplify that he came in the water and in the blood of birth – a literal baptism in both – not just water baptism alone.

This carefully crafted confession refutes the secessionist claim that Jesus Christ came in water only – that is, his incarnation was revealed to the world at his baptism with the descent of the Spirit – or more specifically that the heavenly Christ joined the earthly Jesus at his baptism to proclaim the words of salvation, a gnostic position held by Cerinthus (Irenaeus, *Haer.* 1.26.1–2) and Valentinus (Irenaeus, *Haer.* 3.11.2–3). Nothing beyond these revealed words was necessary for salvation, and, having revealed them, Christ departed Jesus prior to the crucifixion.

Having employed the judgment from Johannine tradition that Jesus Christ came by water and blood, the Elder confirms its truth in v. 6b: "And the Spirit is the one that testifies, for the Spirit is the truth." Previously, the Spirit was characterized as true (4:6), as it is in the Gospel of John (14:17; 15:26; 16:13). The Spirit testifies about Jesus (John 15:26–27) through the Beloved Disciple and the Johannine tradition-bearers that carry on his testimony (John 21:24), which includes the testimony that Jesus Christ, Son of God, came in water and blood.[228] It is also an inward witness derived from the anointing by the Spirit, which the Elder assumes will enable the faithful to recognize that the testimony of the Spirit through the Johannine tradition-bearers is true (2:20–21, 27; 4:13; cf. 3:24). The Spirit's testimony is an external proof that gives further support to the judgment of v. 6a about the coming of Jesus in water and blood.

In 5:7–8 the Elder adds: "There are three that testify: the Spirit and the water and the blood, and these three agree."[229] This is amplification by augmentation of the Christological testimony of the Johannine tradition and the Spirit in 5:6. It lends authority to the testimony because tradition taught that two or three witnesses were needed to verify the truth of any testimony (Deut 17:6; 19:15; cf. John 5:31–40; 8:17–18; Matt 18:16; 1 Tim 5:19). In Jewish thought, testimony can be given by impersonal witnesses

---

[228] Brown, *Epistles of John*, 579–80, 595–98.
[229] About the end of the fourth century, in the midst of the controversies about the Trinity, the "Johannine Comma" was added to vv. 7–8, which supplemented the heavenly witness of the Trinity: the Father, Word, and Holy Spirit. It was included in the King James Version but has been subsequently removed from the text as not original. For a full discussion, see Metzger, *Textual Commentary*, 716–18; Brown, *Epistles of John*, 775–87; Painter, *1, 2, 3 John*, 301–09; Strecker, *Johannine Letters*, 188–91.

such as these three (Gen 31:45-50; Deut 31:28; 1 En. 100:11).[230] The emphatic position of "three" at the beginning of the sentence amplifies the fact that there are three witnesses. The strength of their testimony is underscored by the affirmation that they agree so much as to be one (lit. "the three in the one").[231]

5:9-12: The Testimony of God

Verse 9 contrasts human testimony with God's testimony: "If we receive human testimony, the testimony of God is greater; for this is the testimony of God that[232] he has testified to his Son" (cf. John 3:31-33; 5:31-38; 8:18). The Elder compares external proofs of witnesses (Quintilian, *Inst.* 5.1.7), here lesser human witnesses to the greatest witness of all – God – to the eternal life found in his Son (vv. 10-12). The lesser human testimony is the testimony of the secessionists, who speak only what is from the world, and the greater testimony of God is from the Johannine tradition-bearers, who are aligned with the spirit of truth (1 John 4:4-6). The secessionists may have been citing the testimony of John the Baptist to testify that Jesus was revealed as the Son of God by water at his baptism (John 1:29-34). The Elder draws upon tradition such as that found in John 5:31-38 (cf. 10:38), where Jesus states that John the Baptist's testimony was human testimony that he did not receive (*lambanō*) and his own works from the Father are a greater (*meizō*) testimony.[233] The Elder does not denigrate human testimony itself, but rather argues that such testimony must be undergirded by a greater testimony. In light of the affinities of this section with the *exordium*, the Elder is claiming that his testimony, and that of the Johannine tradition-bearers, is derived from God and true. The secessionists are a source of an incomplete human understanding of the revelation in Christ. God testified to his Son in the life of his Son as witnessed by the Beloved Disciple, a testimony authoritatively interpreted by the Johannine tradition-bearers through the Holy Spirit.

---

[230] Brown, *Epistles of John*, 581.
[231] For discussion of the many interpretations of the precise nature of the three witnesses, see Brown, *Epistles of John*, 573-78; 581-85; Smalley, *1, 2, 3 John*, 281-82.
[232] I understand the second *hoti* to be epexegetical of the preceding predicate. For discussion of the possible understandings of the use of *hoti* here, see Brown, *Epistles of John*, 578-89; Smalley, *Epistles of John*, 283-84.
[233] Brown, *Epistles of John*, 585-86, 599-600.

It is debated whether the content of God's testimony to God's Son is the three witnesses of Spirit, water, and blood just described in vv. 6-8 or is an additional fourth witness added to the three other witnesses.[234] The latter option is supported by v. 11, where God's testimony is defined as eternal life in his Son, and by John 5:31-40, where God's testimony is added to three previous witnesses. Verse 9 is amplification by augmentation using a series that increases in intensity to the highest category (Cicero, *Part. or.* 15.54; Quintilian, *Inst.* 8.4.3-9).

This section is purposefully structured to support the amplification. Twice we see "this is the testimony of God that" (vv. 9, 11) followed by an antithesis of those who accept or reject God's testimony (vv. 10, 12). There is epiphora or the repetition of the endings of successive phrases (Rhet. Her. 4.13.19), for vv. 9, 10, and 11 all end with "his own Son" (*tou huiou autou*) to stress God's testimony. The latter instance is modified to "eternal life, and this life is in his Son" to amplify by augmentation the content of God's testimony to God's Son.

The Elder follows the amplification in 5:9 with an antithesis in 5:10: "Those who believe in the Son of God have the testimony in their hearts. Those who do not believe in God have made him a liar by not believing in the testimony that God has given concerning his Son" (cf. 3:23; 5:13). The antithesis is not exact, for one expects "those who believe in the Son of God" to be negated in the second half of the antithesis but instead finds "those who do not believe God"; that is, the object of the testimony (Son of God) is replaced by the author of the testimony (God). The antithesis is based upon Johannine tradition that also underlies the previous verse: "Whoever has accepted his [Jesus's] testimony has certified this, that God is true" (John 3:33; cf. 1 John 2:22-25). Those believing Jesus is the Son of God have God's testimony in their hearts through the Spirit (2:20, 27). The Spirit is the truth and comes from God (John 15:26; 16:12). To deny God's testimony is to call him a liar and to only receive human testimony, as do the secessionists (v. 9). The Elder has already accused the secessionists of being liars for not confessing that Jesus is the Christ (2:22).

Since its first mention in v. 9, the faithful have been left to anticipate just what is the testimony of God. Now in v. 11 the Elder makes the testimony explicit: "And this is the testimony: God gave us eternal life, and this life is

---

[234] For the former position, see Marshall, *Epistles of John*, 239-40; Smalley, *1, 2, 3 John*, 283-84. For the latter position, see Brown, *Epistles of John*, 586-87; Schnackenburg, *Johannine Epistles*, 238-39.

in his Son." This verse echoes the introduction (*exordium*), where the Johannine tradition-bearers testify to the eternal life that was revealed (1:2-3). The placement of the topic of eternal life in the *exordium* (1:1-3), here at the close of the letter body (*probatio*) and at the beginning and ending of the letter closing (*peroratio*) to follow (5:13, 20), indicates that it is the central topic of the letter.

The Elder concludes the *probatio* in v. 12 with the antithesis: "Whoever has the Son has life; whoever does not have the Son of God does not have life" (cf. v. 10; John 3:15-16, 36; 20:31). The topic of "having" (*echō*) once more refers to the experience of a divine reality. The present participial form of "having" indicates that this eternal life is experienced in the present life of the community. Whereas in 2:23 the divine reality that the faithful experience is the Father obtained by confessing the Son, and in 5:10 it is testimony in their hearts obtained from believing in the Son, here it is eternal life given by confessing the Son. Verse 12 is a corollary of v. 11: Since eternal life is in the Son (v. 11), only those who have the Son have life.

A CLOSER LOOK: WATER AND BLOOD IN 1 JOHN 5:6

There are at least five current interpretations of water and blood in 1 John 5:6.

Water and Blood as Baptism and Eucharist

Several prominent church fathers held – and some modern interpreter hold – a sacramental interpretation of this verse.[235] The anointing of the Spirit within Christians (2:20, 27) testifies to the truth that Jesus Christ is the Son of God through the sacraments of baptism and the Eucharist represented by water and blood, respectively. Jesus Christ is understood as coming "with" the sacraments.[236] The Spirit, water (baptism), and blood (bread and wine) testify that Jesus Christ is the Son of God (5:7).

This interpretation is deficient. The past tense (aorist) is used to describe Jesus Christ as one who came (*erchomai*) by water and blood. The coming is a completed action, but the present tense is needed to

---

[235] Schnackenburg, *Johannine Epistles*, 235-37.
[236] Brown, *Epistles of John*, 575.

express a repetitive action such as observing the sacraments.[237] Also, no one would have been arguing that Jesus came through the water-related baptism and denying that he came through the blood-related Eucharist so that the Elder would have to stress that Jesus came through both sacraments. Besides, by itself blood does not refer to the Eucharist in the New Testament.[238]

Water and Blood as the Baptism and Death of Jesus

A second interpretation is that water and blood refer to the baptism and death of Jesus, respectively.[239] The verb "coming" is understood to refer to Jesus's baptism and death identifying him as the Son of God on a mission of salvation. Clearly, water can refer to Jesus's baptism, for John the Baptist baptized with or in water (John 1:26, 31, 33; Mark 1:8; cf. Acts 1:5; 11:16), and blood can refer to Jesus's death (1 John 1:7; John 19:34; Matt 27:4, 6, 8, 24–25; Acts 5:28). However, the Gospel of John only presupposes the baptism of Jesus and does not give it the weight this interpretation requires (1:6–8, 15, 19–37; 3:22–36). Also, why would only blood refer to the death of Jesus in this letter when the account of his death in Johannine tradition combines blood and water (John 19:34)?

Water and Blood as Jesus's Death

A third interpretation is that water and blood refer to Jesus's death. In the crucifixion account in John's Gospel, when the soldier speared Jesus's side, blood and water flowed out (19:34). This account is the only other place in Johannine literature combining water and blood. First John refers to the blood and death of Jesus (1:7; 2:2; 4:10), so the Elder had the crucifixion on his mind. However, why change the word order from blood and water to water and blood (as in John 19:34) or distinguish between water and blood if they are descriptive of the one event of

---

[237] Strecker, *Johannine Letters*, 182.
[238] Witherington, "Waters of Birth," 160.
[239] Brown, *Epistles of John*, 578; Schnackenburg, *Johannine Epistles*, 232–34; Smalley, *1, 2, 3 John*, 278; Painter, *1, 2, 3 John*, 305–07. Strecker (*Johannine Letters*, 182–86) adds the sacraments as referents since the baptism and death of Jesus are the basis of the sacraments.

crucifixion? More to the point, water and blood describe the coming of Jesus in this context, not his going in death.[240]

Water and Blood as Jesus's Birth

A fourth interpretation is that water and blood refer to the water and blood of birth. This position is not popular, being last supported by G. Richter.[241] Although the Gospel of John is vague about the incarnation, Richter assumed that the language of coming (*erchomai*) refers to it (1:11; 5:43; 16:28). He argued that the Johannine Epistles also refer to the incarnation using the same verb along with the preposition *en* (second reference in 5:6; 4:2; 2 John 7). Associated birth imagery is found in this letter where God is the Father and Jesus is the Son of God (1:3; 2:22–23; 3:8; 4:9–10, 14–15; 5:1, 18), even in the immediate context in 5:5. However, the Spirit, the third witness in 5:6, is associated with the baptism and death of Jesus in Johannine tradition, but never his incarnation.[242]

Water of Birth and Blood of Death

A final interpretation is that water and blood stand for Jesus's birth and death, respectively. This position is also not popular but is supported by B. Witherington. He rightly observes that 1 John contains significant birth references (4:9; 5:18) and that the Gospel of John refers to birth as being in water (3:5). In the Hebrew Scriptures water can refer to semen, amniotic fluid, and birth (Prov 5:15–18; Song 4:12–15), as it does in other Jewish and ancient Near Eastern literature.[243] However, this literature also uses blood to refer to childbirth (Lev 12), so there is no need to see just water as referring to birth. Also, it seems unlikely that only blood would refer to the crucifixion when blood and water both do in John 19:34.

---

[240] Painter, *1, 2, 3 John*, 305–06.
[241] G. Richter, "Blut und Wasser aus der durchbohrten Seite Jesu (Joh 19,34b)," *MTZ* 21 (1970): 1–21; repr. in J. Hainz, ed., *Studien zum Johannesevangelium*, Biblische Untersuchungen 13 (Regensburg: Pustet, 1977), 120–42.
[242] Brown, *Epistles of John*, 576.
[243] Witherington, "Waters of Birth," 155–60; Witherington, *Letters and Homilies*, 544–55.

5:13-21: The Conclusion or Peroratio

BRIDGING THE HORIZONS

This section reminds us of the crucial importance of holding to the central Christian confession that Jesus Christ is the Son of God and that making that confession brings eternal life. In this passage the confession includes accepting the incarnation of the Son of God as Jesus Christ through the water and blood of childbirth as well as his intended mission to shed blood and water at the crucifixion as a redemptive sacrifice for sin (2:2; 4:10). This is God's testimony that the Holy Spirit confirms to be true in the heart of believers. Human testimony would be anything that diminishes this testimony to his full nature as Son of God such as Jesus is my friend, the heavenly Santa Claus, a fine moral example, a historical personage around whom a religion was built, or anything similar. Human testimony makes the testimony of God an overreach, exaggeration, or downright lie, as if God did not know the truth about God's own Son.

5:13-21: THE CONCLUSION OR *PERORATIO*

5:13 I write these things to you who believe in the name of the Son of God, so that you may know that you have eternal life.

5:14 And this is the boldness we have in him, that if we ask anything according to his will, he hears us.

5:15 And if we know that he hears us in whatever we ask, we know that we have obtained the requests made of him.

5:16 If you see your brother or sister committing what is not a deadly sin, you will ask, and God will give life to such a one – to those whose sin is not deadly. There is sin that is deadly; I do not say that you should pray about that.

5:17 All wrongdoing is sin, but there is sin that is not deadly.

5:18 We know that those who are born of God do not sin, but the one who was born of God protects them, and the evil one does not touch them.

5:19 We know that we are God's children, and that the whole world lies under the power of the evil one.

5:20 And we know that the Son of God has come and has given us understanding so that we may know him who is true; and we are in

> him who is true, in his Son Jesus Christ. He is the true God and eternal life.
>
> **5:21 Little children, keep yourselves from idols.**

There is a debate as to whether the "these things" that opens this section in v. 13 refers to the previous section of 5:5–12, making it a transition to what follows, or to the entire epistle, making it the beginning of the conclusion. In support of the former is how 5:13 describes the faithful as having faith in the Son of God and eternal life discussed in 5:11–12. However, support for the latter position is overwhelming. The shift from the third to the first person (last used in 2:26) and the motivation-for-writing formula in 5:13 mark a major transition in letters. The motivation-for-writing formula gives a statement of authorship, reference to the act of writing, and reiteration of the reason for writing.[244] In 1:4 the motivation-for-writing formula marked the transition from the letter opening to the letter body, and now it marks the transition from the letter body to the letter closing. Also indicating transition to the conclusion is the similarity to the first conclusion of the Gospel of John (John 20:31).

The conclusion (*peroratio*) has the twofold division and purpose of recapitulation of the main proofs of the work and emotional appeal and amplification (Aristotle, *Rhet.* 3.19; Cicero, *Inv.* 1.52–56; *Rhet. Her.* 30–31; Quintilian, *Inst.* 6.1). The conclusion of 1 John blends recapitulation and emotional appeal together rather than presenting them separately. The conclusion exhibits three of the four types of recapitulation discussed by the *Rhetorica ad Alexandrum*: "In summing up we shall recapitulate either in the form of a calculation or of a proposal of policy or of a question or of an enumeration" (20.1433b.30ff.; cf. 33.1439b.12ff.; 36.1444b.21ff.). In 1 John, v. 13 is a calculation (considering what has been said), vv. 14–15 and 18–20 are enumerations (giving an accounting of the benefits afforded the Christian), and vv. 16–17 and 21 are proposals of policies (what to do regarding prayer and idolatry).

The conclusion is carefully crafted. The switch of person from third to first and back again is planned. The Elder joins the faithful in the first-person "we" as a fellow beneficiary in the enumerated benefits afforded the Christian (vv. 14–15, 18–20) and remains separate from them using the second-person "you" to propose policies (vv. 16–17, 21). This switch

---

[244] White, *Body of the Greek Letter*, 3, 5, 27, 33, 41, 62–63, 84–86, 97–98; White, *Light from Ancient Letters*, 204–05.

implies that the faithful are spiritually vulnerable to the wiles of the secessionists and need instruction, but he is not spiritually vulnerable and such instruction only applies to them. In the overall structure, the Elder introduces the topics of knowing and asking (vv. 13-15) followed by a specific example of asking (vv. 16-17). He unifies vv. 18-20 using the triple pattern of "we know" beginning each verse. He concludes in v. 21 by warning the faithful not to forsake what they know and follow the secessionists.

5:13: Calculation

The conclusion begins with its sole calculation summarizing what has been said and its ramifications. It is a statement of the intent in writing, functioning as a word of encouragement: "I write these things to you who believe in the name of the Son of God, so that you may know that you have eternal life." Having just discussed the possibilities of either believing in and having the Son and eternal life or not (5:11-12), the Elder affirms that the faithful have both. He typically reassures them after comparing them with the secessionists. He does this in 2:12-14 after the two sections of refutation in 1:5-2:2 and 2:3-11, and he does so again in 2:20-21 after the warning about love of the world and the antichrists in 2:15-19.[245]

Verse 13 is closely connected with the preceding section of 5:5-12, reiterating the related topics of believing in the Son of God (vv. 5, 9-10, 12) and eternal life (vv. 11-12). These topics reappear at the end of the conclusion in v. 20 as well to form an *inclusio*, but in v. 20 they are joined more closely, for there the Son of God himself is identified as eternal life. The topic of life (*zoē*) is a central concern for the Elder. He began the introduction with this topic (1:2-3), developed it in the body of the letter (2:25; 3:14-15), and now amplifies it in the conclusion (vv. 13, 16, 17, 20).

The topic of the name (*onomos*) makes its last appearance and is further developed. In 2:12 the faithful are assured that their sins are forgiven on account of Jesus's name. In 3:23 believing in the name of Jesus Christ is a constituent of the love commandment. Now in v. 13 believing in the name brings eternal life (cf. John 1:12, 2:23). This is also an important reiteration of the related topic of believing (*pisteuō*) because it was introduced in 3:23 with the topic of the name, was developed further, especially with regard to

---

[245] Brown, *Epistles of John*, 633-34.

believing in Jesus as the Son of God (4:1, 16; 5:1, 5, 10), and now appears for the final time with the topic of the name. This intertwining of topics emphasizes that believing is in the name Jesus Christ, a name that affirms that Jesus is fully the Christ.

The Elder writes so that the faithful "may know." This purpose reiterates the topic of knowing (*oida*) found throughout the letter (2:11, 20, 21, 29; 3:2, 5, 14, 15) and initiates an emphasis on knowing in the conclusion (vv. 13, 15, 18–20). The Elder is concerned to assure the faithful of what they know, as is also made apparent by his heavy use of the synonymous topic of knowing (*ginoskō*; 2:3, 4, 5, 13, 14, 18, 29; 3:1, 6, 16, 19–20, 24; 4:2, 6–8, 13, 16; 5:2), which also occurs in the conclusion (5:20). A main focus of epideictic rhetoric is to affirm the audience in the knowledge, values, and traditions it already holds.

5:14–15: Enumeration

In vv. 14–15 the Elder enumerates a blessing enjoyed by the faithful: "And this is the boldness we have in him, that if we ask anything according to his will, he hears us. And if we know that he hears us in whatever we ask, we know that we have obtained the requests made of him." As he does in the other enumerations of blessing in the conclusion (vv. 18–20), the Elder joins the faithful by switching from "you" (v. 13) to "we" as sharing confidence in asking God.[246]

Using the figure of *definitio*, v. 14 defines boldness (*parrēsia*) as being able to ask God and obtain what is requested. Verse 15 says virtually the same thing as v. 14 and constitutes refining of the type in which the idea is repeated in reverse order for amplification (Rhet. Her. 4.43.56). This is not boldness that comes from any self-satisfaction or works aimed at pleasing God. Elsewhere in 1 John boldness is in the face of God's judgment gained by abiding in the Son and living in love (2:28; 4:17). Boldness before God in expecting answers to prayers comes from obeying the commandments and doing what pleases God (3:21–22). Now boldness in prayers being heard and answered comes from asking in God's will (cf. Matt 7:7–11 = Luke 11:9–13; Mark 11:24). Jesus promised to do what the disciples ask in his name (John 14:13–14; 15:16; 16:23–24) while abiding in him (15:7); in other words, when the request is made according to the will of God.

---

[246] It is uncertain whether the prayers are directed to Jesus or God, but typically they are directed to God in Johannine tradition (John 11:22; 15:16; 16:23; 1 John 3:22).

5:16-17: First Proposal of Policy

The Elder now proposes a policy, offering a specific example of asking and receiving from God: "If you see your brother or sister committing what is not a deadly sin, you will ask, and God will give life to such a one – to those whose sin is not deadly. There is sin that is deadly; I do not say that you should pray about that. All wrongdoing is sin, but there is sin that is not deadly" (cf. Jas 5:20). Verse 16 contains the antitheses of life and death, nondeadly and deadly sin. The Elder reiterates the important topic of sin (*hamartia, hamartanō*), especially as developed in 1:5-2:2 and 3:4-10. Whereas Christ intercedes for the sins of the faithful (2:1-2), here the faithful intercede for each other. Taking an intercessory role in the spiritual lives of others within one's community is a Jewish-Christian tradition (Moses – Exod 32:11-14, 30-34; 34:8-9; Christians – Jas 5:15; 1 Clem. 56:1). It is a continuation of the intercessory role of Jesus Christ for believers.[247]

This proposal of policy indicates that in their intercession for one another the faithful need to distinguish between praying for those who have committed nondeadly sin and those who have committed deadly sin.[248] They are instructed to pray for fellow Christians committing nondeadly sin; that is, disobedience to the commandments of God. While seriously affecting the relationship of the sinner with God, such sins do not lead to eternal death for those who have confessed Jesus as the Christ, the Son of God come in the flesh because they have eternal life (5:11-13). Intercession for such sinners reconfirms them in eternal life. This aspect of the proposal assures the faithful that they can be forgiven in light of the Elder's previous statement that sin is incongruous with the Christian life (3:6, 9), a statement he is about to reiterate (5:18).

Intercession is not to be made for those committing deadly sin. Deadly sin is the refusal to believe and confess that Jesus Christ is the Son of God come

---

[247] Schnackenburg, *Johannine Epistles*, 248-49; M. M. Thompson, "Intercession in the Johannine Community: 1 John 5.16 in the Context of the Gospel and Epistles of John," in M. J. Wilkins and T. Paige, eds., *Worship, Theology and Ministry in the Early Church: Essays in Honor of Ralph P. Martin*, JSNTSup 87 (Sheffield: Sheffield Academic Press, 1992), 225-45.

[248] For discussion of the nature of the sins mentioned here, see Brown, *Epistles of John*, 612-19, 636-37; Marshall, *Epistles of John*, 245-51; Schnackenburg, *Johannine Epistles*, 248-51; Smalley, *1, 2, 3 John*, 297-99; Strecker, *Johannine Letters*, 203-08; D. M. Scholer, "Sins Within and Sins Without: An Interpretation of 1 John 5:16-17," in G. F. Hawthorne, ed., *Current Issues in Biblical and Patristic Interpretation* (Grand Rapids: William B. Eerdmans, 1975), 230-46.

in the flesh and to enter eternal life. Such obstinacy, as observed in the secessionists, leaves such a sinner in eternal death and subject to God's eschatological judgment (3:14; John 5:24). They cannot be the subject of intercession because they have not availed themselves of life and the atoning sacrifice of Jesus Christ. The exclusion of intercession for unbelievers or the unrepentant is found in Hebrew tradition (Jer 7:16–20; 11:14; 14:11–12). Withholding prayer was a sign of God's judgment.[249]

An analogous distinction between confessors and nonconfessors and prayer for one group and not for the other is found in the Farewell Discourse of the Gospel of John. There Jesus prays for those who believe in him and are no longer of the world, but he does not pray for those who do not believe in him and remain aligned with the world (John 17:6–9).[250]

5:18–20: Threefold Enumeration

The conclusion continues with a threefold enumeration in vv. 18–20, each beginning with "we know" (*oidamen*), creating epanaphora for amplification (Rhet. Her. 4.13.19). In structure, this beginning is similar to the three secessionist claims starting with "if we say" (*ean eipōmen*; 1:6, 8, 10) and "whoever says" (*ho legōn*; 2:4, 6, 9). These enumerations highlight the dualism of God versus the evil one and the world found throughout the letter. The topic of "knowing" (*oida*) runs throughout the conclusion (vv. 13, 15–16) and probably refers to the instruction the faithful have received throughout their Christian lives. The Elder is pointing to traditional teaching that has great authority because they are past judgments of the community (*kriseis*).

The first enumeration in v. 18 affirms that "We know that those who are born of God do not sin, but the one who was born of God protects them, and the evil one does not touch them" (cf. 1:8, 10). The sinlessness of those born of God reiterates 3:9 (cf. 2:29; 3:6), and both verses are the opposite of 3:8, which states that children of the devil sin. The reason for why the faithful do not sin is that Jesus Christ, the Son born of God (1 John 4:9; 5:1; John 1:14, 18; 3:16, 18), protects them from the evil one (cf. John 10:28; 17:11–12, 15; Rev 3:10). The faithful have conquered the evil one (2:13–14), have conquered the antichrists because the Spirit of God in

---

[249] Thompson, "Intercession in the Johannine Community," 237–42.
[250] Scholar, "Sins Within and Sins Without," 230–46.

them is greater than the spirit of the antichrist (4:4), and have conquered the world through faith (5:4).

The second enumeration in v. 19 is "We know that we are God's children, and that the whole world lies under the power of the evil one" (cf. John 12:31; 14:30; 16:11; 17:14–16). It reiterates two important topics: "to be of God" (*einai ek theou*) and "to be of the world" (*einai ek kosmou*). In 4:4–6 the faithful are said to be of God and to have overcome those of the world because the power in the faithful, the Spirit of God, is greater than the power in the world, the spirit of the antichrist. In 3:8–10 the Elder uses these topics to distinguish between sinners who are of the devil and those not sinning who are children of God.

The third enumeration in v. 20 is "And we know that the Son of God has come and has given us understanding so that we may know him who is true; and we are in him who is true, in his Son Jesus Christ. He[251] is the true God and eternal life." Verse 20 forms an *inclusio* with the beginning of the conclusion in v. 13. There the Elder's stated intention in writing is so the faithful would know that they have eternal life, and now the Son of God is eternal life. Verse 20 also forms an *inclusio* with the introduction. There the Elder affirms that eternal life has been revealed in Jesus Christ (1:2), and now the Son Jesus Christ gives understanding that he is eternal life.

The topic of the Son giving "understanding" (*dianoia*) is part of the Johannine tradition that Jesus reveals God and knowledge of God comes through the Son (John 5:18–19, 30; 10:30, 38; 14:6–7; 17:3, 7, 25). It is probably equivalent to the role of the anointing (*chrisma*) of the Holy Spirit, who provides knowledge of the truth (2:20–21, 27). The designations "know him who is true," "in him who is true," and "true God" amplify the nature of God by repetition as part of the understanding that the Son of God has given God's children. This repetition reiterates the important topics of knowledge (*ginoskō*), truth (*alēthinos*), and "to be in" (*einai en*). In Johannine tradition, God as true and God's word as true (John 7:28; 17:3, 17; Rev 6:10) contrast the evil one, who is a liar (2:22; John 8:44). "Him who is true" (*ho alēthinos*) is a phrase used in Judaism to

---

[251] There is a debate as to whether the referent of "he" (lit. "this one," *houtos*) is God or Jesus. I understand it as a reference to Jesus. To understand God as the referent is to make a tautology: "the true one (God) ... is the true God." Also, in Johannine literature, life is only predicated on Jesus (1:2; 5:11; John 11:25; 14:6; cf. 1 John 5:11). Brown, *Johannine Epistles*, 625–26.

contrast God with idols (Isa 65:16 LXX; 3 Macc 6:18; Josephus, *Ant.* 8.343; Philo, *Embassy* 366; *Spec. Laws* 1.332) and leads naturally into the next verse exhorting the faithful to "keep yourselves from idols" (v. 21).

The Elder makes it clear that the way to know the truth, to know God, and to obtain eternal life is through the Son of God, Jesus Christ (cf. 1:2; 2 John 3; John 14:6; 17:3). Having already affirmed that the secessionists refuse to confess Jesus Christ as the Son of God (2:22–23; 4:3; cf. 5:10), the Elder now excludes them from knowing God, truth, and eternal life. They are "under the power of the evil one" (v. 19).

5:21: Second Proposal of Policy

The Elder concludes the letter in v. 21 with a second proposal of policy: "Little children, keep yourselves from idols." As a shift from the first to the second person indicates, he excludes himself from the need to be exhorted to keep from idols, thus maintaining his authority. This policy recalls the exhortation of 2:15: "Do not love the world or the things in the world," and it complements the preceding verse, where the faithful know the true God (rather than false idols). Guarding against idols is important in light of the Elder's eschatological expectation that he and the faithful are living in the last days (2:18–19; 4:1–6).

A warning about idols at the end of the letter is surprising, especially when there is no indication that either the faithful or the secessionists are in danger of idol worship. While such worship was prevalent in the ancient world and Asia Minor where the Johannine churches are thought to have been located (Acts 14:15; 1 Cor 10:14; 1 Thess 1:9; Rev 13:14-15), the letter has not even alluded to it. The history of interpretation contains many interpretations of idols in this verse, including images of pagan gods, food dedicated to idols, compromise with paganism, mystery religions, gnostic ideologies, anything taking God's place, and secession from the community.[252] The last option in this list – secession – is a viable possibility. The Qumran psalmist describes members who left the community following teachers of lies to be seeking God among idols (1 QH 4:9–11, 15). Here in 1 John idolatry appears to be leaving the Johannine Community to pursue

---

[252] For full discussion, see Brown, *Epistles of John*, 627–29; J.-L. Ska, "'Petits enfants, prenez garde aux idoles' 1 Jn 5,21," *NRTh* 101 (1979): 860-74; J. Hills, "'Little children, keep yourself? from idols': 1 John 5:21 Reconsidered," *CBQ* 51 (1989): 285-310.

a Christology that denies that Jesus is the Christ, Son of God, born of water and blood. It is not to live by the knowledge of the true God given by the Son who is life and instead to remain under the power of the evil one (5:18–20).[253]

The Elder employs allusions to texts of the Old Testament and Judaism and associated polemics that castigate idols. He molds this polemic against idols to vilify the secessionists and instruct the faithful. He is tying the conclusion to the introduction of his letter using the topic of life (*zōē*).[254] In the letter opening, the Elder stresses that the word of life, eternal life, has been heard, seen, looked at, and touched with hands (1:1–2). Biblical writers describe idols as "works of the hands" (Exod 20:4; Lev 19:4; Deut 4:28; 27:15; Pss 115:4; 135:15; Isa 2:8; 17:7–8; Jer 10:1–16; Mic 5:13; Acts 7:41; Rev 9:20). They often mock these works of the hands of craftsmen for not having senses to allow them to see, hear, smell, know, or speak (Deut 4:28; Pss 115:3–8; 135:15–18; Jer 10:5; Dan 5:23; 1 Cor 12:2; Rev 9:20). Eternal life was not made with hands but revealed (1:2). As life was revealed it could be heard, seen, touched, and be in fellowship. The revealed life was touched with hands and was not made by them. It could speak and be heard. The address of Moses to his people in Deuteronomy regarding God's revelation to them includes this contrast between the "senseless" idols who are "made by human hands, objects of wood and stone that neither see, nor hear, nor eat, nor smell" and God who "speaks" out of fire and is "heard" (Deut 4:28, 33, 36).

Prophetic polemic also contrasted the living God with idols that do not have breath in them (Ps 135:15–18; Jer 10:10, 14). The Elder emphasizes that the revealed word is a "word of life," "eternal life" (1:1–2). God gave eternal life in his Son, and to have the Son is to have life (5:11–13, 20). "To keep yourselves from idols" is to keep the testimony of the Johannine tradition-bearers to eternal life that was revealed, that was heard, seen, looked at, and touched. It is not to go after another testimony that is not based on revealed life; that is, idolatry and the testimony of secessionists.

---

[253] Brown, *Epistles of John*, 629.
[254] For more detail, see D. F. Watson, "'Keep Yourselves from Idols': A Socio-Rhetorical Analysis of the *Exordium* and *Peroratio* of 1 John," in D. B. Gowler, L. G. Bloomquist, and D. F. Watson, eds., *Fabrics of Discourse: Essays in Honor of Vernon K. Robbins* (Harrisburg: Trinity Press International, 2003), 281–302.

A CLOSER LOOK: NONDEADLY AND DEADLY SINS

A lot of ink has been spilled trying to determine the distinction between nondeadly and deadly sins. Regarding nondeadly sins, those who have confessed Jesus Christ as the Son of God come in the flesh have moved from darkness to light, death to life, and are born of God (2:22–23; 3:23; 4:2–3, 15; 5:1, 5, 10–13; John 5:24). They now enjoy the eternal life that the Word came to reveal (1:1–2; 2:25; 3:14; 5:20). Ideally, they no longer sin (3:4–10, 5:18), but realistically they still do upon occasion (1:6–2:2). These sins are nondeadly sins, which can be forgiven by repentance through the blood and atoning sacrifice of Jesus Christ (1:7, 9; 2:1–2).

The deadly sin is the refusal to make the confession that Jesus Christ is the Son of God come in the flesh. It leaves the nonconfessor in darkness and subject to the judgment of God, which is eternal death (3:14; 5:10–12; John 5:24). The deadly sin is only committed by nonconfessors. In fact, it is the very sin of not believing! One sign that the deadly sin has been committed is the lack of love for other Christians (2:9–11; 3:14). The secessionists being addressed by the Elder seem to be in view as they do not make the confession (2:18–19, 22–23).

BRIDGING THE HORIZONS

The promise in this section is that we can be confident that all prayers asked in accordance with the will of God will be answered (vv. 14–15). But how do we know that our prayers are according to the will of God? God's will is not fully revealed to us and remains elusive. Clearly, what God has revealed about God's nature and how we should live in light of that nature sets solid parameters regarding what constitutes God's will. Also, being obedient to God and coming to God in prayer opens us up to the mind of God so that our prayers are more in accord with God's will. Still, God's will in any particular situation may not be known by us with certainty. It is hard to know if a prayer is according to God's will, and this uncertainty may undermine our confidence. We are promised that no matter the uncertainties all prayers made according to the will of God will be answered.

The Elder is clear that sin has no place in a Christian's life (3:6, 9; 5:18), but also he is realistic that sin will enter a Christian's life. This is why confession of sin is needed (1:9). Confession is effective because of the atoning sacrifice of Jesus Christ (2:2). Christians should pray for other Christians whose sin is not mortal and God will give them life (vv. 16–17). Life comes through repentance, returning to the light, obedience, and love of others that sin corrupts and destroys. Praying for others makes us advocates for them in an analogous fashion to how Christ is an advocate for us before God. Intercession is part of our role in the priesthood of all believers (1 Pet 2:9).

However, the Elder excludes praying for those with mortal sin. If mortal sin is the failure to confess Jesus Christ as the Son of God come in the flesh, then prayer for those committing that sin has no efficacy. These people remain in darkness and the world. God cannot give life to them until they make the proper confession and enter the eternal life that God gives. Their sinful obstinacy precludes God from giving them life in that state. However, this does not give us license to ignore those who have not made a confession. It does not preclude our prayer for those committing a mortal sin that they come to make the confession that brings them life. It is just that interceding for their sins is not effective until they repent.

Verse 18 promises that Christ protects those who are born of God and prevents the evil one from touching them. But how does this promise work in daily life? We know that even though Christians have eternal life, we still have difficulties and are tempted to do evil. Being born of God through faith does not eliminate these, but it does bring us into a new heavenly family as children of God and gives us victory over the world and the evil one who rules it (2:12–14; 5:4–5). No matter what besets us, no force in this world can harm our new family status or rob us of our victory.

Even so, in v. 21 the Elder still warns us to "keep yourselves from idols"; that is, all that lures us away from obedience and truth to the disobedience and falsehood of the world. This is what the Elder describes as "love of the world" with "the desire of the flesh, the desire of the eyes, the pride of riches" (2:16). Living in a world where so much emphasis is placed on appearance, sex, possessions, money, power, and more, it requires a lot of prayer and obedience not to make priorities of these "idols." Paying attention to all of these is certainly necessary to live wisely in this world, but to make too much of them leads us away from life and back toward the world and death.

The Letter of 2 John

I Introduction to the Letter of 2 John

AUTHOR

The author identifies himself as the "Elder" (*presbyteros*). This Greek word refers to an older man given authority by virtue of having greater life experience (Acts 11:30; 14:23; 15:1–6, 22–23; 20:17; 1 Tim 5:17–19; Titus 1:5; Jas 5:14; 1 Pet 5:1, 5) or a respected male regardless of age given authority in a council of elders (*presbyterion*) as in the Letters of Ignatius (*Eph.* 2.2; 4.1; *Magn.* 2.1; *Trall.* 2.2; 13.2; *Smyrn.* 8.1).[1] The age of the Elder or whether he holds an office cannot be determined from 2 John or the Elder's other letter of 3 John.

We can identify the Elder himself more precisely. Papias, Bishop of Hierapolis in Asia Minor (c. 60–130), makes a distinction between the eyewitnesses (the generation of the apostles and disciples of the Lord) and the elders (the next generation that received the oral tradition from the eyewitnesses): "[B]ut if ever anyone came who had followed the presbyters, I inquired into the words of the presbyters, what Andrew or Peter or Philip or Thomas or James or John or Matthew, or any other of the Lord's disciples, had said, and what Aristion and the presbyter John, the Lord's disciples, were saying" (Eusebius, *Hist. eccl.* 3.39.4). The next generation included a John the Elder to whom Eusebius, Bishop of Caesarea (c. 260–340), attributes the book of Revelation and reports that Papias claimed to have heard speak (*Hist. eccl.* 3.39.5–7).

The Elder of 2 John and 3 John could very well be this John the Elder.[2] However, he is at least "[a] disciple of the disciples of Jesus and thus a

---

[1] Supporting the latter is K. P. Donfried, "Ecclesiastical Authority in 2–3 John," in M. de Jonge, ed., *L'Évangile de Jean: Sources, rédaction, théologie*, BETL 44 (Gembloux: J. Duculot/Leuven: Leuven University Press, 1977), 325–33.

[2] Bultmann (*Johannine Epistles*, 95) concedes that the Elder may be one of the elders Papias mentions.

second-generation figure who served as a transmitter of the tradition that came down from the first generation."[3] The Elder is a disciple of the Beloved Disciple of John's Gospel and an intermediary of the tradition that came down from him (John 21:24; 3 John 12).[4] The Elder addresses this letter to a church as an overseer, not as its founder, and probably not as a holder of a defined office, but by virtue of his authority as a disciple of the Beloved Disciple, the Apostle John. His strong voice in all of the Johannine Letters indicates that he was the main authority among the disciples of the Apostle John.[5]

AUDIENCE AND SITUATION ADDRESSED

There was a schism within the mother church(es) of the Johannine Community (probably in Ephesus) where the Elder is located (1 John 2:18–19; cf. 4:1). Somewhere between AD 90 and 110 the secessionists sent out teachers to proselytize among the Johannine churches (2 John 7–11). The language used in 2 John to describe the secessionists makes their proselytizing intent clear. In v. 7 the verb "to go out" (*exerchomai*) describing the secessionists' travel indicates missionary activity in Johannine usage (1 John 2:19; 4:1; 3 John 7; John 8:42; 13:3). In v. 10 the coordination of the verbs "coming" (*erchomai*) and "bringing" (*pherō*) teaching suggests that the secessionists were coming for the express purpose of disseminating their ideas.[6] Receiving itinerant teachers from the mother church(es) was a customary practice (v. 10; cf. 3 John).

The secessionists modify the Johannine Christology articulated in the Gospel of John in which Jesus is the Christ, a unity of the human and divine (John 1:14; 1 John 1:1–4). They separate Jesus and Christ. They claim that Jesus was a man born of Joseph and Mary and was possessed by the preexistent Christ at his baptism to become the mouthpiece for Christ. Christ was not born of the flesh (vv. 7, 9; 1 John 4:1–3). The knowledge of the teachings of Christ through Jesus is salvific, but the life of Jesus himself does not have ethical implications and is not a model for behavior. This

---

[3] Brown, *Epistles of John*, 650.
[4] Brown, *Epistles of John*, 679–80.
[5] Strecker, *Johannine Letters*, 218–20. J. Lieu (*The Second and Third Epistles of John*, SNTW [Edinburgh: T. & T. Clark, 1986], 52–64) cautions us not to be too specific in our understanding of the Elder based on the scant evidence available to us.
[6] For more discussion of the life setting of 2 John, see Brown, *Epistles of John*, 47–115; Lieu, *Second and Third Epistles of John*, 125–65.

downplay of Jesus's earthly life and elevation of knowledge results in an ethical indifference in opposition to the ethical demands of the love commandment of the Johannine Community (vv. 5–6; 1 John 3:23).

The Elder's authority, the tradition of the Johannine Community that he upholds, and the best interests of this church are constraints that the Elder employs to influence the decisions and actions of the church addressed. He speaks as an authority for the Johannine Community, issuing commands to the church (vv. 8, 10–11), appealing to the tradition of the community in which the church was trained and from which the secessionists have strayed (vv. 1–2, 4–6, 9–11). This church's interests are at stake because veering from the tradition leads to a loss of eternal reward (v. 8) and forfeiture of a relationship with God and Christ (v. 9; cf. 1 John 1:3). Thus, he warns them not to extend hospitality to anyone offering secessionist teachings (v. 10).

LITERARY AND RHETORICAL GENRES

As a Letter

Second John is a letter as indicated by the Elder's reference to writing with paper and ink (v. 12). It probably fit on a standard piece of papyrus, which was 8 by 10 inches or 20 by 25 centimeters. As shown by the language of "lady," "children," and "sister" in the opening and closing (vv. 1, 13) and by the petition (vv. 5–6), 2 John contains elements of a family letter and a letter of petition. However, 2 John is primarily a letter of exhortation and advice that persuades or dissuades the recipients regarding courses of action to take or not to take. This type of letter is primarily positive and often relies upon antitheses and contrasts of virtues and vices for its rhetoric. Its content is usually precepts, the development of moral topics, reminders of what the recipients already know, and reasons for the recommended course of action.[7]

Second John contains the positive exhortation to love, the supporting reason being that love is the founding tradition of the community (vv. 5–6). It incorporates an overall antithesis between the truth of the church addressed and the deception of the secessionists, the virtue of the church and the vice of the secessionists (vv. 4–11). It develops moral topics,

---

[7] S. K. Stowers, *Letter Writing in Greco-Roman Antiquity*, LEC 5 (Philadelphia: Westminster, 1986), 91–94.

especially truth and love (vv. 1–6; cf. v. 11), which the church is reminded it already knows (v. 1–2, 5–6). Reasons are given for the recommended course of action. Following the secessionists means losing full heavenly reward and the Father and Son, as well as participating in the evil deeds of the secessionists (vv. 8–11).

More precisely, 2 John is a subtype of the letter of exhortation and advice known as a paraenetic letter.[8] "A paraenetic style is that in which we exhort someone by urging him to pursue something or to avoid something. Paraenesis is divided into two parts – encouragement and dissuasion."[9] Second John is divided into encouragement to walk according to the commandment to love (vv. 4–6) and dissuasion from association with the secessionists and their teaching (vv. 7–11). Also, a paraenetic letter requires a relationship between the sender and recipients, the sender often being a friend or moral superior.[10] The use of a paraenetic letter indicates that the Elder is on friendly terms with the church and is a moral superior.

As Rhetoric

Second John is best classified as deliberative rhetoric.[11] It is intended to advise an audience regarding courses of action using topics of what is advantageous or harmful and expedient or inexpedient for that audience. The Elder advises that to follow his advice is to maintain the reward of eternal life and the relationship with the Father and the Son. Not to follow his advice is to lose both blessings through the deception of the secessionists and to share in their wicked deeds (vv. 8–11). Paraenetic letters typically employ deliberative rhetoric.[12] As does his choice of writing a paraenetic letter, the use of deliberative rhetoric implies that the Elder is on good terms with the church and the secessionists have not made significant inroads in it.[13]

The Elder assumes that he has authority over the church. He makes no use of extensive examples or formal proofs that following the

---

[8] Stowers, *Letter Writing*, 94–97.
[9] Pseudo Libanius, *Epistolary Styles* 5, as translated by A. J. Malherbe, *Ancient Epistolary Theorists*, SBLSBS 19 (Atlanta: Scholars Press, 1988), 69.
[10] Stowers, *Letter Writing*, 94–96.
[11] For a rhetorical analysis of 2 John, see D. F. Watson, "A Rhetorical Analysis of 2 John According to Greco-Roman Convention," *NTS* 35 (1989): 104–30. This analysis forms the basis of this commentary's rhetorical approach.
[12] Stowers, *Letter Writing*, 93, 95, 107–08.
[13] Stowers, *Letter Writing*, 95.

commandment to love is advantageous, surmising that the church agrees with him. He continually appeals to the Johannine tradition delivered to the church to support his exhortation (vv. 1–2, 4–6, 9–10), assuming that it still holds that tradition to be authoritative and thus it can be used as a tool of persuasion.

The following is a comparison of the epistolary and rhetorical outlines of 2 John:

Epistolary Outline	**Rhetorical Outline**
Letter Opening	
Prescript (vv. 1–2)	
Greeting/Blessing (v. 3)	
Letter Body (vv. 4–11)	
Body Opening (vv. 4–5)	*Exordium and Narratio* (vv. 4–5)
Body Middle (vv. 6–11)	*Probatio* (vv. 6–11)
Body Closing (v. 12)	*Peroratio* (v. 12)
Letter Closing	
Postscript (v. 13)	

II Suggested Readings on the Letter of 2 John

Find commentaries and works on all of the Johannine Epistles in the Suggested Readings on the Letter of 1 John.

C. M. Beasley, "Translating 2 John 12 and 3 John 14." *BT* 71 (2020): 259–64.
K. P. Donfried. "Ecclesiastical Authority in 2–3 John." Pp. 325–33 in *L'Évangile de Jean*. Edited by M. de Jonge. BETL 44. Gembloux: Duculot, 1977.
R. W. Funk. "The Form and Structure of II and III John." *JBL* 86 (1967): 424–30.
T. Griffith. "The Translation of O *Proagōn* in 2 John 9." *TynBul* 67 (2016): 137–44.
M. D. Jensen. "Jesus 'Coming' in the Flesh: 2 John 7 and Verbal Aspect." *NovT* 56 (2014): 310–22.
J. Lieu. *The Second and Third Epistles of John: History and Background*. Edinburgh: T. & T. Clark, 1986.
J. G. Van der Watt, "The Ethical Implications of 2 John 10–11." *Verbum et Ecclesia* 36 (2015): 1–7.
U. C. Von Wahlde. "The Theological Foundation of the Presbyter's Argument in 2 Jn (2 Jn 4–6)." *ZNW* 76 (1985) 209–24.
D. F. Watson. "A Rhetorical Analysis of 2 John According to the Greco-Roman Convention." *NTS* 35 (1989): 104–30.

III Commentary on the Letter of 2 John

VERSES 1-3: LETTER OPENING

1 The elder to the elect lady and her children, whom I love in the truth, and not only I but also all who know the truth,
2 because of the truth that abides in us and will be with us forever:
3 Grace, mercy, and peace will be with us from God the Father and from Jesus Christ, the Father's Son, in truth and love.

Verses 1–3 constitute the letter opening of 2 John. The letter opening is traditionally composed of a prescript naming the sender and recipient (vv. 1–2) and a greeting or health wish (v. 3). Christians often modified these epistolary features for theological purposes. They often added theological descriptors to the sender and recipient, as is the case in 2 John where the relationship between the Elder and the elect lady and her children is described as "love in the truth" that abides forever in them both (vv. 1–2). They also often replaced the greeting or health wish with a blessing, as is also the case in this letter (v. 3).

The letter opening functions like an *exordium*, the opening of Greco-Roman speeches, in introducing key topics to be developed later. Here the topics of love (*agapē*), truth (*alētheia*), abiding (*menō*), and the Father and Jesus Christ the Son are introduced and developed in the body of the letter. Like an *exordium*, the letter opening, as modified theologically by Christians, works to build goodwill with the recipients. Here the positive designation of the recipients and the blessing function in this capacity. The letter opening also functions as a *narratio* of Greco-Roman speeches that gives the background of the matter at hand. Here there is a hint that the matter centers on truth, love, and the Christology that Jesus is the Father's Son.

Verses 1–2: Prescript

The sender begins the letter by identifying himself as the Elder (*presbyteros*), a title of honor denoting a second-generation Christian having authority by virtue of being a disciple of the Beloved Disciple (see "Author" in the Introduction to the Letter of 2 John). He may be the head of the church designated as the "elect sister" that sends greetings in the letter closing (v. 13). The Elder addresses the recipients as "the elect lady and her children." There is debate if the elect lady (*eklektē kyria*) is an individual or a specific church. Some interpreters understand "elect lady" to be a polite address to an anonymous Christian woman since "lady" (*kyria*) is an honorific title in letters. Others see "lady" as a woman's name, "Kyria," but, if so, we would expect a definite article to precede "elect lady."[1] Clement of Alexandria assumed that the recipient of the letter was a Babylonian lady named "Electa," and the children mentioned were her actual children (vv. 1, 4).[2] However, the reference to the "elect sister" (v. 13) would then be a reference to Electa's sister, who would also be named Electa!

It is most likely that the designation "elect lady and her children" refers to an individual house church and its members. This explains the shift from the singular (vv. 1, 4–5) to the plural (vv. 6, 8, 10, 12) and back again (v. 13) depending upon whether the church as a collective or its individual members are addressed. At the beginning of Christian letters, the word "elect" (*eklektos*, v. 1) describes an individual church (Ign. *Trall.* opening formula), a group of churches (1 Pet 1:1–2), and the whole church (Titus 1:1; 1 Clem. 1:1), but not an individual Christian. Also, the word "children" (*tekna*, vv. 1, 4) can refer to members of a church (v. 13; 3 John 4; 1 Cor 4:14, 17; Herm. Vis. 3.9.1; cf. 2 Cor 6:13) and believers in general (1 John 2:1, 28; 3:7, 18).

The family metaphor used to describe the people of God in Jewish and Christian tradition pervades the letter. "The elect lady and her children" (v. 1) and "some of your children" (v. 4) naturally refer to the church addressed, while in the letter closing "the children of your elect sister" (v. 13) refers to the church from which the Elder is writing. This inclusion allows the family metaphor to create a sense of shared identity between the

---

[1] For full discussion of the possible interpretations of the designation "elect lady," see Brown, *Epistles of John*, 651–55; Strecker, *Johannine Letters*, 220–21.
[2] *Hypotyposes* (*Adumbrationes*) GCS 17, 215.

Elder's church and the church he addresses. This inclusion also naturally blends into the broader metaphor of the church as the children of God, a metaphor common to Johannine tradition (1 John 2:29–3:2; 3:10; 5:1–2).

The Elder's designation of the church members as "elect" (*eklektos*) reminds them that Jesus has chosen them (John 6:70; 13:18; 15:16, 19). Their new identity requires a new faith and practice. They must affirm that Jesus Christ has come in the flesh (v. 7), walk in the truth (v. 4), obey the love commandment (vv. 4–6; John 13:34; 15:12), and abide in the teachings of Christ (v. 9). The Elder exemplifies this new faith and practice when he identifies the church as those "whom I love in the truth."

Truth (*alētheia*) is a key topic in 2 John and is repeated five times in vv. 2–4. It is the revelation of God through Jesus Christ come in the flesh (2 John 7; 1 John 2:21–22). It is the revelation of God's love through Jesus Christ, a love that obligates and enables Christians to love one another (1 John 3:11–22; 4:7–21; John 13:34–35). "Truth" used without an article, as in this instance, can be adverbial meaning "truthfully" as in "truly love" or have the theological meaning "love in the sphere of the truth." The latter is the meaning here. The Elder is doing more than affirming the truth of his love for the church. He loves its members within the sphere of truth. Truth is the sphere in which love is demonstrated (3 John 1) and Christians assured that they are in the truth when they love (1 John 3:18–22).[3]

Not only does the Elder love the church in truth, but "all who know the truth" do as well. Some interpreters restrict the content of "truth" here to just teaching, since "walking in the truth" (v. 4; 3 John 3–4) is equivalent to "abiding in the teaching" of the Johannine tradition (v. 9), especially against the false teachers.[4] However, based on the theological use of truth in Johannine literature, it is probably to be taken in a theological sense. To know the truth is not simply to have knowledge of teaching, but to express truth in mutual love. To know the truth is to surrender the will to love, the love that God demonstrated in Christ and was exemplified by Christ.[5] To obey the commandments, especially to love, is to know one belongs to the truth (1 John 3:18–22).

---

[3] Brown, *Epistles of John*, 655–56.
[4] Strecker, *Johannine Letters*, 221–22; R. Bergmeier, "Zum Verfasserproblem des II. und III. Johannesbriefes," *ZNW* 57 (1966): 93–100.
[5] Schnackenburg, *Johannine Epistles*, 90–95; Smalley, *1, 2, 3 John*, 319; Strecker, *Johannine Letters*, 222–26.

In v. 2 the Elder assures the church that he and others who know the truth can love them in the truth (v. 1) because truth abides in Christians and will be with them forever. Truth motivates to love, empowers love, and manifests itself in love. Truth abiding "forever" in Christians is part of the Johannine theology that divine realities are the possession of Christians forever (John 4:13-14; 6:51, 58; 8:51-52; 10:28-29; 11:26; 14:16; 1 John 2:17). Christians know the truth (John 8:31-32; 1 John 2:21) and truth is in them, and they are in the truth (cf. 1 John 1:8; 2:4). The truth abiding within Christians is virtually equivalent to the anointing of the Holy Spirit, the Spirit of Truth, who enters the lives of Christians at conversion and guides them in the truth (John 14:15-17; 16:13; 1 John 2:20-27).

The Elder describes himself and the church as being in the truth four times and the truth being in them one time in vv. 1-4. Rhetorically this amplification by repetition contrasts them with the secessionists who do not have the truth, but are deceivers, do not confess Jesus Christ come in the flesh, are antichrists, and perform evil deeds (vv. 7, 11). They did not abide in the truth, the teaching of God, and therefore do not have God (v. 9; cf. v. 2).

Verse 3: Greeting/Blessing

In the greeting of a Greco-Roman letter the sender typically extends a health wish or blessing to the recipient(s). Here in the greeting of v. 3 the Elder makes unusual modifications to the conventional greeting. Rather than extend a blessing to the church, he assures its members that they will be blessed, and includes himself in that blessing. His assurance unites him with the church as recipients of blessing and works to increase their mutual goodwill.

The blessing is threefold – grace, mercy, and peace – and derives from God the Father and from Jesus Christ his Son. Grace (*charis*) replaces the usual "greeting" (*chairein*) and is the undeserved love of God (John 1:14-17). Mercy (*eleos*) is God's faithfulness to covenant commitments, including forgiveness. Peace (*eirēnē*) is well-being in all aspects of life, specifically eternal life mutually experienced by Christians in this life and the next (John 14:27; 16:33; 20:19, 21, 26).

The Elder and the church will experience the blessings of grace, mercy, and peace from the Father and Son if they remain in truth and love; that is, loving one another (vv. 5-6) and holding the proper Christology (vv. 7-9). It is by abiding in truth and love that grace, mercy, and peace, and even the

Father and Son, are experienced (cf. v. 9). The inclusion that frames the prescript amplifies this reality: The Elder and others love the church in the truth (v. 1) and the Elder and the church need to abide in truth and love (v. 3).

The Elder continues to use the family metaphor that runs throughout the prescript and letter to describe the relationship of Christians and churches (vv. 1, 4, 13), but he applies it to the divine. God is the Father and Jesus is the Father's Son, a relationship central to the confession and practice of faithful Christians (v. 9; 1 John 1:3, 7; 2:22–24; 3:23; 4:14–15; 5:1, 10–12, 20). This metaphor anticipates the heretical Christology addressed in v. 7 that denies that Jesus is God's Son.

VERSES 4–5: EXHORTATION TO OBEY THE LOVE COMMANDMENT

4 I was overjoyed to find some of your children walking in the truth, just as we have been commanded by the Father.

5 But now, dear lady, I ask you, not as though I were writing you a new commandment, but one we have had from the beginning: let us love one another.

Verses 4–5 constitute the body opening of the letter. They allude to matters shared by both the sender and the recipients that provide a common basis for deliberation ("the love commandment"), give the reason for writing and the matter(s) upon which the recipients are to respond ("the need to keep the commandment"), present a request or petition ("love one another"), and express joy ("I was overjoyed"). The request is in standard form: v. 4 providing the background for the request introduced by the joy formula (*echarēn*); and v. 5 providing the request itself using a typical verb of asking (*erōtan*), a direct address to the recipients in the vocative using an expression of courtesy ("dear lady") and specifying the action desired ("love one another").[6]

Verses 4–5 further develop the major theological themes of the truth and love introduced in the letter opening (vv. 1–3) and to be developed further in the body of the letter in vv. 6–11. Verses 4–5 function rhetorically as the *exordium* or introduction, setting forth the main concern, the subjects to

---

[6] White, *Body of the Greek Letter*, 18–23, 39–41; White, *Light from Ancient Letters*, 195, 204, 207–11; R. Funk, "The Form and Structure of II and III John," *JBL* 86 (1967): 425–27; T. Y. Mullins, "Petition as a Literary Form," *NovT* 5 (1962): 46–47.

be discussed, and a call for a hearing.[7] The Elder's concern is that the church members walk in the truth as commanded by the Father; that is, that they love one another (vv. 4–6; 1 John 3:23; 4:21; 5:2–3).

In v. 4 the Elder rejoices that some members of the church are walking in the truth. This joy in the welfare of the church functions like a thanksgiving that was expected at this point in Greco-Roman letters after the letter opening (vv. 1–3). Senders typically express thanks for aspects of their relationship with the recipients. The Elder's formula "I was overjoyed" (*echaren lian*) is functionally equivalent to "I thank" (*eucharisteō*) used to open thanksgivings in Pauline and other early Christian letters (Rom 1:8; 1 Cor 1:4; Phil 1:3; Col 1:3, 1 Thess 1:2; 2 Thess 1:3).[8] The thanksgiving functions like an *exordium* in enabling the Elder to elicit positive pathos or emotion from the church. The more positive the emotions between the Elder and the church, the more likely its members are to respond to his petition to love one another according to the love commandment (v. 5).

That the Elder finds "some" of the church walking in the truth implies that "others" are not. I am giving the partitive genitive "some of your children" (*ek ton teknon sou*) its full force, implying that a second group exists within the church that is not obeying the truth.[9] If everyone were walking in the truth, why would the Elder need to petition them in the next verse to follow the love commandment? I am also giving full force to the verb "I find" (*heurēka*), which implies that the Elder has full knowledge of the community through personal visits, visitors from the church, or informed sources.

Verse 4 provides the background for the petition and v. 5 provides the petition itself. The petition of the body opening of a letter corresponds to the rhetorical *narratio* in providing the principle occasion of the letter and the point upon which the writer wants the recipients to render a decision.[10] The Elder petitions the church to continue to obey the love commandment that derives from the Old Testament and Jesus himself (John 13:34–35; 15:12, 17) and is central to the Johannine Community's self-understanding

---

[7] Cf. Watson, "Rhetorical Analysis of 2 John," 110–13.
[8] Funk, "Form and Structure," 425–27; J. A. du Rand, "Structure and Message of 2 John," *Neot* 13 (1979): 103–04; Brown, *Epistles of John*, 661, 791–92.
[9] Bultmann, *Johannine Epistles*, 110; Painter, *1, 2, 3 John*, 347; Smalley, *1, 2, 3 John*, 323; Strecker, *Johannine Letters*, 228; *contra* Brown, *Epistles of John*, 661; Lieu, *I, II, III John*, 249; Marshall, *Epistles of John*, 65.
[10] Watson, "Rhetorical Analysis of 2 John," 116–18.

(1 John 2:7-8; 3:11, 23; 4:7, 11-12, 21). Love is the advantageous, honorable, and beneficial choice for doctrine and practice within the community; that is, the typical virtues espoused in deliberative rhetoric (Aristotle, *Rhet.* 1.3.1358b.5; [*Rhet. Alex.*] 1.1421b.21ff; Cicero, *Inv.* 2.4.12; 2.51.155-58.176; *Part. or.* 24.83-87; *Top.* 24.91; Rhet. Her. 3.2.3-5.9; Quintilian, *Inst.* 3.8.1-6, 22-35).

The Elder's parenthesis "not as though I were writing you a new commandment, but one we have had from the beginning" emphasizes the traditional character of the love commandment. It not only has its source in the Father (v. 4), but stems from the beginning, from the origins of this church as a part of the Johannine Community (v. 6; 1 John 2:7-8, 24; 3:11) and Jesus himself (1 John 1:1; John 13:34; 15:12). It was part of the original preaching that founded the Johannine Community in general and the church addressed. Tradition is a strong authority in the Greco-Roman world and strengthens the Elder's petition in the face of the teaching of the secessionists, which he emphasizes is not traditional (v. 9).

The Elder does not assert his authority in an overbearing way. He uses an official petition beginning with the verb "to ask" (*erōtaō*) rather than a commandment. This is a petition indicating a personal concern used when the one petitioning considers himself to share the same social status as the ones petitioned.[11] He includes himself in the petition as one needing to love the church as much as it needs to love him and each other.

VERSES 6-11: BEWARE THE DANGERS OF THE SECESSIONIST DECEIVERS

6 And this is love, that we walk according to his commandments; this is the commandment just as you have heard it from the beginning - you must walk in it.

7 Many deceivers have gone out into the world, those who do not confess that Jesus Christ has come in the flesh; any such person is the deceiver and the antichrist!

8 Be on your guard, so that you do not lose what we have worked for, but may receive a full reward.

9 Everyone who does not abide in the teaching of Christ, but goes beyond it, does not have God; whoever abides in the teaching has both the Father and the Son.

---

[11] Mullins, "Petition," 47-48.

10 If anyone comes to you and does not bring this teaching, do not receive and welcome this person into your house,

11 for to welcome is to participate in the evil deeds of such a person.

The body middle of the letter develops topics introduced in the letter body opening and introduces other topics of equal importance.[12] It is often difficult to delineate, but there are two strong indications that this section is the body middle. One indication is an opening formula like "and this is" (*kai hautē estin*) found here. It is a Johannine formula often introducing an explanation for a previously mentioned concept.[13] The Elder seeks to persuade the church members to love one another according to the love commandment as just given in the petition of the body opening (v. 5) and introduces the new topic of the secessionists developed in this section, which makes loving one another even more essential. A second indication of the body middle is the presence of responsibility statements.[14] The Elder directs the church members on how to deal with the secessionists. They are to be on guard for them (v. 8) and not to offer them hospitality (vv. 10–11). The body middle functions rhetorically as the *probatio* of a persuasive work, providing elaboration, amplification, and proof of propositions in the *narratio* and introducing new and related matters.[15]

Verse 6 elaborates the topic of love immediately preceding (vv. 4–5). It is constructed as a double tautology, for each half says the same thing in reverse or chiastic order: Love is walking by the commandments and the commandment is walking in love (lit. "it").[16] Within the chiasm the shift from the plural commandments to the singular commandment is refining of the idea (*expolitio*), which, while repeating an idea, adds new meaning (Rhet. Her. 4.42.54–44.58). The commandments are the teachings of the Johannine Community encapsulated by the comprehensive, singular love commandment (1 John 3:23; John 15:10–12).[17]

In the first part of the chiasm the Elder defines love as both he and the church walking according to the commandments, something he just

---

[12] White, *Body of the Greek Letter*, 39–40.
[13] Brown, *Epistles of John*, 664–65.
[14] White, *Body of the Greek Letter*, 7–9.
[15] Watson, "Rhetorical Analysis of 2 John," 118–28.
[16] Some interpreters see the referent of "it" as "walking in the truth" in v. 4, but this proposed referent is inordinately distant and thus grammatically unlikely.
[17] Watson, "Rhetorical Analysis of 2 John," 120–21.

petitioned both himself and the church to do in v. 5. Now in the second part of the chiasm he excludes himself and it is the church that must walk in the love commandment. This insinuates that he is walking in the love commandment and not in danger of doing otherwise. The threat to walking in the love commandment that he is about to discuss is only a threat to the church addressed. This insinuation supports giving full weight to the partitive genitive in v. 4 – "some" within the church are not walking in the truth, and now they must also be exhorted to walk in the love commandment.

Walking according to the commandment(s) is to walk in the truth (v. 4) and love one another (v. 5). Love is obedience to God's commands (1 John 5:3) and expresses itself in action (1 John 2:3–6; 3:10–22; 4:7–5:3). The love of Christians for one another is rooted in God's love for them as revealed in the giving of God's Son as a sacrifice for sin (1 John 4:7–21). The love commandment is amplified by the description "from the beginning," which, as in the previous verse, once again reminds the church that the love commandment is central to its origins (1 John 2:7, 24; 3:11) and braces its members to beware of secessionists who would deceive them to abandoning their beginnings (vv. 7–11).

Verses 7–9 describe the secessionist example of not walking according to the old-new commandment to love one another. Verse 7 provides the motivation for v. 6. Walking according to the commandment of love is now more important than ever because many deceivers have gone out into the world. They do not confess that Jesus Christ has come in the flesh. This false Christology threatens the Johannine Community's walk in love. The love of Christians for one another is rooted in God's love for them as revealed in the incarnation, life, and sacrificial death of God's Son, Jesus Christ. That love is only experienced and understood with a proper confession of the nature of Jesus as the Son of God (1 John 4:7–11, 14–16). Love is exercised in the truth (vv. 1, 4), and if the truth is abandoned, love has no example, context, or purpose.

The confession being denied is "Jesus Christ has come in the flesh." It is literally "Jesus Christ coming in the flesh" (cf. 1 John 4:2). The verb "come" (*erchomai*) is a present participle ("is coming"), with the denial being "Jesus Christ is coming in the flesh." This translation could refer to the denial of either the legitimacy of the expectation of the incarnation that has already occurred or the future coming of Jesus. This has led to speculation that the controversy here is not so much Christological as eschatological. The secessionists would not be denying the legitimacy of the incarnation but the second coming of Jesus and the future millennial reign of Christ on earth.[18]

While the present participle "is coming" would seem to refer more naturally to the future coming or parousia of Jesus than to his past incarnation, understanding the referent to be the incarnation is preferred. This confession is an example of the Johannine use of the present participle to refer to Jesus's incarnation as "the one who is coming" (John 1:15, 27; 3:31; 6:14; 11:27; 12:13).[19] The expectation of the arrival of the already present secessionist antichrists is described as "coming" using the present infinitive of the verb (1 John 2:18; 4:3).[20] Even the past tense of the verb (perfect participle) in the confession in 1 John 4:2 ("Jesus Christ has come in the flesh") has a present aspect and refers to the incarnation, further indicating that the incarnation is the verb's primary referent in Johannine literature.[21] Also, denying the second coming of Jesus is not an issue in Johannine literature, and typically in the New Testament the second coming is expressed as Jesus Christ coming "in glory," not "in the flesh" (Phil 3:21; Col 3:4; Titus 2:13; 1 Pet 4:13).[22]

The Elder understands the secessionists' modification of Christology to be a deception. "Deceivers" (*hoi planoi*) can also be translated as "those who lead astray."[23] Both translations are appropriate because the Elder is creating an antithesis for the topic of walking in the truth from vv. 4 and 6. Whereas the Elder and the church have the truth (vv. 1–4), the secessionists deceive (v. 7). Whereas the Elder is exhorting the church to walk in truth and in the commandment of love (vv. 4–6), the secessionists are trying to lead the church astray (v. 7 [*planos*]; 1 John 2:26 and 3:7 [*planaō*]; 4:6 [*planē*]). Which confession the church chooses is crucial because confession determines spiritual allegiance. To confess with traditional Christology is to belong to God, while to confess with "new" Christology is to belong to the antichrist (1 John 2:22–23; 4:2–3, 15). The deceit of the false Christology that denies Jesus Christ come in the flesh belongs to the

---

[18] Schnackenburg, *Johannine Epistles*, 284–85; Strecker, *Johannine Letters*, 233–36.
[19] Cf. Lieu, *Second and Third Epistles of John*, 86–87.
[20] Bultmann, *Johannine Epistles*, 112; Brown, *Epistles of John*, 669–70, 685–86; Smalley, *1, 2, 3 John*, 328–30.
[21] M. D. Jensen, "Jesus 'Coming' in the Flesh: 2 John 7 and Verbal Aspect," *NovT* 56 (2014): 310–22.
[22] Bultmann, *Johannine Epistles*, 112; Schnackenburg, *Johannine Epistles*, 284.
[23] BDAG, 822.

secessionists, the liar, the deceiver, the devil, and the antichrist (v. 7; 1 John 2:22; 4:1–6; cf. 3:7–8).

These deceivers have "gone out into the world" (v. 7). The aorist tense of the verb indicates a specific time when the schism occurred within this church. The verb "to go out" (*exerchomai*) used to describe the secessionists' activity indicates proselytizing in Johannine usage (1 John 2:19; 4:1; 3 John 7; John 8:42; 13:3). The Gospel of John describes Judas leaving the Last Supper to betray Jesus as "he went out" (*exēlthen*). The secessionists have left the sphere of truth, the Johannine Community. They have chosen the world, the sphere of deceit and evil ruled by the devil (1 John 2:15–17, 19). They are the false prophets who have gone out into the world with the spirit of error (1 John 4:1, 6). The description here of "many deceivers" who are proselytizing and the reference to "many" antichrists affecting the Johannine Community in 1 John 2:18 indicate that the secessionists have been successful.

To amplify his vilification of the secessionists, the Elder identifies the "many deceivers" who propagate the false Christology as "the deceiver and the antichrist." The shift from the plural to the singular indicates that by their confession the secessionists individually and as a group are the deceiver/antichrist of apocalyptic expectation. The same point is made in 1 John 2:18 that the antichrist is found in the secessionist antichrists of the Johannine Community.

In Johannine tradition the appearance of the secessionist antichrists is a sign of the last days (1 John 2:18; 4:3), a tradition aligned with New Testament eschatological expectation that false teachers and prophets will arise, deceiving and leading the faithful astray (Matt 24:3–5, 11, 24; Mark 13:5–6; 21–23; Rev 12:9; 19:20). In light of the appearance of the secessionists, in v. 8 the Elder warns the church to "be on your guard" (*blepete*), a warning often used in eschatological contexts (Mark 13:33; Eph 5:15–16; Heb 10:25), particularly those pertaining to the appearance of deceptive false teachers (Matt 24:4–5; Mark 13:5–6, 21–23; Luke 21:8). Since it is the last days and deceivers have come who are the antichrist(s) (v. 7; 1 John 2:18; 4:3), the church needs to be on its guard so as not to lose what it has worked for and receive less than a full heavenly reward.

"What has been worked for" is not explicitly stated, but eternal life is implied, especially considering the next verse where failure to abide in the teaching of Christ results in the loss of a relationship with the Father and Son. In Johannine tradition, correct Christology is a work of God that allows the believer to receive eternal life (1 John 2:21–25).[24] However, how can a reward be less than full if it is eternal life? Reward (*misthos*) in the New Testament designates heavenly reward (Matt 5:12; 10:41–42; Mark 9:41; 1 Cor 3:8–9, 14; Rev 11:18; 22:12), which, once a person has eternal life, can be less or more (cf. 1 Cor 3:10–15).[25] The Elder warns the church members to be on their guard to maintain their Christology and full heavenly reward.

The pronoun "we" of "we have worked for" is not distinctive of the apostles who founded the church or the Johannine tradition-bearers who work to maintain the Johannine churches, but of the entire Johannine Community. The Elder does not include himself in his exhortation to be on guard in order not to lose heavenly reward but does include himself as one who has worked in truth and love. This strategy allows him to speak as an authority that is in no danger of falling prey to secessionist deceit while emphasizing the mutuality of the work of truth and love shared by all members of the Johannine Community.[26]

Verse 9 provides further motivation for the exhortation in v. 8 to vigilance against losing heavenly reward. The church must abide in the teachings that came from Christ or lose its relationship with the Father and Son that such teachings provide (1 John 2:21–25). The secessionists do not abide in the teachings that came from Christ.[27] They deny the truth that abides in them through the anointing of the Holy Spirit (v. 2; 1 John 2:20, 27). They no longer walk in the truth as commanded by God (v. 4) and do

---

[24] Brown, *Epistles of John*, 672.
[25] Painter, *1, 2, 3 John*, 353.
[26] I am adopting the first-person plural reading "we have worked for" (*eirgasametha*) rather than the second-person plural "you have worked for" (*eirgasasthe*). The other three verbs in the verse are second-person plural. It is likely that scribes changed the first-person plural reading to the second-person plural to create uniformity. Metzger, *Textual Commentary*, 721. The inconsistency of person can also be explained by the Elder's rhetorical strategy as described above.
[27] I am taking "of Christ" (*tou christou*) as a subjective rather than as an objective genitive. It refers to Christ's teachings (e.g., the love commandment of vv. 5–6) rather than teachings about Christ (e.g., that Jesus Christ has come in the flesh of v. 7). Granted, the reference in v. 7 to other teachings about Christ and the parallel verses in 1 John 2:21–25 pertaining to denying or confessing Christ favor the objective genitive here. However, in Johannine usage "teaching" (*didachē*) is used with the subjective genitive of Christ's teachings (John 7:16–17; 18:19). Also, Johannine tradition affirms that all true teachings derive from Christ (John 16:14–15). Brown, *Epistles of John*, 674–75; Schnackenburg, *Johannine Epistles*, 286; contra Bultmann, *Johannine Epistles*, 113; Smalley, *1, 2, 3 John*, 332; Strecker, *Johannine Letters*, 242 n. 53; Painter, *1, 2, 3 John*, 354; Lieu, *I, II, III John*, 258–59.

not demonstrate love as taught by Christ (vv. 5-6). To "go beyond" (*proagō*) the teachings of Christ is not to abide by walking according to truth and love, but to be led astray. The Elder subtly appeals to authority and insinuates that the tradition of the Johannine Community came directly from Christ, so not abiding in the tradition is to follow the deceiver and the antichrist (v. 7).

The verb "go beyond" (*proagō*) is often thought to refer to advancing Christology in a Gnostic direction; that is, minimizing the earthly Jesus and his redemptive death in favor of a heavenly Christ as revealer of knowledge. However, the focus of the verse is simply "not abiding" (*menō*) in the Christology of the Johannine Community. *Proagō* used without a direct or indirect object as here in this verse never means "to progress." That idea is expressed with the verb *prokoptō*, which is the verb typically used when referring to Gnostic thought. Within Gnosticism, *proagō* referred to emanations that progress from a deity, not those that progress in doctrine. Interpreters are importing the Christology of v. 7 – the denial that Jesus Christ has come in the flesh – to create a "progressive" translation for *proagō* in v. 9 and provide the content of this assumed theological advance. The emphasis in v. 9 is failure to abide in the Christology of the Johannine Community with no sense of "progress" in Christology of any kind, including Gnostic Christology.[28]

Expressions urging responsible behavior occur in the body of the letter toward the closing, most often in letters from social superiors to social inferiors and in administrative correspondence.[29] In v. 10 the Elder exhorts the church to be responsible and not welcome secessionist proselytizers, thus allowing them to disseminate the teaching that is other than the teaching of Christ (v. 9). This is a practical application of the Elder's warning to the church to be on its guard against deceivers with false Christology (v. 8).

The reason for the exhortation to shut out the secessionists is that giving them a voice is to participate in their evil deeds (v. 11). In Johannine thought evil deeds belong to Cain, who was from the evil one (1 John 3:12), and are characteristic of the world, which prefers darkness over light (John 3:19-21; 7:7); a world that belongs to the evil one (1 John 5:18-19). The seriousness of welcoming the secessionists is revealed when v. 11 is translated literally: "The one saying to him, 'Greetings,' fellowships in his evil

---

[28] T. Griffith, "The Translation of *Ho Proagōn* in 2 John 9," *TynBul* 67 (2016): 137-44.
[29] White, *Light from Ancient Letters*, 206.

works." Even the simple greeting to a false teacher implicates the greeter in the evil deeds of that teacher!

Given that hospitality was a virtue and necessity in the Greco-Roman world and the Johannine emphasis upon loving one another (John 13:34-35; 1 John 3:11; 4:7-21), the Elder's strong exhortation to inhospitality would be quite a surprise to the church addressed. However, it is in league with similar warnings in the early church about withholding hospitality from those spreading false doctrine (Ign., *Smyrn.* 4.1) and the broader concern of this time to prevent members of a group from saying or doing something to disturb its cohesion to its detriment, even to the point of exclusion.[30]

The Elder fears contamination by association. Ideas of the secessionists appealed to the people of that age – the downplaying of the physical body, the elevation of things spiritual, and the ability to claim to be Christian and yet return to pagan ways. The New Testament speaks of being mindful around sinful Christians (Jude 22-23) and avoiding Christians who knowingly continue in sin (Matt 18:17; 1 Cor 5:3-5, 9-11; Titus 3:10-11). Jesus told his disciples not to have fellowship with those who refuse to hear their words (Matt 10:14-15; Luke 10:10-12). This practice of not allowing traveling false teachers to have a voice continued in the early church (Did. 11:1-2; Ign., *Eph.* 7.1; 9:1; *Smyrn.* 4.1; 7.1-2). The *Didache*, a late first- or early second-century church manual, requires the church to test the teaching of itinerants coming to it: "Let everyone who 'comes in the Name of the Lord' be received; but when you have tested him you shall know him, for you shall have understanding of true and false" (12.1). The Elder will not even allow a test of the teachers here in 2 John!

VERSE 12: BODY CLOSING

12 Although I have much to write to you, I would rather not use paper and ink; instead I hope to come to you and talk with you face to face, so that our joy may be complete.

Verse 12 is the body closing of the letter, which presents the motivation for writing, forms a bridge to further communication, gives notification of a coming visit, and accentuates the message by noting it has many more facets

---

[30] J. Van der Watt, "The Ethical Implications of 2 John 10-11," *Verbum et Ecclesia* 36 (2015): 1-7.

that are better discussed in person.[31] This verse also functions as the rhetorical *peroratio* in recapping key points and building positive emotion toward the speaker. The Elder began the body of the letter by expressing his joy that some of the church members were walking in the truth (v. 4). Now he closes the body of the letter by adding that visiting the church and talking with its members face to face will complete both his and their own joy. The completion (*pleroō*) of joy found within the Christian life is a Johannine theme. Hearing the voice of Jesus completed the joy of John the Baptist (John 3:29). The joy of Christians is complete when asking and receiving in Jesus's name (John 16:24) and receiving his teachings (John 17:13). The joy of the Elder and the recipients of 1 John is complete by sharing the letter (1 John 1:4).

It cannot be inferred that the Elder has any real intention to visit the church since mention of a visit is an epistolary convention akin to "see you later" (3 John 13). Curiously, the idiom "face to face" (*stoma pros stoma*) is not used to describe a visit in early letters. Remarkably, it is found in similar form (*stoma kata stoma*) in Num 12:8 (LXX), where God describes Moses as having conversed directly with God, seeing God's glory (cf. 3 John 11). The Elder may insinuate that he plans a visit to deliver the very words of God in person, thus providing a strong rhetorical and theological constraint for the recipients to adhere to the Johannine tradition.[32] With secessionist missionaries influencing outlying areas of the Johannine Community and the Elder's immediate response limited to letter writing, he may very well intend to visit. Such an expressed visit would constrain the congregation from welcoming the secessionist missionaries, for certainly the Elder would discover this disregard for his instruction once he arrived. Mention of a visit in letters of this period could function as a threat.[33]

VERSE 13: LETTER CLOSING

13 The children of your elect sister send you their greetings.

Verse 13 is a standard letter closing with the typical verb "to greet" (*aspazomai*) introducing the greeting from a third party.[34] The postscript reintroduces the family metaphor, with the elect lady and her children

---

[31] White, *Body of the Greek Letter*, 5, 25, 27, 29–31, 39–41; White, *Light from Ancient Letters*, 202, 205.
[32] C. M. Beasley, "Translating 2 John 12 and 3 John 14," *BT* 71 (2020): 259–64.
[33] White, *Light from Ancient Letters*, 202.
[34] White, *Light from Ancient Letters*, 202.

(v. 1) now greeting an elect sister's children. The introduction of another elect house church within the Johannine Community forms an inclusion with v. 1, where the church addressed is also designated as "elect." While conventional, the postscript serves to remind the church that it is part of the Johannine Community and that there is a sister church still faithful to the Elder and the tradition he upholds.

A CLOSER LOOK: LETTER WRITING

Most people at this time were illiterate, and some could read but not write. To send a letter, they hired an amanuensis or scribe to write it for them. Literate people also often preferred to use a scribe even if they could write. The sender of the letter would dictate to the scribe, who would write in shorthand on a wax tablet. Also, the sender could give the scribe the basic idea of what needed to be included in the letter and give him freedom to compose it as he saw fit. Once the letter content was finalized, the scribe would write the letter on papyrus. He would cut a piece of papyrus to size from larger rolls and write using a sharpened reed dipped in an ink made of soot and tree gum.

Paul used a scribe in writing his letters, one of whom, Tertius, even refers to himself by name (Rom 16:22). As was customary, Paul mentions writing in his own hand at the end of several letters, indicating that he composed the content of the letter, but it was written on papyrus by a scribe (1 Cor 16:21; Gal 6:11; 2 Thess 3:17; Col 4:18; cf. Phlm 19). The Elder who authored the letters of John most likely hired a secretary for 2 and 3 John, and he most certainly did so for the complex work of 1 John, which required numerous wax tablets and the expense of time and materials.

BRIDGING THE HORIZONS

In our time when truth is so often considered relative and "false news" is perpetuated for personal, financial, and political gain, 2 John reminds us that truth is not something we can dilute or dismiss. The truth is that Jesus Christ came in the flesh and revealed God's love to us (2 John 7; 1 John 2:21–22). Truth is known by obeying the commandments of God, especially the commandment to love (vv. 4–6). Truth is known by surrendering ourselves in love for others with the same love that God showed us in surrendering Jesus Christ in love for us and Jesus Christ expressed for us in his self-sacrifice. Love for others assures us that we are in the truth (1 John 3:18–20).

Divine love obligates, models, and enables us to love one another (John 13:34–35; 1 John 3:11–22; 4:7–21). Accepting the truth of God's love creates a community where we can embrace God's love for us and others. Truth and love are exercised, realized, and enjoyed in the community of the beloved. This reality, this truth, shines a light on the need to be part of Christian community and for that community to be loving.

We are always thinking about our personal happiness and fulfillment. How can I be wanted, needed, and relevant? How can I find peace and contentment? Peace is well-being rooted in the grace-filled and merciful gift of eternal life that God and Jesus Christ give to Christians to enjoy now and forever (2 John 3; John 14:27; 16:33; 20:19, 21, 26). We experience this peace by loving one another (vv. 5–6) and holding to a true understanding of the person and work of Jesus Christ (vv. 7–9). We are back again to the centrality of community, here in personal and corporate peace.

The understanding of Jesus Christ passed down in tradition and its ethical implications are worthy of profound respect. This does not preclude reexamining and recontextualizing Christology throughout the ages so that it relates to changing contexts. However, 2 John reminds us that its main affirmations are not for us individually or corporately to dismiss, dilute, or alter (vv. 7–9). Community and culture will change, but the testimony about Jesus Christ rooted in eyewitness tradition is the bedrock of truth.

The Letter of 3 John

I Introduction to the Letter of 3 John

AUTHOR

The author of 3 John is the Elder who also wrote 2 John. He is an authoritative tradition-bearer of the Johannine Community and is probably located in the mother church in Ephesus in Asia Minor (Modern Turkey; see Introduction to the Letter of 1 John).

AUDIENCE AND SITUATION ADDRESSED

The Elder sent a written work with emissaries to an outlying church of the Johannine Community headed by a man named Diotrephes (v. 9). The writing may have been a recommendation of his emissaries so that Diotrephes would provide hospitality and their message would be heard.[1] Regardless of the nature of this writing, Diotrephes refused to extend hospitality to the emissaries, even refusing to allow others in his church to show them hospitality under threat of expulsion from the church (vv. 9-10). Diotrephes's refusal to extend hospitality has a serious practical side. Travelers relied upon the hospitality of those they visited for food, shelter, and protection.

The emissaries had to rely on the hospitality of a man named Gaius, to whom 3 John is addressed.[2] Gaius is unknown outside of this letter and, due to the common nature of this name, probably should not be identified with others sharing this name in the New Testament (Acts 19:29, 20:4; Rom 16:23; 1 Cor 1:14). It does not appear that Gaius was expelled from

---

[1] Bultmann, *Johannine Epistles*, 100; Schnackenburg, *Johannine Epistles*, 296; Lieu, *I, II, III John*, 110; Painter, *1, 2, 3 John*, 363.

[2] For more on the situation, see Brown, *Epistles of John*, 47-115; U. C. von Wahlde, *The Gospel and Letters of John. Volume 3: Commentary on the Three Johannine Letters, Eerdmans Critical Commentary* (Grand Rapids: Eerdmans, 2010), 278-87.

the church of Diotrephes for extending hospitality to the Elder's emissaries, for if Gaius had been expelled, it seems likely that the Elder would express his dismay about it – and he does not. Gaius apparently lived in the region of Diotrephes's church and was probably a member of it or even a leader of another Johannine church (vv. 3–8). The Elder now writes to thank Gaius for his hospitality in the past (vv. 3–8) and to urge him to host his present and future emissaries, perhaps including Demetrius if he is the bearer of this letter (v. 12). The ability to host others in their homes and to absorb the expense of extending hospitality indicates that both Gaius and Diotrephes are householders and have some excess economic means.[3]

The exact situation addressed by 3 John is unknown, but it likely centers on theology, leadership, or both (see the commentary on vv. 9–10 for a more nuanced discussion). Regardless of the details, the situation poses a serious challenge to the Elder's authority. By refusing to extend hospitality to the Elder's emissaries and his subsequent spreading of false rumors about the Elder and the other Johannine tradition-bearers, Diotrephes affronted the honor of the Elder and his emissaries (vv. 9–10). Gaius honored the Elder's emissaries by extending hospitality and thus honored the Elder as well – and the Elder commends him for it. The Elder is trying to address this affront to his honor by reinforcing the honor he already has with Gaius and by threatening a face-to-face riposte with Diotrephes (v. 10).

LITERARY AND RHETORICAL GENRES

As a Letter

The Elder refers to the process of writing 3 John with his reference to writing with "pen and ink" (v. 13). Third John conforms in length and content to private letters of the period and probably fit on a standard piece of papyrus that was 8" by 10" or 20 by 25 cm. From the great variety of ancient letters, many have identified 3 John as a letter of recommendation. They assume that the Elder is writing to recommend to Gaius his emissary and carrier of the letter, Demetrius, so that Gaius will extend him hospitality.[4] Such a letter

---

[3] J.-M. Carman, "Scaling Gaius and Diotrophes: Socio-Economic Stratification in 1 and 3 John," *JSNT* 43 (2020): 28–43.

[4] Brown, *Epistles of John*, 748–49; Parsenios, *First, Second, and Third John*, 148–49, 154–55; J. Polhill, "The Setting of 2 John and 3 John," *SBJT* 10(3) (2006): 36–37; Stowers, *Letter Writing*, 156; A. J. Malherbe, "Inhospitality of Diotrephes," in J. Jervell and W. A. Meeks, eds., *God's Christ and His People: Studies in Honour of Nils Alstrup Dahl* (Oslo: Universitetsforlaget, 1977), 222–32; repr. in his *Social Aspects of Early Christianity*, 2nd revised edition (Philadelphia: Fortress, 1983), 92–112.

lessens or eliminates the need for the prospective host to test the suitability of visitors before extending hospitality.[5]

In vv. 5–10 the language of recommendation letters is prominent, particularly of seeking hospitality for the ones carrying the recommendation letter and sending them on to their next stop. The Elder's petition to "send on" (*propempō*) the emissaries (v. 6) refers to sending on a traveler for whom you have extended hospitality to their next destination with moral and material support (Acts 15:2–3; 20:38; 21:5; Rom 15:23–24; 1 Cor 16:6, 11; 2 Cor 1:16; Titus 3:13). The sender often designates the addressee as a "coworker" (*synergoi*) as the Elder does Gaius (v. 8). The sender's request to the recipient is often to "support" (*hypolambanō*) the one sent, which Gaius is asked to do (v. 8). Typically, another verb for "receive" is used (*dechomai* and cognates; Mark 6:11; Acts 15:4; 17:7; 18:27; 21:17; 28:7; Col 4:10), and it appears twice here (*epidechomai*) to describe the negative behavior of Diotrephes in not receiving the Elder's emissaries (vv. 9–10). Concern is expressed that the ones sent will be able to "testify" (*martyreō*) to the one that sent them about that hospitality that was extended, as the Elder's emissaries have done for the gracious Gaius (vv. 3, 6).[6]

However, it is not accurate to label 3 John as primarily a letter of recommendation. Letters of recommendation consistently exhibited three conventions at this time: a short opening and closing, a request to welcome someone, and a promise to repay the favor.[7] These conventions are not present in 3 John. The opening and closing are elaborate, and the Elder does not directly ask Gaius to welcome Demetrius or in any way promise to repay the favor.[8]

Most letters in the Greco-Roman world were mixed letters; that is, they have characteristics of several letters in their more abstracted, pure forms.[9] Third John is just such a private, mixed letter. It has characteristics of the friendly, requesting, advisory or paraenetic, commendatory, praising, encouraging, vituperative, and accusing letters. Friendly letters were usually exchanged between those that were personally acquainted and social equals, but those in a prominent position (perhaps the Elder) could address those subject to their authority (perhaps Gaius) with a friendly letter in an effort to maximize the chances that the recipients will respond as desired.[10] In letters of request there is an entreaty for services and goods (like

---

[5] Malherbe, "Inhospitality of Diotrephes," 277; B. J. Malina, "The Received View and What It Cannot Do: III John and Hospitality," *Semeia* 35 (1986): 187.
[6] Parsenios, *First, Second, and Third John*, 152–56.
[7] White, *Light from Ancient Letters*, 194.
[8] L. Marulli, "A Letter of Recommendation?: A Closer Look at Third John's 'Rhetorical' Argumentation," *Bib* 90 (2009): 204–06.
[9] Ps. Lib. 45, 92; White, *Light from Ancient Letters*, 197–98.
[10] Ps. Dem. 1; Ps. Lib. 11, 58; Stowers, *Letter Writing*, 58–70.

hospitality; vv. 5–8),[11] and friendly letters often lay the basis for a request (like Diotrephes's inhospitality).[12]

An advisory or paraenetic letter steers the recipient toward or away from some action on the basis of honor (e.g., hospitality, v. 5). Its contents contain virtues and vices (hospitality, inhospitality; vv. 5–10), examples held up for imitation or revulsion (Diotrephes versus Demetrius; vv. 9–10, 12), reminders of what the recipient has already done (Gaius's hospitality; vv. 5–8), and justification for the action recommended (emissaries need support; vv. 7–8).[13] A letter of commendation (recommendation, introduction) praises individuals carrying the letter in preparation for a hospitable reception and to aid their work (possibly Demetrius; v. 12).[14] A letter of praise encourages someone for a singular action or virtue (Gaius for hospitality; vv. 5–8).[15] A letter of encouragement praises people to strengthen them to do more of what makes them praiseworthy (Gaius needs encouragement if he is under pressure in any way from Diotrephes; v. 10).[16] In a letter of vituperation, the evil nature of a third party is the focus (Diotrephes's inhospitality; vv. 9–10).[17] A letter of accusation criticizes someone for impropriety (Diotrephes's rebuff of the Elder and his emissaries; vv. 9–10).[18]

As Rhetoric

Third John is primarily epideictic rhetoric, the rhetoric of praise and blame.[19] This is expected since letters of friendship, commendation, praise, vituperation, and accusation are typically epideictic rhetoric by nature.[20] Such rhetoric is intended to increase the audience's adherence to honorable values and virtues it already holds.[21] The Elder praises Gaius for his virtue of

---

[11] Ps. Lib. 7.
[12] Ps. Dem. 1; Stowers, *Letter Writing*, 59.
[13] Ps. Dem. 11; Ps. Lib. 5, 52; Stowers, *Letter Writing*, 94–106.
[14] Ps. Dem. 2; Ps. Lib. 8, 55; Stowers, *Letter Writing*, 153–65; White, *Light from Ancient Letters*, 193–94; B. Olsson, "Structural Analyses in Handbooks for Translators," *BT* 37 (1986): 124–25.
[15] Ps. Dem. 10; Ps. Lib. 30, 77; Stowers, *Letter Writing*, 77–85.
[16] Ps. Lib. 36, 83; cf. Ps. Dem. 10.
[17] Ps. Dem. 9; Stowers, *Letter Writing*, 85–90.
[18] Ps. Dem. 17; Stowers, *Letter Writing*, 166–73.
[19] D. F. Watson, "A Rhetorical Analysis of 3 John: A Study in Epistolary Rhetoric," *CBQ* 51 (1989): 479–501; Marulli, "Letter of Recommendation?" 205.
[20] Stowers, *Letter Writing*, 52, 77.
[21] Some have argued that the letter is deliberative rhetoric (B. L. Campbell, "Honor, Hospitality and Haughtiness: The Contention for Leadership in 3 John," *EvQ* 77 (2005): 329–30), ignoring the fact that the Elder is encouraging Gaius to continue an action, not persuade him to pursue a new one, which is more typical of deliberative rhetoric.

hospitality (vv. 3-8) and blames Diotrephes for his vice of inhospitality and evil words (vv. 9-10). The Elder wants Gaius to hold strongly to hospitality in the face of Diotrephes's inhospitality; that is, to adhere to his current values.

Third John is secondarily deliberative rhetoric, that rhetoric which seeks to persuade or dissuade an audience from a particular course of action. It advocates what is advantageous and expedient and what is not. Here the physical needs of traveling emissaries have to be addressed, and Gaius is praised and Diotrephes blamed in part to ensure that Gaius will continue to meet those needs since Diotrephes will not (vv. 3-12). What epideictic rhetoric praises, deliberative rhetoric advises, and the two support each other (Quintilian, *Inst.* 3.7.28).

The threefold repetition of the vocative "beloved" (*agapete*) in vv. 2, 5, and 11 is an epistolary transition.[22] It divides the letter into three parts: letter opening (vv. 2-4), letter body opening (vv. 5-8), and letter body closing (vv. 11-12). This repetition helps define the *exordium* that obtains audience goodwill and the *narratio* that introduces the situation and the topics to be addressed (vv. 2-4) and the *probatio* that works out the topics introduced in the *exordium* and *narratio* (vv. 5-12), as well as a transition to exhortation within the *probatio* (v. 11).

The following is a comparison of the epistolary and rhetorical outlines of 3 John[23]:

Epistolary Outline	Rhetorical Outline
Letter Opening	
Prescript (v. 1)	
Health Wish (v. 2)	*Exordium* and *Narratio* (vv. 2-4)
Thanksgiving (vv. 3-4)	
Letter Body (vv. 5-12)	*Probatio* (vv. 5-12)
Opening (vv. 5-8)	
Middle (vv. 9-10)	
Closing (vv. 11-12)	
Letter Closing (vv. 13-15)	*Peroratio* (vv. 13-15)
Reference to Writing (v. 13)	
Intended Visit (v. 14)	
Peace Wish, Greetings from Third Parties (v. 15)	

---

[22] White, *Body of the Greek Letter*, 15-16, 41; Funk, "Form and Structure," 429.
[23] For a similar epistolary outline, see J. A. du Rand, "The Structure of 3 John," *Neot* 13 (1979): 121-31; Klauck, *Ancient Letters*, 27-40.

II Suggested Readings on the Letter of 3 John

Find commentaries and works on all of the Johannine Letters in the Suggested Readings for the Letter of 1 John.

S. L. Adams. "An Examination of Prayer in 3 John 2 and the Farewell Discourse in Light of the Mission of God." *Neot* 54 (2020): 187–207.
B. L. Campbell. "Honor, Hospitality and Haughtiness: The Contention for Leadership in 3 John." *EvQ* 77 (2005): 321–41.
J.-M. Carman. "Scaling Gaius and Diotrephes: Socio-economic Stratification in 1 and 3 John." *JSNT* 43 (2020): 28–43.
J. Lieu. *The Second and Third Epistles of John: History and Background*. Edinburgh: T. & T. Clark, 1986.
A. J. Malherbe. "The Inhospitality of Diotrephes." Pp. 222–32 in *God's Christ and His People: Studies in Honour of Nils Alstrup Dahl*. Edited by J. Jervel and W. A. Meeks. Oslo: Universitetsforlaget, 1977. Repr. pp. 92–112 in his *Social Aspects of Early Christianity*. 2nd revised edition (Philadelphia: Fortress, 1983).
B. J. Malina. "The Received View and What It Cannot Do: III John and Hospitality." *Semeia* 35 (1986): 171–94.
L. Marulli. "A Letter of Recommendation? A Closer Look at Third John's 'Rhetorical' Argumentation." *Bib* 90 (2009): 203–23.
M. M. Mitchell. "'Diotrephes Does Not Receive Us': The Lexicographical and Social Context of 3 John 9–10." *JBL* 117 (1998): 299–320.
D. F. Watson. "A Rhetorical Analysis of 3 John: A Study in Epistolary Rhetoric." *CBQ* 51 (1989): 479–501.

III Commentary on the Letter of 3 John

VERSES 1–4: LETTER OPENING

1 The elder to the beloved Gaius, whom I love in truth.
2 Beloved, I pray that all may go well with you and that you may be in good health, just as it is well with your soul.
3 For I was overjoyed when some of the brothers and sisters arrived and testified to your faithfulness to the truth, namely how you walk in the truth.
4 I have no greater joy than this, to hear that my children are walking in the truth.

Verses 1–4 are the letter opening. They describe the relationship between the sender and recipient ("beloved," "love in the truth," vv. 1–2), provide a health wish (*hygiainō*, v. 2), and express joy over news about the welfare of the recipient (*lian echarēn*, vv. 3–4).[1] These verses also constitute the *exordium* and the *narratio*, the former of which seeks to obtain the audience's attention, receptivity, and goodwill, and the latter of which introduces the situation addressed and topics to be discussed.

Verse 1: Letter Prescript

As a prescript, v. 1 names the sender and recipient, and, as in early Christian letters, provides some theological description of them as well. The Elder is a leader of the Johannine Community centered in Ephesus in Asia Minor (Turkey), while Gaius is a member of the house church of Diotrephes or a member or leader of a house church in the vicinity of that church. Gaius was a common name at that time, and this Gaius does not

---

[1] White, *Light from Ancient Letters*, 198–202; Funk, "Form and Structure," 424–28.

need to be identified with three other men named Gaius in the New Testament: Gaius of Corinth (1 Cor 1:14; Rom 16:23), Gaius of Macedonia (Acts 19:29), and Gaius of Derbe (Acts 20:4).

The Elder addresses Gaius as "beloved" (*agapētos*), an address often found in letters between family and friends.[2] This address occurs elsewhere in the letter in the plural to include the members of Gaius's church (vv. 2, 5, 11). The Elder also explicitly describes Gaius as "whom I love in truth." These loving designations are modeled on the relationship between Jesus and God in which Jesus is God's "beloved" (John 3:35; 10:17; 15:9; 17:23), and, through Jesus, Christians are God's beloved as well. If God and Jesus love Christians, then Christians ought to love one another (1 John 3:11, 23; 4:7-21; 2 John 5; John 13:34; 15:12). The Elder is exhibiting his close relationship to and love for Gaius within the Johannine Community.

The Elder loves Gaius "in truth" (*en alētheia*). This statement not only affirms that the Elder genuinely loves Gaius, but that they share a spiritual unity in the truth. To believe in Christ who is the truth (John 14:6) is to enter the realm of truth and to have the truth abide within (1 John 3:18; 2 John 1, 4). The Elder exercises his love of Gaius in the sphere of truth in which all Johannine Christians are united (vv. 3-4, 8, 12).

The letter prescript enhances the relationship between the sender and recipient. Here the honor in which the Elder holds Gaius and their shared Christian life in the truth enhances their bond. The letter prescript also introduces key topics, here being love (vv. 1, 6) and truth (vv. 3-4, 8, 12) in relationship to hospitality.

Verses 2-4: Health Wish and Expression of Joy

These are typically found in the letter opening. Verse 2 constitutes the standard health wish that is often converted to a blessing in early Christian letters (as in 2 John 3). Three key verbs common to the letter tradition are used. The first is "I pray" (*euchomai*), which also means "wish" and expresses the sender's wish for the health and good welfare of the recipient. The second is "to prosper, succeed" (*euodoomai*), and the third is "to be in good physical health" (*hygiainō*). These three verbs, while conventional, do testify to the Elder's affection for Gaius and contribute to building positive pathos or emotion between them.[3] The first (*euchomai*) can be understood

---

[2] White, *Light from Ancient Letters*, 200.
[3] Brown, *Epistles of John*, 703.

as more than wishing, but as praying, so that all of v. 2 is a prayer in league with Johannine tradition that prayer should be in the name of Jesus for his glory and the glory of God (John 14:12–14; 15:7–8). The Elder prays for the good health and prosperity of Gaius because such a prayer when fulfilled will benefit those who will rely on his hospitality for their mission.[4]

Wishing that Gaius's physical health be as good as his soul's health does not distinguish the body and soul as two components of the human person. While such a distinction is found in the New Testament (Matt 10:28), in Johannine thought "soul" (*psychē*) is used of life that can be laid down (John 10:11; 13:37–38; 15:13; 1 John 3:16) as differentiated from eternal life (*zoē*). One example is "Those who love their life (*psychē*) lose it, and those who hate their life (*psychē*) in this world will keep it for eternal life (*zoē*)" (John 12:25). Here in 3 John the comparison is between physical health (*hygiainō*) and life as a whole (*psychē*), both physical and spiritual; that is, life in relationship to God in Christ. The Elder's health wish reflects the belief of that time (and increasingly in our own) that physical health and spiritual health are related (1 Cor 11:27–32; Jas 5:13–16).

As the preposition "for" (*gar*) beginning v. 3 indicates, vv. 3–4 provide the reason why the Elder can affirm that Gaius's soul is well (v. 2) and for his own joy. That reason is that brothers and sisters testified about Gaius's faithfulness to the truth – that he walks in the truth by showing hospitality to the Elder's emissaries (vv. 5–8). An expression of joy was common in ancient private letters as is true of the Johannine Letters (1 John 1:4; 2 John 4; 3 John 3–4). Joy in Christian letters often relates to the spiritual well-being of the church(es) addressed (Rom 16:19; 2 Cor 7:16; Col 2:5; 1 Thess 3:8–9). The joy topic functions rhetorically to build positive pathos or emotion between the Elder and Gaius, and it makes these verses function like the epistolary thanksgiving of ancient letters that is typically found after the health wish.[5]

These brothers and sisters who testify about Gaius may be the emissaries of vv. 5–6 that the Elder had previously sent and to whom Gaius offered hospitality after Diotrephes refused to do so. They may be others of the Johannine Community who knew this situation and/or had also benefited from Gaius's hospitality. The Elder summarizes the friends' testimony as: "your faithfulness to the truth, namely how you walk in the truth." It has

---

[4] S. L. Adams, "An Examination of Prayer in 3 John 2 and the Farewell Discourse in Light of the Mission of God," *Neot* 54 (2020): 187–207.
[5] Funk, *Form and Structure*, 425–26.

been proposed that "your faithfulness to the truth" (lit. "being in the truth") is the actual report received, and "namely how you walk in the truth" is the Elder's independent affirmation of the report.[6] A more precise explanation is that the Elder uses the figure of refining (*expolitio*), in which repetition in a new form adds fuller meaning (Rhet. Her. 2.42.54–44.58). The Elder adds "walking in the truth" to define "faithfulness to the truth" that was reported to him. This refining helps clarify and amplify the positive report received.

"Truth" (*alētheia*) is used in the Johannine Letters for correct Christology as found in Johannine tradition (1 John 2:21–23; 5:20; 2 John 7) or as a principle of behavior (1 John 1:6; 2:4; 3:18–19). It is the revelation of the Father and Son, particularly the love of the Father and the Son (1 John 3:16–18; 4:10–11; 2 John 4). "Walking" (*peripateō*) is a metaphor for the ethical life. Thus "walking in the truth" expresses the ethical life implied in "faithfulness to the truth" (1 John 1:6–7; 2:6, 11; 2 John 4, 6). The Elder is praising Gaius for his ethical behavior exhibited in the truth – extending hospitality to the traveling emissaries. The hospitality and love described in vv. 5–6 illustrate "walking in the truth."

As noted, in v. 4 the Elder notes his joy that the Christians he oversees are walking in the truth (cf. 2 John 4), which builds positive pathos between the Elder and Gaius. He even uses an emphatic, double comparison meaning "more greater" (*meizoteros*) joy (Quintilian, *Inst.* 8.4.9–14). The Elder has had greater joy and now has joy that tops even that! Also working to build a positive relationship, as well as community identity, is the family metaphor. The Elder presents himself as having children (v. 4). "My children" are all those Johannine Christians who respect the Elder as a Johannine tradition-bearer and who adhere to the truth as he teaches it (*teknia*, 1 John 2:1, 12, 28; 37, 18; 4:4, 5:21; *tekna*, 2 John 1, 4; 3 John 4). It does not refer specifically to Gaius or the Elder's own converts. Unlike Paul, who refers to his converts as his children (1 Cor 4:14–15; Gal 4:19; Phil 2:22; Phlm 10), in Johannine theology only God begets Christians – not evangelists (John 1:13; 3:3, 5).[7] The Elder has children in the sense that he guides the children born of God.

---

[6] Brown, *Epistles of John*, 706; Smalley, *1, 2, 3 John*, 347.
[7] Brown, *Epistles of John*, 707; Schnackenburg, *Johannine Epistles*, 293; cf. Painter, *1, 2, 3 John*, 370.

Rhetorical Function as *Exordium* and *Narratio*

In correlation with their epistolary roles, vv. 2–4 have the rhetorical role of *exordium* or introduction.[8] They attempt to elicit goodwill and receptivity from the audience and introduce topics that will be discussed going forward. The *exordium* of epideictic rhetoric, like 3 John, is usually based on praise and blame (Aristotle, *Rhet.* 3.14.1414b.1–1415a.4). Here the Elder praises Gaius by affirming that he is faithful to the truth and twice affirming that he is walking in the truth (*alētheia, alēthēs*, vv. 3–4). This topic is further developed both positively and negatively. Gaius's hospitality for the friends enables the Johannine Christians to work together in truth (vv. 5–8) and is antithetical to the inhospitality of Diotrephes, who also spreads false charges about the Elder and the Johannine tradition-bearers (vv. 9–10). Demetrius, the emissary being sent, received testimony from the truth itself and from the true witness of the Johannine School (v. 12). This last usage of the topic of truth is related to the topic of testifying or witnessing (*martyreō, martyria*) to the truth of someone's life. The friends testified to the truth of Gaius's life (v. 3) and his love (v. 6), while the threefold testimony of everyone, the truth itself and the Johannine tradition-bearers now testify favorably to Demetrius (v. 12).

Verses 3–4, as well as vv. 5–6 to follow, also function somewhat like a rhetorical *narratio*, which describes the situation and the main issue on which the rhetor wants the audience to focus.[9] Epideictic rhetoric, like 3 John, typically does not use a *narratio*, but if it does it should recount actions or deeds that relate to the main issue (Aristotle, *Rhet.* 3.16.1416b.1–3; Rhet. Her. 3.7.13). This is exactly what the Elder is doing in recounting Gaius's hospitality to the Elder's emissaries – hospitality that he wants him to continue to extend. Also, the *narratio* in general should begin with praise of someone on the side of the rhetor (Quintilian, *Inst.* 4.2.129–31), and here the Elder praises Gaius's walk in the truth, hospitality, and love for his emissaries and the church.

VERSES 5–8: THE HOSPITALITY OF GAIUS

5 Beloved, you do faithfully whatever you do for the brothers and sisters, even though they are strangers to you;

---

[8] Watson, "A Rhetorical Analysis of 3 John," 486–91.
[9] Watson, "A Rhetorical Analysis of 3 John," 491–93.

> 6 they have testified to your love before the church. You will do well to send them on in a manner worthy of God;
>
> 7 for they began their journey for the sake of Christ, accepting no support from nonbelievers.
>
> 8 Therefore we ought to support such people, so that we may become coworkers with the truth.

The transitional vocative "beloved" (*agapēte*) in v. 5 indicates a shift to the body opening of the letter (vv. 5–8), which provides a common basis between the sender and recipient (the welfare of the Elder's emissaries), a response to information received (about Gaius), a positive response to an action of the recipient (praise for extending hospitality), a petition using the formula "you will do well" (*kalōs poiein*, provide hospitality), and the main reason for writing (extend more hospitality).[10]

Verses 5–6 form the background for the petition (vv. 5–6a) and the petition itself (v. 6b). The background for the petition is a description of Gaius's past hospitality and the love he showed to the Elder's emissaries. The background of the petition begins with the formula "you do faithfully" (*piston poieis*; lit. "you do a faithful thing"), which is the Christian equivalent of the formula "to do good" (*kalos poiein*) that typically begins the petition in the body opening of a letter.[11] The formula has been Christianized so that the focus is not on good in general, but on being faithful within the tradition of the Johannine Community. Also, the letter opening (vv. 2–4) serves as further background for the petition because it too describes Gaius's faithfulness.[12]

Gaius has already been hospitable to those who have come to him, and they reported this fact to the Elder (v. 6; cf. v. 3). Traveling Christian workers testify to Gaius's truth before the church of the Elder (v. 3) and now testify to his love. Truth and love are interdependent in Johannine theology (1 John 2:3–6; 3:18–19; 4:20–21). Since love is obedience to the highest commandment to love others, Gaius's hospitality and love for the emissaries are outward manifestations of the truth that characterizes his life (vv. 3–4) and why the Elder can affirm that all is well with Gaius's soul (v. 2).

---

[10] White, *Body of the Greek Letter*, 17–25, 39–41; White, *Light from Ancient Letters*, 207–11; Funk, "Form and Structure," 427–28.
[11] Funk, "Form and Structure," 427.
[12] Funk, "Form and Structure," 429.

In the background of the petition the Elder confirms that what Gaius does (lit. "works," *ergazomai*, v. 5) for the emissaries he does (*poieō*) faithfully. This affirmation introduces the important topic of work. Those like Gaius who extend hospitality will become coworkers (*synergoi*) with the truth (v. 8). By contrast, what Diotrephes is doing (lit. his "works," *erga*) includes evil words, refusal to extend hospitality and preventing others from doing the same (v. 10). The work topic culminates in the exhortation to do good (*agathopoieō*) and be from God, and not do evil (*kakopoieō*) having not seen God (v. 11).

The petition of v. 6b is the main issue that the Elder wants Gaius to consider: "you will do well to send them [the Elder's emissaries] on in a manner worthy of God." The formula "you will do well" (*kalōs poiēseis*) is often used in the body opening of a letter to introduce the petition or request pertaining to the main issue that the sender addresses.[13] In the petition, the command "send them on" (*propempō*) has an almost technical sense of providing itinerants you are hosting with supplies that enable them to journey to their next stop (Acts 15:2-3; 20:38; Rom 15:23-24; 1 Cor 16:6, 11; 2 Cor 1:16; Titus 3:13; Polycarp, *Phil.* 1:1). Sending out emissaries is to be done "in a manner worthy of God." This may describe the quality of the preparations that Gaius is to make as he sends the emissaries out. Demetrius is introduced in v. 12, and the Elder intimates that he would like Gaius to extend Demetrius hospitality.

In vv. 7-8 the Elder provides a reason Gaius why should further support the emissaries. He uses an enthymeme, a conclusion with one premise stated and the other premise suppressed. It is the only formal proof in 3 John.

> Premise: The itinerants' journey is for Christ and they accepted no support from nonbelievers (v. 7).
> Unstated premise: Those who journey for Christ and accept no support from nonbelievers should be supported by believers.
> Conclusion: The itinerants ought to receive support from believers (v. 8).

The opening phrase, "they began their journey," is literally "they went out" (*exerchomai*). It is a verb denoting itinerant ministry and indicates that these emissaries who received hospitality from Gaius were itinerant Christian workers. It is the same verb used of the secessionist missionaries

---

[13] Funk, "Form and Structure," 427-28; White, *Light from Ancient Letters*, 208, 211.

who left the Johannine Community (1 John 2:19; 4:1; 2 John 7) and of Paul and Silas in their missionary travels (Acts 14:20; 15:40).

These itinerants have gone out "for the sake of Christ" (lit. "for the sake of the name"). The name can be the name of God or Christ. On the one hand, similar phraseology is used with the name of Christ for evangelism (Rom 1:5) and preaching (Ign., *Eph.* 7.1) and the name of Christ and God separately for inner-church ambassadorship (Ign., *Phld.* 10.1–2). The exact nature of the name given Jesus in missionary practice is unknown. Possibilities include Lord, I AM, Son of Man, and Son of God. The expression "for the sake of the name" is probably rooted in the baptismal formula, "baptized in the name of Jesus" (Acts 8:16; cf. 1 Cor 1:13, 15) or the formula of salvation, "believing in the name" (John 1:12; 3:18; Acts 4:12; cf. John 2:23).[14] On the other hand, in Johannine theology Jesus reveals the name of God (John 5:43; 17:6, 11–12, 26), and this verse follows a reference to supplying hospitality in a manner worthy of God (v. 6). Thus, the reference here is probably to the name of God.[15]

With a cause worthy of hospitality (the name of God or Christ), these emissaries have not accepted support from nonbelievers (lit. "Gentiles") – only from fellow Christians. This may be their practice for several reasons. Jesus taught that those who preach the gospel deserve support from other Christians (Matt 10:5–15; Mark 6:6–13; Luke 10:1–12), and the early Church obeyed that teaching (1 Cor 9:14; 1 Tim 5:18; Did. 13:1). This practice of hospitality keeps the proclamation of the gospel free for the Gentiles. It also keeps Christian proclamation distinct from missionaries of pagan religions and assorted philosophers who charged for their messages and were known to exploit their hosts.

The practice of accepting support only from one's own group may also be part of a very sectarian mindset in the Johannine Community that its members could and should expect support from fellow Johannine Christians. Compare the practice of the Essenes:

> On the arrival of any of the sect from elsewhere, all the resources of the community are put at their disposal, just as if they were their own; and they enter the houses of men whom they have never seen before as though they were their most intimate friends. Consequently, they carry

---

[14] Brown, *Epistles of John*, 711–12.
[15] Lieu, *I, II, & III John*, 271–72; Schnackenburg (*Johannine Epistles*, 295) identifies the referent as Christ. Brown (*Epistles of John*, 712) argues for both the name of Christ and God simultaneously since Jesus is one with God.

nothing whatever with them on their journeys, except arms as a protection against brigands. In every city there is one of the order expressly appointed to attend to strangers, who provides them with raiment and other necessaries. (Josephus, *J.W.* 2.8.4.124–25)

Based on the preceding statement about the emissaries' activity being for the sake of Christ and without support from nonbelievers, in v. 8 the Elder provides a conclusion or implicit exhortation: Gaius and other Johannine Christians ought to support them. He uses the verb "ought" (*opheilō*), which in Johannine literature refers to an obligation of being a Johannine Christian, often to the obligation to love based on the love given by Christ (1 John 3:16; 4:11).

In v. 8b the Elder provides a reason for his conclusion that Gaius and other Johannine Christians should actively support the emissaries: to become coworkers in the truth. The dative "in the truth" can be a dative of advantage meaning "on behalf of" or "in the service of" the truth and refer to Gaius working with the emissaries in the service of the truth. It can also be an associate dative "with" and refer to Gaius working with the truth itself as are the emissaries. The latter is probably meant, for in Johannine thought truth is often personified as working alongside the believer (John 8:32).[16] Also, truth is personified in v. 12 as witnessing to the truth of Demetrius's life.

As its personification indicates, "truth" is not a mere equivalent to the gospel being proclaimed by the emissaries. In Johannine thought, truth is a broad Christological concept. Here in v. 8 truth could refer to Jesus (John 14:6) or the Spirit (1 John 5:6) and/or the revelation in Jesus appropriated by faith. The truth that is Jesus the Christ is appropriated internally by the Christian (1 John 1:8; 2:4; 2 John 2) so that the Spirit of Truth abides in the anointed believer (John 14:17; 1 John 2:20–21, 27) and bears witness to the truth alongside the believer (John 15:26–27).[17] The Elder is exhorting himself and Gaius, and probably their associates as well, of the need to put hospitality into action and demonstrate that they are coworkers with the Truth–Jesus–Spirit (1 John 3:18).

Epideictic rhetoric is used to praise people for their honorable work in order to increase their assent to that work (Aristotle, *Rhet.* 1.3.1358b.5; [*Rhet. Alex.*] 3.1425b.36–39; Cicero, *Inv.* 2.4.12; 2.51.155–56; *Top.* 24.91;

---

[16] Brown, *Epistles of John*, 714; Smalley, *1, 2, 3 John*, 352–53; Lieu, *I, II, & III John*, 273. Contra Bultmann, *Johannine Epistles*, 99.
[17] Brown, *Epistles of John*, 715.

Rhet. Her. 3.6.10). Here Gaius is praised to increase his assent to the value of hospitality that he already holds and as an honorable course of action that makes him a coworker with the truth. With the shift to the first-person plural in v. 8, the Elder includes himself as one who wants to continue to offer hospitality and be a coworker with the truth. He does not stand aloof but shoulder to shoulder with Gaius – a stance with persuasive impact.

VERSES 9–10: THE INHOSPITALITY AND HOSTILITY OF DIOTREPHES

> **9 I have written something to the church, but Diotrephes, who likes to put himself first, does not welcome us.**
>
> **10 So if I come, I will call attention to what he is doing in spreading false charges against us. And not content with those charges, he refuses to welcome the brothers and sisters and even prevents those who want to do so and expels them from the church.**

The letter body middle of 3 John is composed of vv. 9–10. The body middle of a letter both develops topics introduced in the body opening and introduces new and related matters. The body middle is indicated by a reference to writing (using *graphō*, v. 9), a conditional clause using "if" (*ean*), and the subjunctive marking a move to a current or new subject (v. 10).[18] The body middle continues to function rhetorically as the *probatio*, which shares the same functions of developing topics introduced previously and introducing new topics for development. In epideictic rhetoric (like 3 John) the *probatio* uses amplification to develop topics rather than formal proofs (Quintilian, *Inst.* 3.7.1–6), and this portion of 3 John is highly amplified using repetition and amplification by augmentation.[19]

In v. 9 the Elder refers to a letter that he sent with some emissaries to the church led by Diotrephes – a letter Diotrephes did not receive well.[20] It is unlikely to have discussed heretical doctrine as do 1 and 2 John, for no doctrinal issues are raised in 3 John. It is likely to have discussed extending

---

[18] White, *Body of the Greek Letter*, 13–15, 33–35, 38–39, 41.
[19] See Watson, "A Rhetorical Analysis of 3 John," 49–99.
[20] For *ti* ("something"), some manuscripts substitute the particle *an* denoting contingency with the meaning "I would have written" to imply that no letter was ever actually written. Some manuscripts substitute "you have written" (*egrapsas*) to imply that Gaius is the one who wrote the letter. Having a high regard for apostolic authority, scribes probably changed the original in disbelief that an apostolic letter was ignored.

hospitality since that is the issue just elaborated in vv. 3–8. It may have been a letter of recommendation for the emissaries to whom Gaius extended hospitality (v. 10).

The description of Diotrephes as one "who likes to put himself first" is literally "who likes to be first among them." This reference to "among them" implies that Gaius is not a member of the church of Diotrephes. Otherwise, it would read "among you." Also, if Gaius were a member of Diotrephes's church, he would not need the Elder to report of events at that church. Gaius's independence from Diotrephes best explains how he can offer hospitality to the emissaries sent from the Elder in spite of Diotrephes's prohibition of such action (v. 10).

What Are the Dynamics of the Situation?

The NRSV translation "does not accept our authority" is part of a widespread faulty translation. The verb (*epidechomai*) derives from diplomatic contexts and refers to "welcoming" or "receiving" emissaries in a hospitable fashion (cf. v. 10). To receive or reject emissaries is to receive or reject the sender, especially if a letter of recommendation is proffered.[21] However, there is no implication in the verb as to the motive of the action taken. Thus, here in v. 9 the NRSV translation oversteps its bounds to assume that Diotrephes's rejection of the Elder's emissaries is motivated by a rejection of the Elder's authority.[22] The translation should be "does not receive us" as corrected by the updated edition of the NRSV. This translation lacks any surmise about why Diotrephes rejected the Elder's emissaries (v. 10), and the nature of Diotrephes's action rightfully remains speculative.

One possible scenario for Diotrephes's actions is misguided leadership. Perhaps he received instruction from the Elder like that in 2 John to refuse to accept secessionists who lacked a proper Christology. Diotrephes may have been overly cautious, basically putting his church under quarantine until he could sort out the issues.[23] Denying hospitality to the emissaries must have seemed reasonable to his church since expelling members from the church who extended hospitality to the emissaries required community

---

[21] A. J. Malherbe, *Social Aspects of Early Christianity*, revised and enlarged edition (Philadelphia: Fortress, 1983), 106–07.
[22] M. M. Mitchell, "'Diotrephes Does Not Receive Us': The Lexicographical and Social Context of 3 John 9–10," *JBL* 117 (1998): 299–320.
[23] Brown, *Epistles of John*, 738; Painter, *1, 2, 3 John*, 362–63.

action (Matt 18:15–20; 1 Cor 5:1–5). However, this scenario assumes Diotrephes's complete lack of faith in the Elder and the Johannine Community. If Diotrephes were trying to keep his church loyal to Johannine tradition, would he not at least receive and read the letter that the Elder had sent, especially if it is a letter of recommendation (v. 9)? Would he not be able to determine for himself with just a brief theological exchange on the doorstep whether or not the emissaries were faithful Johannine Christians or secessionists? Why would Diotrephes go as far as to speak evil words about the Elder and the Johannine School if he were simply protecting his church from possible corruption through isolation? Diotrephes quarantining his church is not a convincing scenario of interpretation here.

Another scenario is usurping authority. The Elder may have expected Diotrephes to extend hospitality to his emissaries as one of the duties of a church elder (1 Tim 3:2; Titus 1:8), but Diotrephes refused. Perhaps Diotrephes no longer acknowledges the authority of the Elder and the Johannine School and was usurping sole authority over his church. He forbids hospitality by members of his church to cut the bonds with the Johannine Community, for receiving emissaries would only reinforce those bonds. He spreads evil words to further undermine the ethos of the Elder and his compatriots. The verb "does not welcome" (*epidechomai*) is in the present tense, indicating that Diotrephes's negative attitude continues at the time of writing of this letter. Diotrephes dishonors the Elder, his gospel, and his emissaries by withholding hospitality, especially if the Elder sent a letter of recommendation with the emissaries (v. 9).[24] A weakness of this position is that Diotrephes's church would have to be convinced to change leadership, and strongly enough to ignore social conventions and withhold hospitality. Would a leadership change be enough to leave emissaries from the former leadership out in the cold?

A theological scenario is that Diotrephes rejects the Elder's emissaries because he is a leader among the secessionists and is at theological odds with the Elder. Diotrephes is the leader of a former Johannine Church that is now in secession and bears the wrong Christology (1 John 2:18–27; 4:1–3; 2 John 7). He does not recognize the authority of the Elder and the Johannine School, refusing to receive their emissaries and further

---

[24] B. L. Campbell, "Honor, Hospitality and Haughtiness: The Contention for Leadership in 3 John," *EvQ* 77 (2005): 321–41.

undermining their authority.[25] However, if theology was a central issue, why is there no theological discussion in the letter? Why is there no reference to Diotrephes's errant Christology? With the centrality of Christology and ethics in 1 and 2 John related to the same secession, it is strange that the issue in 3 John is hospitality, not theology. The Elder has been trying to communicate with the church of Diotrephes through emissaries, not dismiss it as secessionist.[26]

Some have argued the opposite: that Diotrephes is faithful to the Johannine tradition and the Elder is the secessionist with errant Christology and ethics.[27] If so, why was this letter included in the canon? The overall construction of the history and theology of the Johannine Community understands the Community under the leadership of the Apostle John and the Johannine School as a bulwark against a secessionist understanding. More facets of the Johannine Letters are accounted for in the traditional interpretation than in a reconstruction based on the reverse.

It is reading too much into the situation to conclude that Diotrephes represents the new position of a monarchical bishop that exercised authority over a body of churches – an office emerging in the early second century.[28] If Gaius were nearby, he would attend a house church supervised by the monarchical bishop in the vicinity, who could be Diotrephes, yet he acts independently.

Honor Challenge and Possible Visit

In v. 10 the Elder suggests that he might visit to address the actions of Diotrephes. He is probably referring to visiting Diotrephes's own church. Whether the Elder is really intending to visit is not known. In v. 14 he expresses a wish to visit Gaius, but this is a standard epistolary phrase like "see you later" and does not necessarily imply an actual visit. However, in light of the fact that Diotrephes continues to challenge the honor of the Elder and the Johannine tradition-bearers, it is possible that the Elder plans a visit to redeem his honor in the eyes of Diotrephes's church. This would

---

[25] Painter, *1, 2, 3 John*, 364–65.
[26] Parsenios, *First, Second, and Third John*, 160.
[27] Bultmann, *Johannine Epistles*, 101; Strecker (*Johannine Letters*, 261–63) traces this position through German scholarship: E. Käsemann, "Ketzer und Zeuge," *ZTK* 48 (1951): 292–311.
[28] Schnackenburg (*Johannine Epistles*, 299) sees this episode as indicative of a transition to the monarchical bishop.

be the appropriate action in an honor culture. If he did not redeem his honor, the tradition he upholds would also suffer dishonor.

Diotrephes is doing three things that challenge the Elder's honor: spreading false charges against the Elder and the Johannine tradition-bearers, refusing hospitality to their emissaries, and expelling members of his own house church who extend hospitality to these emissaries. This trio of evil works is listed in an escalating fashion in which each successive evil is more unbelievable than the preceding one. This is amplification by augmentation in which something of a high degree is topped by something of an even higher degree (Quintilian, *Inst.* 8.4.3–9). While disparaging the Elder is not enough, Diotrephes tops that by refusing his emissaries and forbidding anyone else from extending them hospitality. This figure amplifies the evil nature of Diotrephes's actions.[29]

Diotrephes's trio of evil works contrasts the good works of Gaius. The contrast begins in the introduction of the trio when the Elder promises that he will "call attention to what he [Diotrephes] is doing." This is literally "his works that he makes" (*autou ta erga ha poiei*), an expression that contrasts his previous praise of Gaius, "you do faithfully whatever you do" (*piston poieis ho ean ergasē*, v. 5). The contrast continues in the description of Diotrephes's evil work: "spreading false charges against us." "Spreading" (*phlyareō*) is literally "talk nonsense about" and implies that these charges of Diotrephes have no basis in fact. "False charges" (*logoi ponēroi*) is literally "evil words." Spreading false charges is not to walk in the truth. Unlike Diotrephes, Gaius walks in the truth (vv. 3–4), and the emissaries and those who show them hospitality are coworkers with the truth (v. 8).

Epideictic rhetoric favors the topics of the noble–disgraceful and virtue–vice; that is, what is to be praised or blamed (Rhet. Her. 3.6–8). When praising someone, it is most effective to emphasize character and virtuous deeds that are the exercise of that character. The praise should show that the person is one of the few to exercise the virtue, it was exercised for the sake of others, and it had good results (Quintilian, *Inst.* 3.7.15–16). The Elder focuses on Gaius's good character and the virtue of hospitality, that he was the only one to extend it, that he performed it for the sake of strangers, and that it had desired results (vv. 3–8). The Elder focuses on Diotrephes's bad character of the vice of inhospitality, that he worked for himself first, and that it had undesirable results of stranding the emissaries

---

[29] Watson, "A Rhetorical Analysis of 3 John," 496.

(vv. 9-10). This makes a rhetorical contrast of the examples of Gaius and Diotrephes, further amplifying the praise of Gaius and the blame of Diotrephes.

VERSES 11–12: EXHORTATION TO IMITATE GOOD VERSUS EVIL AND A RECOMMENDATION OF DEMETRIUS

> 11 Beloved, do not imitate what is evil, but imitate what is good. Whoever does good is from God; whoever does evil has not seen God.
>
> 12 Everyone has testified favorably about Demetrius, and so has the truth itself. We also testify for him, and you know that our testimony is true.

Verses 11–12 form the letter body closing, as indicated by the transitional vocative "beloved" (*agapete*) that structures the letter (vv. 2, 5), and a responsibility statement of what the recipients should do (v. 11).[30] The latter is the exhortation that often ends a letter. The exhortation draws together the informal comparison of the behavior of Gaius (vv. 5–8) and Diotrephes (vv. 9–10) and anticipates the good example of Demetrius to follow (v. 12). The Elder indirectly asks Gaius to respect his authority and provide hospitality to his emissaries; that is, do what is good and be from God. He asks Gaius to do what he has already praised him for doing and assumes he will continue to do: Walk in the truth (v. 3), do faithfully (v. 5), and do well (v. 6).

The exhortation of v. 11 is rhetorically sophisticated. It has the chiastic order of evil-good-good-evil that amplifies the evil nature of Diotrephes at either end. Also, the repetition of evil allows some refining. We expect "whoever does good is from God" to be followed by "whoever does evil is not from God," but instead find "has not seen God." Johannine thought links love and doing right to being from God, being born of God, and knowing God (1 John 2:29; 3:9–10; 4:7; cf. 4:20). However, *no one*, either good or bad, has ever seen God in any physical sense (John 1:18; 5:37; 6:46; 1 John 4:12, 20). The Elder means that those who believe have seen the Father spiritually through Jesus (John 1:18; 14:9) and those doing evil cannot because they hate the light (John 3:19–21). This exhortation is an outworking of 1 John 3:6: "No one who abides in him sins; no one who sins has either seen him [Jesus] or known him."[31]

---

[30] White, *Body of the Greek Letter*, 7–9, 15–16, 41.
[31] Brown, *Epistles of John*, 721.

In v. 12 the Elder recommends Demetrius to Gaius. Demetrius brought this letter to Gaius and needs hospitality, will be coming in the near future, or is simply an example worthy of imitation. This man is unknown outside this passage. He is not Demetrius the silversmith of Ephesus who opposed Paul (Acts 19:23-27) or Demas (short form of Demetrius) who was coworker of Paul (Col 4:14; 2 Tim 4:10; Phlm 24). He is not one of the missionaries that has already returned to the Elder from Gaius (vv. 3, 5-8). If this were so, Gaius would have no need for the Elder to recommend him since Gaius would already know him. Demetrius is probably an emissary sent from the Elder to the church to which Gaius belongs or to Diotrephes's own church and will have to stay with Gaius because of Diotrephes's hostile attitude. In the New Testament, letters of recommendation accompanied Christians to help ensure they would be received, supported, and heard (Acts 18:27; Rom 16:1-2; 1 Cor 16:3; 2 Cor 3:1; Phil 2:25-30; Col 4:7-9).

To put a finer point on it, we note that letter carriers were designated as such in the letters they carried, and their roles in bringing the letter were specified, whether informing, bringing goods, or representing the sender. This is not the case in 3 John, indicating that Demetrius may not be the letter carrier. Also, he is introduced with the passive voice "everyone has testified" (*martyreō*) which is how the New Testament introduces people worthy of imitation, not bearers of letters in need of hospitality. Demetrius may simply be a praiseworthy individual known to Gaius.[32] It has been proposed that Demetrius may be an expelled member of Diotrephes's church to whose welfare the Elder is asking Gaius to attend.[33] However, if Demetrius were a member of Diotrephes's church, he would have his own lodging nearby and not need hospitality.

Three sources testify favorably to Demetrius, a number that fulfills the rhetorical use of threes for emphasis and the Jewish use of two or three witnesses to verify the truth (Deut 19:15; 1 John 5:7-8). First, it is from "everyone," that is all those who are in fellowship (*koinonia*) with the Elder and the Johannine tradition-bearers (1 John 1:3) and know Demetrius, including the church from which the Elder is writing. Second, testimony is "from the truth itself." Truth is personified as giving testimony that

---

[32] Lieu, *Second and Third Epistles of John*, 117-19; Lieu, *I, II, & III John*, 279-81; Marulli, "Letter of Recommendation," 206-07.

[33] I. Lorencin, "Hospitality versus Patronage: An Investigation of Social Dynamics in the Third Epistle of John," *AUSS* 46 (2008): 173-74.

Demetrius lives according to its direction. It is the truth that abides in Christians (2 John 2) and to which Christians belong (1 John 3:19). It is a truth about Jesus that has been imputed through faith and manifests itself in the ethical walk, especially in love (1 John 3:18–19; 2 John 4; 3 John 3–6). Third, testimony is from those whose "testimony is true"; that is, the Elder and the Johannine tradition-bearers. It is not the object of the testimony that is stressed to be true – the life of Demetrius – but the source of the testimony that is true – the testimony of the Johannine tradition-bearers. This testimony is to the truth received from John the Apostle (1 John 1:1–3; John 19:35; 21:24). Earlier in the letter the friends testified to the truth and the love of Gaius (vv. 3, 6). Now three witnesses testify to the truth and love of Demetrius. In other words, Demetrius, like Gaius, is a true Johannine Christian in his theology and ethics.

VERSES 13–14: LETTER CLOSING

13 I have much to write to you, but I would rather not write with pen and ink;

14 instead I hope to see you soon, and we will talk together face to face.

Verses 13–14 constitute the letter closing, which gives a reference to writing and other things better discussed in person (v. 12) and a notification of a coming visit (v. 13; 2 John 12).[34] The reference to a visit is conventional and no real visit may be planned soon or otherwise. However, early letters do not use the idiom "face to face" (*stoma pros stoma*) to express this convention, but a similar form (*stoma kata stoma*) is found in Num 12:8 (LXX), where God describes Moses as having spoken directly with God, seeing God's glory (cf. 3 John 11). By using this idiom, the Elder may be insinuating that he will visit to deliver God's words in person, thus providing strong rhetorical and theological constraints to continue to recognize the authority and teachings of the Johannine tradition-bearers.[35]

In addition, in light of the honor challenge that Diotrephes has posed by not accepting the Elder's authority or his emissaries, it is quite possible that the Elder plans a visit to restore his honor – and soon (cf. 2 Cor 12:14; 12:20–13:4). A visit to call attention to what Diotrephes is doing is alluded

---

[34] White, *Light from Ancient Letters*, 202.
[35] Beasley, "Translating 2 John 12 and 3 John 14," 259–64.

to earlier (v. 10). In this period, if an honor challenge was not met, there is permanent dishonor for the one challenged and the tradition he or she upholds. Not only is the honor of the Elder challenged, but also of all the Johannine tradition-bearers (v. 12).

The letter closing functions rhetorically as a *peroratio* that recapitulates main topics previously discussed and appeals to the audience's emotion.[36] The *peroratio* of epideictic rhetoric is truncated because the amplification found throughout the rhetoric makes both recapitulation and emotional appeal superfluous at the conclusion (Rhet. Her. 3.8.15). This is true in 3 John, which is highly amplified throughout, but not in the conclusion, which contains epistolary conventions that are formulaic and concise with little appeal to the emotions.

VERSE 15: LETTER POSTSCRIPT

15 Peace to you. The friends send you their greetings. Greet the friends there, each by name.

The letter postscript contains typical closing greetings (*aspazomai*), including extension of greetings from a third party and the request to extend greetings to others, each by name,[37] as well as the typical Christian addition of a benediction in the form of a peace wish. A peace wish and expressions of peace, often in benedictions as here, normally close Jewish and Pauline letters (Rom 16:20; 2 Cor 13:11; Gal 6:16; Eph 6:23; Phil 4:9; 1 Thess 5:23; 2 Thess 3:16; 1 Pet 5:14). Besides being typical of letter closings, this peace wish is probably influenced by Johannine tradition that included the risen Christ's greeting to his disciples, "Peace be with you" (John 20:19, 21, 26; cf. John 14:27).

"Friends" (*philoi*) used here and "beloved" (*agapetoi*) used earlier (vv. 2, 5, 11) are theological designations meaning "those loved by God." This love cannot be limited just to God, for love also comes from others in the Johannine Community who love other Christians as God loves them (John 15:12–15; 1 John 4:11). As Gaius is "beloved" (*agapetoi*, vv. 2, 5, 11), so is a group of faithful friends of the Elder and Gaius. Gaius is to extend greetings to all the friends in his church individually by name, which would be a realistic request for a member of a small house church.

---

[36] Watson, "A Rhetorical Analysis of 3 John," 499–500.
[37] White, *Light from Ancient Letters*, 202.

A CLOSER LOOK: THE VIRTUE OF HOSPITALITY

Hospitality was a virtue in the Greco-Roman world. While there was lodging of varying quality available for travelers, it was often not clean or safe. Bed bugs, prostitution, and theft were common. It was expected that travelers who came to your home late in the day would be fed, housed overnight, and given enough food to get to the next stop on their journey. Homeowners became temporary patrons and travelers became temporary clients under their protection. There were social norms in place to test the suitability of the stranger to be a guest and expectations for both host and guest to meet to maintain the honor of both. Disregarding these expectations and affronting the honor of either host or guest resulted in the two becoming enemies of one another.

The early church considered hospitality to fellow Christians to be a virtue and expression of mutual love (Rom 12:9-13; Heb 13:1-2; 1 Clem. 10-12; Clement of Alexandria, *Strom.* 2.9). It expected hospitality for its traveling evangelists, teachers, and prophets (Matt 25:35; Acts 16:14-15; Rom 12:13; 15:23-24; 16:1-2; 1 Tim 3:2; 5:9-10; Titus 1:8; 3:13; Heb 13:2; 1 Pet 4:9; 3 John 5-8; 1 Clem. 1.2; 10.7; 11.1; 12.1; Did. 11-13; Herm. Mand. 8.10; Herm. Sim. 8.10.3; 9.27.2).[38] Such hospitality was rooted in Jewish practice and in Jesus's practice of sending out his own disciples in mission and expecting them to rely on hospitality (Mark 6:10-11; Luke 10:1-12). Christians were to receive travelers as they would Jesus himself (Matt 10:40; Mark 9:37).

This custom of hospitality could be abused by travelers staying too long or by misrepresenting who sent them, so the early church created guidelines (Did. 11-13). Letters of recommendation, some elements of which are contained in 3 John, directly addressed the problem by informing the potential hosts about the legitimacy of the one seeking hospitality.

---

[38] B. J. Malina, "The Received View and What It Cannot Do: III John and Hospitality," *Semeia* 35 (1986): 171-94, esp. 181-87.

BRIDGING THE HORIZONS

At first read, it does not seem that there are any natural bridges from 3 John to the present. How does a conflict between two church leaders over extension of hospitality to the emissaries of the one by the other provide us with guidance today? There is also a lack of apparent theological or ethical direction, except to extend hospitality in ways foreign to our culture (if not simply dangerous). Nonetheless, we can build some abutments for our bridge.

The conflict in 3 John offers us examples of leadership. Whatever his motives, Diotrephes offers a negative example of leadership. He did not provide for the physical needs of Christians sent to him by a well-known colleague (probably even with a letter of recommendation), dictated how Christians under his leadership were to respond to these visitors, and continuously vilified the Elder. Whatever the precise nature of the dispute, Diotrephes lacked compassion, limited rather than guided those in his spiritual charge, and bad-mouthed his colleague. He demanded that those he led neglect the needs of others. He did not give them the freedom to decide for themselves what their Christian response should be. Diotrephes dishonored the Elder, his emissaries, and the message they brought from him without giving them a hearing.

As a positive example of leadership, Gaius was willing to provide for the needs of those sent by the Elder. As such, he honored the Elder, his emissaries, and the message they brought from him. Gaius illustrates walking in the truth, assessing the situation and acting according to the love commandment that especially governed the Johannine Community. His actions are born out of a continuous attempt to be obedient to the truth in word and deed. This was a spiritual approach that has come to characterize his life.

The Elder also provides a model of leadership. He is aware that the rejection of his emissaries is also a rejection of himself and his message. He, his colleagues, and his message have been dishonored. While we do not live in an honor culture, vestiges of it are still in place. Sometimes leaders have to defend themselves because what they stand for is so closely associated with their own personhood. False personal accusations need to be addressed or the message is tarnished. True accusations need to be addressed as well for the same reason.

As a leader, the Elder also affirms the right behavior of Gaius and encourages him to exhibit more in the future. Unlike Diotrephes, he leads Gaius without restricting how he must respond. He is an encouraging and guiding leader rather than a dictatorial one.

Also, the Elder does not reciprocate the vilification of Diotrephes. He only describes his actions and only insinuates that his actions are evil. He sets an example that defending ourselves does not mean we have to stoop to the level of those trying to bring us down.

Theologically the letter upholds the truth that is Jesus Christ, his teaching, his example, and the truth given by Spirit in the Christian life. Gaius is praised for his faithfulness to the truth and walking in the truth (vv. 3–4) and encouraged to offer hospitality as a way to be a coworker with the truth (v. 8). It is a truth that can testify to the believer through the Holy Spirit and is upheld by faithful adherence to tradition (v. 12).

Index of Greek and Roman Rhetorical Handbooks

Aristotle
[Rhetorica ad Alexandrum]
  1.1421b.21ff, 167
  3, 9, 28, 68, 81
  3.1425b.36–39, 195
  3.1426b.17ff, 28
  5.1427b.31ff, 11
  6.1428a.1ff, 28, 81
  12, 44, 99
  12.1430b.30ff, 68
  13, 31, 42, 82
  20.1433b.30ff, 142
  29.1437b.33ff, 18
  33.1439b.12ff, 142
  34.1440a.5ff, 29, 42
  34.1440a.20ff, 67
  34.1440a.21–25, 82
  35, 9
  36.1443b.25ff, 29, 31
  36.1444b.21ff, 142
Rhetorica
  1.2.1356a.3–4, 8
  1.2.1356a.4, 18
  1.2.1356b.8, 8
  1.2.1357b.16–17, 44, 99
  1.3.1358b.5, 167, 195
  1.8.1366a.6, 8
  1.9, 9, 28
  1.9.1367b.30–31, 67
  1.9.1367b.35–1368a.37, 28, 82
  1.9.1368a.36–37, 62
  1.9.1368a.38–40, 10, 28, 68, 81
  1.9.1368a.40, 28
  2.1.1377b.1–1378a.7, 96
  2.18.1392a.5, 28, 81
  2.22.1396a.8, 28, 63
  2.23.1400b.30, 63
  2.25.1402a.1–1402b.7, 31, 42
  2.26.1403a.3–4, 31, 42
  3.9.1410a.8, 81
  3.14.1414b.1–1415a.4, 18, 191
  3.14.1415a.7, 18
  3.16.1416b.1–3, 191
  3.17.1417b.3, 27, 28, 68, 81
  3.17.1418a.11–1418b.12, 27, 50, 82
  3.17.1418b.13, 63
  3.17.1418b.13–15, 29, 31
  3.17.1418b.14, 31, 42
  3.17.1418b.15, 29
  3.19, 142

Cicero
De oratore
  2.19.80, 57
  2.43.182, 96
  2.43.182–84, 8
  2.53.215, 31, 42
  2.77.311–12, 57
  2.84–85, 28
  3.40.60–61, 100
  3.53.203, 97, 100
  3.54.207, 97
De Inventione rhetorica
  1.9.12, 12
  1.15.21, 18
  1.16.22, 72
  1.30.48, 68, 131
  1.31–41, 8
  1.42.78, 29
  1.42.79, 31, 42
  1.42.79–43.80, 82
  1.51.97, 57
  1.52–56, 142
  1.53.89–90, 82
  2.4.12, 167, 195

208

Index of Greek and Roman Rhetorical Handbooks

2.51.155-56, 195
2.51.155-58.176, 167
Orator ad M. Brutum
  4.12, 28
  11.37, 62, 82
  12.38, 28, 63, 82
  37.128, 8
  39.135, 85
  40.137, 97, 100
  40.138, 90
Partitiones oratoriae
  12.44, 29, 31, 42, 82
  13.47, 72, 129
  15.54, 46, 69, 72, 83
  16.55-56, 75
  17.58, 28
  21-23, 28
  21.71, 28, 68, 81
  21.72, 10
  24.83-87, 167
Topica
  8, 72
  24.91, 167, 195
Demetrius
  De elocutione
    2.78, 100
    4.211-14, 59
    4.214, 60
Longinus
  De sublimitate
    12.2, 64
    23.1, 59
    32.5, 100
Quintilian
  Institutio oratoria
    3.4.6-9, 10
    3.4.16, 11
    3.7, 9
    3.7.1-6, 196
    3.7.4-6, 27, 62
    3.7.6, 28, 68
    3.7.15-16, 200
    3.7.28, 11, 185
    3.8.1-6, 167
    3.8.12-14, 10
    3.8.22-35, 167
    3.9.7, 27
    4.1.7, 18
    4.1.20-22, 84
    4.1.23-27, 21

4.1.49, 49
4.1.62, 18
4.2.54, 27
4.2.79, 27
4.2.129-31, 191
4.3.12-17, 57
4.4.1, 27
4.5.1-28, 27
5.1-14, 27
5.1.7, 136
5.9.2-7, 44
5.9.3-7, 47
5.10.1-8, 51
5.10.2, 9
5.11.3-5, 129
5.11.5, 72
5.11.36, 22
5.11.36-44, 68
5.11.37, 131
5.11.42-44, 131
5.12.9, 18
5.12.12, 69
5.13.11-15, 29
5.13.15, 82
5.13.15-16, 31, 42
5.13.16, 31, 42
5.13.27, 29
5.13.28, 29, 31, 42
5.14.2, 9
5.14.5-24, 51
6.1, 142
6.2.11, 96
6.2.21, 96
6.2.24, 96
7.4.1-3, 11
8.4.3-9, 72, 137, 200
8.4.9-14, 190
8.4.26-27, 64
8.6.6, 100
8.6.19, 35
9.1.29, 97, 100
9.1.35, 97
9.2.6-16, 72
9.2.7, 97, 100
9.2.14, 97
9.2.16-18, 49
9.2.26-27, 69, 85
9.3.23, 85
9.3.23-26, 22
9.3.28, 59

Quintilian (cont.)
    9.3.28–29, 132
    9.3.65, 132
    9.3.66–75, 132
    9.3.67, 132
    9.3.68, 49
    9.3.69, 132
    9.3.82, 132
    9.3.90, 97
    9.3.97, 69, 85
    9.3.98, 100
Rhetorica ad Herennium
    1.5.8, 72
    2.18.28–29.46, 63
    2.30–31, 142
    2.42.54-44.58, 190
    3.2.3-5.9, 167
    3.6–8, 9, 28, 200
    3.6.10, 196
    3.6.11–12, 18

    3.7.13, 27, 191
    3.8.15, 28, 68, 204
    4.13.19, 137, 146
    4.14.21, 49
    4.15.22, 69, 85, 100
    4.15.22–16.24, 72
    4.21.29–23.32, 132
    4.23.33–24.34, 72
    4.25.35, 64
    4.26.36, 49
    4.28.38, 59, 132
    4.34.45, 100
    4.35.47, 58
    4.38.50, 97
    4.42.54, 34, 44, 47, 92, 113, 117, 126, 129, 132
    4.42.54–44.58, 168
    4.43.56, 45, 73, 76, 83, 87, 103, 123, 144
    4.43.56–44.58, 99
    4.45.58, 81

Index of Deuterocanonical and Early Christian Writings

1 Enoch
  22:13, 122
  22:4, 122
  45:6, 122
  98:8, 122
  100:4, 122
  100:11, 136
1QH
  4.9–11, 148
  4.15, 148
1QS
  1.18–2.25, 39
  3.3–4, 39
  3.11–12, 39
  3.13–4.26, 113
  3.17–22, 39
  3.18–21, 108
2 Baruch
  36–40, 77
2 Clement
  6.7, 123
  16.3, 122
3 Maccabees
  6:18, 148
4 Ezra
  7:112–15, 122
Apocalypse of Abraham
  24:5, 97
Barnabas
  19:10, 122
CD
  20.14–15, 73
Clement of Alexandria
  Stromateis
    2.9, 205
Didache
  1–7, 39

  11.1–2, 174
  11.6–8, 108
  11–13, 205
  13.1, 194
  16.3, 109
  16.4, 75
Diognetus
  9.2, 123
Eusebius
  Historia ecclesiastica
    3.39.4, 155
    3.39.5–7, 155
Gregory of Nazianzus
  Oratio in laudem Basilii
    39.14, 20
Ignatius
  To the Ephesians
    2.2, 155
    4.1, 155
    7.1, 174, 194
    9.1, 174
  To the Magnesians
    2.1, 155
  To the Philadelphians
    7.1–2, 108
    10.1–2, 194
  To the Smyrnaeans
    4.1, 174
    7.1–2, 174
    8.1, 155
  To the Trallians
    opening formula, 162
    2.2, 155
    13.2, 155
Irenaeus
  Adversus haereses
    1.26.1–2, 135

Irenaeus (cont.)
    3.11.2–3, 135
    5.1.1, 20
Josephus
   Jewish Antiquities
    1.52–59, 97
    8.343, 148
   Jewish War
    2.8.4.124–25, 195
Philo
   On the Embassy of Gaius
    366, 148
   Questions and Answers on Genesis
    1.59, 97
   On the Special Laws
    1.332, 148
Polycarp
   To the Philippians
    1:1, 193
    9:1, 20
Psalms of Solomon
    15:12, 122

Shepherd of Hermas
   Mandates
    8.10, 205
    11.7, 108
   Similitudes
    8.10.3, 205
    9.18.1, 123
    9.27.2, 205
   Visions
    3.9.1, 162
Testament of Benjamin
    7:3–5, 97
Testament of Judah
    14:8, 113
    19:4, 113
    20:1, 113
    20:1–2, 108
    23:1, 113
    25:3, 113
Testament of Moses
    8, 77

Index of Scripture and the Apocrypha

Old Testament
  Genesis
    1:26, 87
    3:5, 87
    4:1–16, 96
    8:21, 37
    31:45–50, 136
    32:29, 104
  Exodus
    10:9, 58
    19:10–11, 88
    20:4, 149
    32:11–14, 145
    32:30–34, 145
    33:19, 104
    34:8–9, 145
  Leviticus
    12, 140
    16, 39
    17:11, 35
    19:4, 149
    19:14, 53
    19:18, 50
  Numbers
    8:21, 88
    12:8, 175, 203
    19:12, 88
  Deuteronomy
    4:28, 149
    4:33, 149
    4:36, 149
    7:9, 36
    13:1–5, 108
    17:6, 135
    18:15–22, 108
    19:15, 135, 202
    27:15, 149
    31:28, 136
    32:4, 36
  Joshua
    6:21, 58
    24:7, 20
  1 Samuel
    12:20, 102
    24:5, 102
    25:25, 104
  1 Kings
    8:46, 37
    22:22–23, 108
  2 Chronicles
    15:1, 108
  Job
    15:14–16, 37
    36:10–12, 43
  Psalms
    1:1, 34
    11:7, 87
    15:2, 34
    17:15, 87
    24:4, 102
    27:1, 32
    32:5, 36
    33:5, 36
    34:11, 37
    36:9, 32
    89:1–4, 36
    104:2, 32, 34
    115:3–8, 149
    115:4, 149
    135:15, 149
    135:15–18, 149
    145:17, 36
  Proverbs
    4:10, 37

Index of Scripture and the Apocrypha

Old Testament (cont.)
    5:1, 37
    5:15–18, 140
    7:24, 37
    20:9, 37
Song of Songs
    4:12–15, 140
Isaiah
    1:3–4, 43
    2:5, 34
    2:8, 149
    5:11–13, 43
    10:17, 32
    17:7–8, 149
    20:4, 58
    53: 4, 89
    53:11–12, 89
    53:6, 37
    60:19–20, 32
    61:1–2, 108
    64:6, 37
    65:16, 148
Jeremiah
    6:26, 48
    7:16–20, 146
    9:6, 43
    10:1–16, 149
    10:5, 149
    10:10, 149
    10:14, 149
    11:14, 146
    14:11–12, 146
    14:13–16, 108
    31:20, 48
    31:33–34, 43
    31:34, 36
Ezekiel
    2:2, 108
    9:6, 58
Daniel
    2:2, 34
    5:23, 149
    11:36, 77
Hosea
    4:1–2, 43
Joel
    3:4, 122
Amos
    2:10–11, 20

Micah
    3:8, 108
    5:13, 149
    7:8, 32
    7:18–20, 36
Habakkuk
    2:14, 43
Zechariah
    7:12, 108
Apocrypha
Tobit
    4:3, 37
    12, 37
    13, 37
Sirach
    2:1, 37
    3:1, 37
2 Maccabees
    12:6, 36
New Testament
Matthew
    5:8, 87
    5:12, 172
    5:37, 61
    5:48, 46
    6:2–4, 101
    6:13, 61
    7:7–11, 144
    7:15–23, 109
    7:21, 65
    10:5–15, 194
    10:14–15, 174
    10:15, 122
    10:28, 189
    10:32–33, 73
    10:40, 205
    10:41–42, 172
    11:22, 122
    11:24, 122
    11:27, 43
    11:30, 128
    12:36–37, 122
    13:13–15, 53
    13:19, 61
    13:36–43, 122
    13:38–39, 61
    16:22, 39
    16:23, 53
    18:7, 53

Index of Scripture and the Apocrypha

18:15–20, 198
18:16, 135
18:17, 174
18:19, 103
19:21, 46
21:22, 103
22:34–40, 125
23:35, 97
24:3, 83
24:3–5, 171
24:4–5, 73, 171
24:11, 75, 109, 171
24:24, 75, 109, 171
25:35, 205
25:46, 123
27:4, 139
27:6, 139
27:8, 139
27:24–25, 139
Mark
  1:5, 36
  1:8, 139
  6:6–13, 194
  6:10–11, 205
  6:11, 183
  8:38, 82
  9:37, 205
  9:41, 172
  10:21, 101
  10:23–27, 64
  11:24, 144
  12:28–34, 125
  13:5–6, 75, 171
  13:21–22, 109
  13:21–23, 171
  13:22, 75
  13:33, 171
Luke
  3:11, 101
  6:24, 64
  10:1–12, 194, 205
  10:10–12, 174
  10:22, 43
  11:9–13, 144
  11:22, 61
  12:13–21, 64
  12:32–34, 64
  12:33, 101
  16:15, 102

16:19–31, 64
18:13, 39
21:8, 171
John
  1:1, 18, 23, 38
  1:4–5, 33
  1:49, 131
  1:4–9, 32
  1:7–9, 33
  1:9, 32, 51
  1:11, 140
  1:12, 86, 143, 194
  1:12–13, 52, 126
  1:13, 190
  1:14, 18, 20, 23, 87, 110, 117, 146, 156
  1:14–17, 164
  1:15, 131, 170
  1:17, 34
  1:18, 87, 117, 118, 146, 201
  1:19, 31
  1:26, 139
  1:27, 131, 170
  1:29, 65, 89
  1:29–31, 91
  1:29–34, 133, 136
  1:31, 83, 139
  1:34, 131
  1:36, 89
  1:49, 131
  2:4, 69
  2:11, 23, 87
  2:23, 143, 194
  3:1–10, 93
  3:3, 190
  3:5, 134, 190
  3:6, 64
  3:13, 119
  3:14, 25
  3:14–16, 120
  3:15–16, 138
  3:16, 25, 45, 65, 75, 85, 107, 117, 146
  3:16–17, 65, 116, 117, 120
  3:17, 119
  3:17–21, 84
  3:18, 6, 104, 117, 146, 194
  3:19, 32, 65
  3:19–21, 32, 33, 51, 173, 201
  3:20–21, 34
  3:21, 23

New Testament (cont.)
   3:29, 175
   3:31, 112, 170
   3:31–32, 20
   3:31–33, 136
   3:33, 137
   3:34, 86
   3:35, 188
   3:36, 74, 75, 120, 138
   4:13–14, 164
   4:14, 120
   4:19, 131
   4:21, 68
   4:23, 68
   4:25, 33
   4:42, 65, 119, 131
   5:14, 38
   5:18–19, 147
   5:23, 73
   5:24, 6, 25, 75, 84, 99, 146, 150
   5:25, 68
   5:25–29, 69
   5:28, 68
   5:30, 147
   5:31–38, 136
   5:31–40, 135, 137
   5:37, 87, 118, 201
   5:43, 140, 194
   6:14, 170
   6:33, 65
   6:35, 25
   6:36, 90
   6:39–40, 69, 87
   6:40, 25, 75
   6:44, 69, 87
   6:46, 87, 118, 201
   6:47, 25, 74, 75
   6:48, 25
   6:50, 99, 131
   6:50–51, 25
   6:51, 65, 110, 164
   6:54, 69, 87
   6:56, 54, 92
   6:57–58, 117
   6:58, 131, 164
   6:63, 64
   6:66–67, 70
   6:68, 25
   6:69, 71, 88, 121, 131
   6:70, 61, 163

   7:4, 23
   7:7, 65, 173
   7:18, 5, 89
   7:28, 147
   7:30, 69
   7:40, 131
   7:41, 131
   8:12, 25, 32, 33, 34, 49, 52, 65
   8:17–18, 135
   8:18, 136
   8:19, 73, 90
   8:20, 69
   8:26–27, 112
   8:28–29, 103
   8:31, 74
   8:31–32, 37, 121, 164
   8:32, 195
   8:42, 156, 171
   8:44, 37, 61, 62, 72, 73, 91, 147
   8:46, 6
   8:47, 70, 112
   8:50, 5
   8:51, 65
   8:51–52, 26, 164
   8:55, 73
   9:3, 23
   9:22, 36
   9:39, 65, 120
   9:41, 35
   10:10, 25, 74, 75
   10:11, 189
   10:11–18, 100
   10:17, 188
   10:18, 44, 55
   10:26, 70
   10:28, 74, 75, 86, 146
   10:28–29, 164
   10:30, 73, 147
   10:38, 121, 136, 147
   11:9–10, 33, 34, 53
   11:24, 69
   11:25, 25, 117
   11:25–26, 25, 99
   11:26, 164
   11:27, 131, 170
   11:40, 5
   11:52, 86
   12:13, 131, 170
   12:23, 69
   12:25, 189

12:25-26, 26
12:27, 69
12:31, 61, 62, 65, 111, 129, 130, 147
12:35-36, 32, 33, 34, 53
12:37-46, 90
12:38-40, 53
12:41, 87
12:42, 36
12:44-45, 73
12:45, 87, 118
12:46, 32, 33, 52, 65
12:47, 65, 119
12:48, 69
12:49-50, 33, 44, 55
13:1, 69
13:2, 61
13:3, 156, 171
13:10, 6
13:14, 100
13:15, 47
13:18, 163
13:23, 48
13:27, 61
13:30-31, 70
13:33, 37
13:34, 44, 47, 48, 49, 50, 51, 55, 86, 104, 125, 163, 167, 188
13:34-35, 6, 55, 96, 101, 116, 163, 166, 174, 177
13:37-38, 189
14:6, 25, 34, 148, 188, 195
14:6-7, 147
14:6-11, 24, 73
14:7, 90
14:7-10, 121
14:8-9, 87
14:9, 5, 22, 87, 201
14:12-14, 189
14:13-14, 103, 144
14:15, 6, 44, 45, 55, 128
14:15-17, 9, 54, 105, 164
14:16, 38, 164
14:16-17, 71
14:17, 45, 54, 65, 76, 113, 135, 195
14:19, 117
14:21, 44, 45, 55, 128
14:23-24, 128
14:24-26, 38
14:26, 33, 76
14:27, 164, 177, 204

14:30, 61, 62, 65, 111, 129, 147
14:31, 44, 55, 128
15:1-10, 74
15:1-11, 92
15:4, 75
15:4-7, 54
15:7, 74, 75, 92, 103, 144
15:7-8, 189
15:9, 188
15:10, 6, 44, 45, 55, 128
15:10-12, 48, 55, 168
15:12, 6, 44, 47, 48, 50, 51, 55, 56, 96, 101, 104, 116, 125, 163, 166, 167, 188
15:12-15, 204
15:13, 189
15:16, 124, 144, 163
15:16-17, 103
15:17, 6, 47, 50, 55, 96, 101, 104, 116, 125, 166
15:18-19, 101, 117
15:18-21, 86
15:18-25, 98
15:19, 65, 66
15:22, 35
15:23, 73
15:24, 35
15:26, 71, 76, 113, 135, 137
15:26-27, 9, 19, 20, 38, 135, 195
15:27, 23
16:1-4a, 98
16:2, 65
16:3, 73, 86
16:5-15, 38
16:8-10, 93
16:8-11, 90
16:8-9, 37
16:11, 61, 65, 108, 111, 130, 147
16:12, 137
16:12-15, 71, 76
16:13, 9, 113, 135, 164
16:13-15, 33
16:23-24, 144
16:23-26, 103
16:24, 175
16:25, 68
16:28, 109, 140
16:33, 61, 65, 112, 128, 129, 164, 177
17:1, 69
17:2-3, 26, 75
17:3, 22, 43, 44, 73, 74, 147

New Testament (cont.)
   17:5, 5, 87
   17:6, 194
   17:6–9, 146
   17:7, 147
   17:8, 121
   17:10–11, 22
   17:11–12, 146, 194
   17:13, 175
   17:14, 65, 101, 109, 117
   17:14–16, 98, 147
   17:14–19, 66
   17:15, 61, 146
   17:15–16, 61, 62
   17:17, 88, 147
   17:18, 65, 109
   17:19, 88
   17:20–21, 24
   17:20–23, 74
   17:21, 22, 47
   17:22, 87
   17:22–23, 75
   17:23, 188
   17:24, 5, 87, 118
   17:25, 147
   17:26, 194
   18:37, 70, 72, 112
   19:11, 35
   19:26, 48
   19:34, 133, 134, 139, 140
   19:35, 90, 203
   20:19, 164, 177, 204
   20:21, 164, 177, 204
   20:22–23, 6
   20:26, 164, 177, 204
   20:26–29, 20
   20:29, 90
   20:31, 25, 72, 127, 138, 142
   21:1, 24
   21:14, 24
   21:17, 103
   21:20, 48
   21:24, 135, 156, 203
Acts
   1:5, 139
   2:17, 59
   2:20, 122
   2:37, 102
   4:12, 194
   5:28, 139

   7:41, 149
   8:16, 194
   11:16, 139
   11:30, 155
   14:15, 148
   14:20, 194
   14:23, 155
   15:1–6, 155
   15:2–3, 183, 193
   15:4, 183
   15:22–23, 155
   15:40, 194
   16:14–15, 205
   17:7, 183
   18:27, 183, 202
   19:18, 36
   19:23–27, 202
   19:29, 181, 188
   20:3, 193
   20:4, 181, 188
   20:17, 155
   20:38, 183
   21:5, 183
   21:17, 183
   26:18, 39
   28:7, 183
   28:25–27, 53
Romans
   1:5, 194
   1:8, 166
   3:3–4, 36
   3:21–26, 39
   3:22–24, 37
   3:25, 35, 39
   5:15, 59
   6, 38
   6:4, 34
   8:4, 34
   8:10, 54
   8:16–17, 119
   8:27, 102
   8:34, 38
   10:9, 36
   11:9, 53
   12:9–13, 205
   12:13, 205
   12:21, 61
   13:5, 102
   14:13, 53
   14:15, 34

Index of Scripture and the Apocrypha

15:23–24, 183, 193, 205
16:1–2, 202, 205
16:19, 189
16:20, 204
16:22, 176
16:23, 181, 188
1 Corinthians
  1:4, 166
  1:9, 36
  1:13, 194
  1:14, 181, 188
  1:15, 194
  1:23, 53
  2:6, 46
  3:8–9, 172
  3:10–15, 172
  3:14, 172
  4:3–5, 103
  4:14, 59, 162
  4:14–15, 190
  4:17, 162
  5:1–5, 197
  5:3–5, 174
  5:5, 122
  5:9, 59
  5:9–11, 174
  5:11, 59
  7:31, 65
  8:7, 102
  9:14, 194
  9:15, 59
  10:13, 36
  10:14, 148
  10:25, 102
  11:27–32, 189
  12:2, 149
  12:3, 110
  13:12, 87
  14:20, 46
  14:37, 59
  15:23, 83
  16:3, 202
  16:6, 183, 193
  16:11, 183, 193
  16:21, 176
2 Corinthians
  1:16, 183, 193
  2:3, 25
  2:3–4, 59
  2:9, 59

3:1, 202
3:18, 87
6:13, 162
6:14, 88
7:12, 59
7:13, 25
7:16, 189
11:10, 54
12:14, 203
12:20–13:4, 203
13:5, 54
13:10, 59
13:11, 204
Galatians
  1:20, 59
  1:22, 54
  2:20, 54
  3:28, 54
  4:19, 190
  5:6, 54, 104
  5:11, 53
  6:11, 59, 176
  6:16, 204
Ephesians
  2:1–2, 108
  4:13, 46
  5:6–11, 39
  5:15–16, 171
  6:16, 61
  6:23, 204
Philippians
  1:3, 166
  1:4, 25
  1:6, 122
  1:10, 122
  2:9–11, 60
  2:16, 122
  2:22, 190
  2:25–30, 202
  3:21, 170
  4:9, 204
Colossians
  1:13–14, 39
  1:28, 46
  2:5, 189
  3:4, 170
  4:7–9, 202
  4:10, 183
  4:14, 202
  4:18, 176

New Testament (cont.)
  1 Thessalonians
    1:1, 54
    1:2, 166
    1:9, 148
    2:4, 102
    2:14, 54
    2:19, 83
    3:8–9, 189
    3:9, 25
    4:16, 54
    5:2, 122
    5:18, 54
    5:23, 204
  2 Thessalonians
    1:3, 166
    2:1–12, 77
    2:8–12, 73
    3:16, 204
    3:17, 176
  1 Timothy
    3:2, 198, 205
    3:14, 59
    4:1, 75
    5:1–2, 59
    5:9–10, 205
    5:17–19, 155
    5:18, 194
    5:19, 135
    6:15–16, 34
  2 Timothy
    1:13, 73
    4:3, 76
    4:8, 36
    4:10, 202
  Titus
    1:1, 162
    1:5, 155
    1:8, 198, 205
    2:13, 170
    2:1–8, 59
    3:10–11, 174
    3:13, 183, 193, 205
  Philemon
    10, 190
    19, 59, 176
    21, 59
    24, 202
  Hebrews
    2:17, 39
    7:25, 38
    8:12, 39
    9:22, 35
    10:19–23, 39
    10:23, 36
    10:25, 171
    11:4, 97
    11:11, 36
    13:1–2, 205
    13:2, 205
  James
    1:25, 46, 101
    2:15–17, 101
    4:4, 66
    5:13–16, 189
    5:14, 155
    5:15, 145
    5:16, 36
    5:20, 145
  1 Peter
    1:1–2, 162
    1:18–19, 39
    2:8, 53
    2:9, 151
    4:9, 205
    4:13, 170
    5:1, 155
    5:1–5, 59
    5:5, 155
    5:12, 59
    5:14, 204
  2 Peter
    1:21, 108
    2:1, 76
    2:1–3, 109
    2:9, 122
    2:12–22, 6
    3:1, 59
    3:2, 73
    3:7, 122
    3:10, 122
    3:12, 122
  Jude
    3, 73
    6, 122
    17, 73
    20, 73
    22–23, 174
  Revelation
    2:7, 62, 129

2:10–11, 62
2:11, 129
2:14, 53
2:17, 62, 129
2:23, 102
2:26", 129
2:26–28, 62
3:5, 36, 62, 129
3:10, 146
3:12, 62, 129
3:21, 62, 129
5:5, 129
5:6, 98
5:9, 98
5:12, 98
6:4, 98
6:9, 98
6:10, 147

9:20, 149
11:18, 172
12:9, 75, 171
12:11, 62
13:1–10, 77
13:3, 98
13:8, 98
13:11–18, 108
13:14–15, 148
16:13, 108
16:13–14, 109
18:24, 98
19:20, 108, 171
20:10, 109
21:7, 62
21:8, 99
22:4, 87
22:12, 172